The Fast Forward MBA in Finance

SECOND EDITION

THE FAST FORWARD MBA SERIES

The Fast Forward MBA Series provides time-pressed business professionals and students with concise, one-stop information to help them solve business problems and make smart, informed business decisions. All of the volumes, written by industry leaders, contain "tough ideas made easy." The published books in this series are:

The Fast Forward MBA Pocket Reference, Second Edition
(0-471-22282-8)
by Paul A. Argenti

The Fast Forward MBA in Selling
(0-471-34854-6)
by Joy J.D. Baldridge

The Fast Forward MBA in Financial Planning
(0-471-23829-5)
by Ed McCarthy

The Fast Forward MBA in Negotiating and Dealmaking
(0-471-25698-6)
by Roy J. Lewicki and Alexander Hiam

The Fast Forward MBA in Project Management
(0-471-32546-5)
by Eric Verzuh

The Fast Forward MBA in Business Planning for Growth
(0-471-34548-2)
by Philip Walcoff

The Fast Forward MBA in Business Communication
(0-471-32731-X)
by Lauren Vicker and Ron Hein

The Fast Forward MBA in Investing
(0-471-24661-1)
by John Waggoner

The Fast Forward MBA in Hiring
(0-471-24212-8)
by Max Messmer

The Fast Forward MBA in Technology Management
(0-471-23980-1)
by Daniel J. Petrozzo

The Fast Forward MBA in Marketing
(0-471-16616-2)
by Dallas Murphy

The Fast Forward MBA in Business
(0-471-14660-9)
by Virginia O'Brien

The Fast Forward MBA in Finance

SECOND EDITION

JOHN A. TRACY

John Wiley & Sons, Inc.

Published by John Wiley & Sons, Inc., New York.
Published simultaneously in Canada.

This publication is designed to provide accurate and authoritative information in regard to the subject matter covered. It is sold with the understanding that the publisher is not engaged in rendering professional services. If
professional advice or other expert assistance is required, the services of a
competent professional person should be sought.

Wiley also publishes its books in a variety of electronic formats. Some content that appears in print may not be available in electronic books.

ISBN: 0-471-20285-1

Printed in the United States of America.

10 9 8 7 6 5 4 3 2 1

for
Richard and Robert, my dog track buddies,
who have helped me more than they know.

CONTENTS

PREFACE   xiii

PART 1
FINANCIAL REPORTING OUTSIDE
AND INSIDE A BUSINESS

CHAPTER 1—GETTING DOWN TO BUSINESS   3

Accounting Inside and Out   4
Internal Functions of Accounting   6
External Functions of Accounting   6
A Word about Accounting Methods   8
End Point   9

CHAPTER 2—INTRODUCING FINANCIAL STATEMENTS   11

Three Financial Imperatives, Three Financial
    Statements   11
Accrual-Basis Accounting   13
The Income Statement   16
The Balance Sheet   18
The Statement of Cash Flows   21
End Point   24

CHAPTER 3—REPORTING PROFIT TO MANAGERS   27

Using the External Income Statement
    for Decision-Making Analysis   27
Management Profit Report   31
Contribution Margin Analysis   35
End Point   36

CHAPTER 4—INTERPRETING FINANCIAL STATEMENTS   39

A Few Observations and Cautions   39
Premises and Principles of Financial Statements   41
Limits of Discussion   46
Profit Ratios   47
Book Value Per Share   49
Earnings Per Share   51
Market Value Ratios   53
Debt-Paying-Ability Ratios   55
Asset Turnover Ratios   58
End Point   59

PART 2
ASSETS AND SOURCES OF CAPITAL

CHAPTER 5—BUILDING A BALANCE SHEET   63

Sizing Up Total Assets   63
Assets and Sources of Capital for Assets   66
Connecting Sales Revenue and Expenses
    with Operating Assets and Liabilities   69
Balance Sheet Tethered with Income Statement   75
End Point   76

CHAPTER 6—BUSINESS CAPITAL SOURCES   79

Business Example for This Chapter   80
Capital Structure of Business   81
Return on Investment   86
Pivotal Role of Income Tax   89
Return on Equity (ROE)   91

Financial Leverage   92
End Point   95

CHAPTER 7—CAPITAL NEEDS OF GROWTH   97

Profit Growth Plan   98
Planning Assets and Capital Growth   99
End Point   105

PART 3
PROFIT AND CASH FLOW ANALYSIS

CHAPTER 8—BREAKING EVEN
AND MAKING PROFIT   109

Adding Information in the Management Profit Report   109
Fixed Operating Expenses   112
Depreciation: A Special Kind of Fixed Cost   113
Interest Expense   116
Pathways to Profit   116
End Point   122

CHAPTER 9—SALES VOLUME CHANGES   125

Three Ways of Making a $1 Million Profit   126
Selling More Units   129
Sales Volume Slippage   133
Fixed Costs and Sales Volume Changes   134
End Point   136

CHAPTER 10—SALES PRICE
AND COST CHANGES   139

Sales Price Changes   139
When Sales Prices Head South   144
Changes in Product Cost and Operating Expenses   146
End Point   148

CHAPTER 11—PRICE/VOLUME TRADE-OFFS   149

Shaving Sales Prices to Boost Sales Volume   150
Volume Needed to Offset Sales Price Cut   154
Thinking in Reverse: Giving Up Sales Volume
     for Higher Sales Prices   157
End Point   159

CHAPTER 12—COST/VOLUME TRADE-OFFS AND SURVIVAL ANALYSIS   161

Product Cost Increases: Which Kind?   161

Variable Cost Increases and Sales Volume   163

Better Product and Service Permitting Higher Sales Price   165

Lower Costs: The Good and Bad   166

Subtle and Not-So-Subtle Changes in Fixed Costs   169

Survival Analysis   170

End Point   177

CHAPTER 13—PROFIT GUSHES: CASH FLOW TRICKLES?   179

Lessons from Chapter 2   179

Cash Flow from Boosting Sales Volumes   180

Cash Flows across Different Product Lines   185

Cash Flow from Bumping Up Sales Prices   185

End Point   188

PART 4
CAPITAL INVESTMENT ANALYSIS

CHAPTER 14—DETERMINING INVESTMENT RETURNS NEEDED   191

A Business as an Ongoing Investment Project   191

Cost of Capital   192

Short-Term and Long-Term Asset Investments   195

The Whole Business versus Singular Capital Investments   196

Capital Investment Example   197

Flexibility of a Spreadsheet Model   206

Leasing versus Buying Long-Term Assets   206

A Word on Capital Budgeting   210

End Point   210

Chapter Appendix   211

CHAPTER 15—DISCOUNTING INVESTMENT RETURNS EXPECTED   213

Time Value of Money and Cost of Capital   214

Back to the Future: Discounting Investment Returns   215

Spreadsheets versus Equations   217
Discounted Cash Flow (DCF)   218
Net Present Value and Internal Rate of Return (IRR) 222
After-Tax Cost-of-Capital Rate   224
Regarding Cost-of-Capital Factors   226
End Point   227

PART 5
END TOPICS

CHAPTER 16—SERVICE BUSINESSES   231

Financial Statement Differences of Service
    Businesses   232
Management Profit Report for a Service
    Business   234
Sales Price and Volume Changes   237
What about Fixed Costs?   239
Trade-off Decisions   239
End Point   241

CHAPTER 17—MANAGEMENT CONTROL   243

Follow-through on Decisions   244
Management Control Information   244
Internal Accounting Controls   247
Independent Audits and Internal Auditing   249
Fraud   250
Management Control Reporting Guidelines   252
Sales Mix Analysis and Allocation of Fixed Costs 262
Budgeting Overview   270
End Point   273

**CHAPTER 18—MANUFACTURING
ACCOUNTING**   275

Product Makers versus Product Resellers   275
Manufacturing Business Example   276
Misclassification of Manufacturing Costs   280
Idle Production Capacity   283
Manufacturing Inefficiencies   285

Excessive Production   287

End Point   289

APPENDIX A GLOSSARY FOR MANAGERS   291

APPENDIX B TOPICAL GUIDE TO FIGURES   313

INDEX   315

This book is for business managers, as well as for bankers, consultants, lawyers, and other professionals who need a solid and practical understanding of how business makes profit, cash flow from profit, the assets and capital needed to support profit-making operations, and the cost of capital. Business managers and professionals don't have time to wade through a 600-page tome; they need a practical guide that gets to the point directly with clear and convincing examples.

In broad terms this book explains the tools of the trade for analyzing business financial information. *Financial statements* are one primary source of such information. Therefore financial statements are the best framework to explain and demonstrate how managers analyze financial information for making decisions and keeping control. Surprisingly, most books of this ilk do not use the financial statements framework. My book offers many advantages in this respect.

This book explains and clearly demonstrates the indispensable analysis techniques that street-smart business managers use to:

- Make profit.
- Control the capital invested in assets used in making profit

and in deciding on the sources of capital for asset investments.

- Generate cash flow from profit.

The threefold orientation of this book fits hand in glove with the three basic financial statements of every business: the profit report (income statement), the financial condition report (balance sheet), and the cash flow report (statement of cash flows). These three "financials" are the center of gravity for all businesses.

This book puts heavy emphasis on cash flow. Business managers should never ignore the cash flow consequences of their decisions. Higher profit may mean lower cash flow; managers must clearly understand why, as well as the cash flow timing from their profit.

The book begins with a four-chapter introduction to financial statements. Externally reported financial statements are prepared according to generally accepted accounting principles (GAAP). GAAP provide the bedrock rules for measuring profit. Business managers obviously need to know how much profit the business is earning.

But, to carry out their decision-making and control functions, managers need more information than is reported in the external profit report of the business. GAAP are the point of departure for preparing the more informative financial statements and other internal accounting reports needed by business managers.

The "failing" of GAAP is *not* that these accounting rules are wrong for measuring profit, nor are they wrong for presenting the financial condition of a business—not at all. It's just that GAAP do not deal with presenting financial information to managers. In fact, much of this management information is very confidential and would never be included in an external financial report open to public view.

Let me strongly suggest that you personalize every example in the book. Take the example as your own business; imagine that you are the owner or the top-level manager of the business, and that you will reap the gains of every decision or suffer the consequences, as the case may be.

If you would like a copy of my Excel workbook file of all the figures in the book contact me at my e-mail address: tracyj@colorado.edu.

As usual, the editors at John Wiley were superb. Likewise, the eagle-eyed copy editors at North Market Street Graphics polished my prose to a much smoother finish. I would like to mention that John Wiley & Sons has been my publisher for more than 25 years, and I'm very proud of our long relationship.

John A. Tracy
Boulder, Colorado
March, 2002

PART 1

Financial Reporting Outside and Inside a Business

CHAPTER 1

Getting Down to Business

Every business has three primary financial tasks that determine the success or failure of the enterprise and by which its managers are judged:

- *Making profit*—avoiding loss and achieving profit goals by making sales or earning other income and by controlling expenses

- *Cash flow*—generating cash from profit and securing cash from other sources and putting the cash inflow to good use

- *Financial health*—deciding on the financial structure for the entity and controlling its financial condition and solvency

 *To continue in existence for any period of time, a business has to make profit, generate cash flow, and stay solvent.*

Accomplishing these financial objectives depends on doing all the other management functions well. Business managers earn their keep by developing new products and services, expanding markets, improving productivity, anticipating changes, adapting to new technology, clarifying the business model, thinking out clear strategies, hiring and motivating people, making tough choices, solving problems, and arbitrating conflicts of interests between different constituencies (e.g., customers who want lower prices versus employees who want higher wages). Managers should act ethically, comply with a myriad of laws, be responsible members of society, and not harm our natural environment—all the while making profit, generating cash flow, and avoiding insolvency.

KEY CONCEPT   ACCOUNTING INSIDE AND OUT

Ask people to describe accounting and the most common answer you'll get is that accounting involves a lot of record keeping and bookkeeping. Which is true. The accounting system of a business is designed to capture and record all its transactions, operations, activities, and other developments that have financial consequences. An accounting system generates many documents, forms, and reports. Even a small business has hundreds of accounts, which are needed to keep track of its sales and expenses, its assets and liabilities, and of course its cash flows. Accounting systems today are computer-based. The accounts of a business are kept on the hard disks of computers, which should be backed up frequently, of course.

The primary purpose of an accounting system is to accumulate a complete, accurate, and up-to-date base of data and information needed to perform essential functions for a business. Figure 1.1 presents a broad overview of the internal and external functions of business accounting. Note the Janus, or two-faced, nature of an accounting system that looks in two different directions—internal and external, or inside and outside the business.

In addition to facilitating day-to-day operating activities, the accounting department of a business has the responsibility of preparing two different kinds of *internal reports*—very detailed reports for management control and much more condensed reports for decision making. Likewise, the accounting department prepares two different kinds of *external reports*—financial reports for owners and lenders and tax returns for tax authorities. Accountants have a relatively free hand in designing control and decision-making reports for managers. In sharp contrast, external reporting is *compliance-driven*. External financial reports must comply with authoritative standards and established accounting rules. And, as I'm sure you know, tax returns must comply with tax laws.

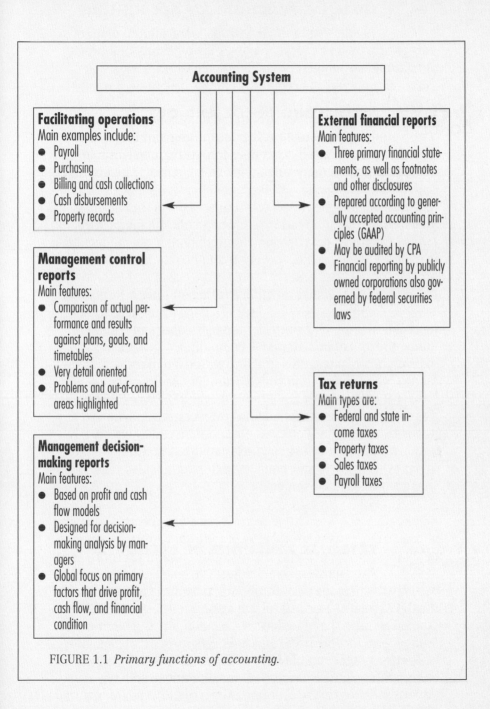

Accounting System

Facilitating operations
Main examples include:
- Payroll
- Purchasing
- Billing and cash collections
- Cash disbursements
- Property records

Management control reports
Main features:
- Comparison of actual performance and results against plans, goals, and timetables
- Very detail oriented
- Problems and out-of-control areas highlighted

Management decision-making reports
Main features:
- Based on profit and cash flow models
- Designed for decision-making analysis by managers
- Global focus on primary factors that drive profit, cash flow, and financial condition

External financial reports
Main features:
- Three primary financial statements, as well as footnotes and other disclosures
- Prepared according to generally accepted accounting principles (GAAP)
- May be audited by CPA
- Financial reporting by publicly owned corporations also governed by federal securities laws

Tax returns
Main types are:
- Federal and state income taxes
- Property taxes
- Sales taxes
- Payroll taxes

FIGURE 1.1 *Primary functions of accounting.*

KEY CONCEPT — INTERNAL FUNCTIONS OF ACCOUNTING

In addition to the day-to-day operational demands (preparing payroll checks, paying bills on time, sending out invoices to customers, etc.), Figure 1.1 reveals two other internal functions of accounting: the preparation of management control reports and reports for management decision making. Management control demands attention to a very large number of details; quite literally, thousands of things can go wrong. Management decision making, in contrast, focuses attention on relatively few key factors. Decision making looks at the forest, not the trees. For decision-making purposes, managers need accounting reports that are condensed and global in nature—that present the big picture. These reports should resonate with the business model and should be structured according to the profit and cash flow models of the business.

In passing, I should mention that accounting information seldom comprises the whole set of information needed for decision making and control. Managers use many, many other sources of information—competitors' sales prices, delivery problems with suppliers, employee morale, and so on. Nonaccounting data comes from a wide diversity of sources, including shopping the competition, sales force reports, market research studies, personnel department records, and so on. For example, customer files are very important, and they usually include both accounting data (past sales history) and nonaccounting data (sales reps assigned to each customer).

KEY CONCEPT — EXTERNAL FUNCTIONS OF ACCOUNTING

Accountants have two primary external reporting responsibilities: the preparation of tax returns and external financial reports (see Figure 1.1 again). Exceedingly complex and constantly changing laws, rules, and forms govern state and federal income taxes, payroll taxes, property taxes, and sales taxes. Accountants have their hands full just keeping up with tax regulations and forms. Accountants also have to stay abreast of changing accounting standards to prepare external financial reports.

External Financial Reports

In the next chapter I present an overview of external financial reports. Please bear in mind that this book does not examine in any great detail the external financial reports of business.* This book is mainly concerned with internal reports to managers and how managers analyze the information in these reports for making decisions and for controlling the financial performance of the business. Only a few brief comments about external financial reporting of particular importance to managers are mentioned here.

The financial statements of a business that are the core of the external financial reports sent to its shareowners and lenders must conform with *generally accepted accounting principles* (GAAP). These are the authoritative guidelines, rules, and standards that govern external financial reporting to the outside investors and creditors of a business. The main purpose of having financial statements audited by an independent CPA firm is to test whether the statements have been prepared according to GAAP. If there are material departures from these ground rules of financial statement accounting and disclosure, the CPA auditor says so in the audit opinion on the financial statements.

External financial reports include footnotes that are an integral addendum to the financial statements. Footnotes are needed because the external financial report is directed to outside investors and creditors of the business who are not directly involved in the day-to-day affairs of the business. Managers should already know most of the information disclosed in footnotes. If managers prefer to have certain footnotes included in their internal accounting reports, the footnotes should be included—probably in much more detail and covering more sensitive matters than footnotes presented in external financial reports.

An external financial report includes three primary financial statements: One summarizes the profit-making activities of the business for the period; one summarizes the cash inflows and outflows for the same period; and one summarizes the assets of the business at the end of the period that are balanced by the claims against, and sources of, the assets.

*Without too much modesty, I can recommend my book, *How to Read a Financial Report,* 5th ed. (New York: John Wiley & Sons, 1999).

The three primary financial statements do not come with built-in analysis. Rather, the financial statements provide an organized source of information. It's up to the users to extract the vital signals and messages from the statements. As I explain later, managers need much more information than are reported in the external financial statements.

For example, suppose you're about ready to lower sales prices 10 percent because you think sales volume will increase more than enough to make this a smart move. You'd better know which profit and cash flow analysis tools to use to test the impact of this decision on your business. The external profit report does not provide the information you need. Rather, you need the type of internal profit report explained in Chapter 3 to analyze just how much sales volume would have to increase in order to increase profit. You might be surprised by how much sales volume would have to increase. If you think sales volume would have to increase by only 10 percent, you are dead wrong!

A WORD ABOUT ACCOUNTING METHODS

GAAP have been developed to standardize accounting methods for measuring net income (bottom-line profit), for presenting financial condition and cash flow information, and to provide financial disclosure standards for reporting to external investors and lenders to business. Over the years GAAP have come a long way, but have not yet resulted in complete uniformity and consistency from one business to the next, or even among companies in the same industry. Businesses can choose from among different but equally acceptable accounting methods, which can cause a material difference in the profit (net income) reported for the year and in the values of certain assets, liabilities, and owners' equity accounts reported in the financial statements of a business.

Profit depends on how it's measured—in particular, on which accounting methods have been selected and how the methods are applied in practice. I'm reminded of the old baseball joke here: There's an argument between the batter and the catcher about whether the pitch was a ball or a strike. Back and forth the two go, until finally the umpire settles it by saying "It ain't nothing until I call it." Likewise, someone has to decide how to "call" profit for the period; profit depends on how the "strike zone" is determined, and this depends heavily on which particular accounting methods are selected to measure profit.

External financial reports are the primary means of communication to fulfill the *stewardship fiduciary function* of management—that is, to render a periodic accounting of what has been done with the capital entrusted to management. The creditors and shareowners of a business are the sources of, as well as having claims on, the assets of the business. Therefore, they are entitled to a periodic accounting by their stewards (*agents* is the more popular term these days).

DANGER! Please keep in mind that managers have a fiduciary responsibility to the outside world. They are responsible for the fairness and truthfulness of the financial statements. There's no doubt that top management has the primary responsibility for the business's financial statements—this cannot be shifted or "outsourced" to the CPA auditor of its financial statements. Nor can legal counsel to the business be blamed if top management issues misleading financial statements, unless they were a party to a conspiracy to commit fraud.

Because external financial reports are public in nature, disclosure is limited, especially in the profit performance report of a business. Disclosure standards permit the business to withhold information that creditors and external investors probably would like to know. The theory of this, I believe, is that such disclosure would reveal too much information and cause the business to lose some of its competitive advantages. The internal accounting profit report presented in the next chapter contains confidential information that the business wouldn't want to reveal in its external financial report to the outside world.

Publicly owned corporations are required to include a *management discussion and analysis* (MD&A) section in their annual financial reports to stockholders, which deals with the broad factors and main reasons for the company's profit performance. Generally speaking, these sections are not too specific and deal with broad issues and developments over the year.

END POINT

The book analyzes how to make profit. So it seems a good idea in conclusion to say a few words in defense of the profit motive. Profit stimulates innovation; it's the reward for taking risks; it's the return on capital invested in business; it's compensation for hard work and long hours; it motivates efficiency; it weeds out products and services no longer in demand; it keeps pressure on companies to maintain their quality of customer service and products.

In short, the profit system delivers the highest standard of living in the world. Despite all this, it's no secret that many in government, the church, and society at large have a deep-seated distrust of our profit-motivated, free enterprise, and open market system—and not entirely without reason.

It would be naive to ignore the abuses and failings of the profit system and not to take notice of the ruthless profit-at-any-cost behavior of some unscrupulous business managers. Unfortunately, you don't have to look very far to find examples of dishonest advertising, unsafe products, employees being cheated out of their pensions, dangerous working conditions, or deliberate violation of laws and regulations.

Too many companies travel the low moral and ethical road. A form of Gresham's law* seems to be at work. Dirty practices tend to drive out clean practices, the result being a sinking to the lowest level of tolerable behavior. Which is very sad. No wonder profit is a dirty word to so many. No wonder business gets bad press. Ethical standards should be above and ahead of what the law requires.

Many businesses have adopted a formal code of ethics for all employees in the organization. It goes without saying that managers should set the example for full-faith compliance with the code of ethics. If managers cut corners, what do they expect employees to do? If managers pay only lip service to the code of ethics, employees will not take the code seriously.

---

*You may recall that Sir Thomas Gresham was a sixteenth-century economist who is generally credited with the important observation that, given two types of money circulating in the economy, the one perceived as more dear or of higher quality will be kept back and spent last; the cheaper or lower-quality money will be offered first in economic exchange. Thus, the cheaper money will drive out the higher-quality money. Even though we have only one currency in the American economy, you may have noticed that most of us tend to pass the currency that is in the worst shape first and hold back the bills that are in better condition.

Introducing Financial Statements

This chapter introduces the financial statements that are included in periodic financial reports from a business to its shareowners and lenders. They are called *external* financial statements to emphasize that the information is released outside the business. Let me stress the word *introducing* in the chapter title. One brief chapter cannot possibly cover the waterfront and deal in a comprehensive manner with all aspects of external financial statements. This chapter's objective is more modest and more focused.

My main purpose is to explain the basic content and structure of each financial statement in order to provide stepping-stones to later chapters, which develop models of profit, cash flow, and financial condition for management decision-making analysis. External financial statements are not designed for *management* use; they are designed for outside investors and lenders who do not manage the business. External financial statements report results, but not how and why the results happened.

THREE FINANCIAL IMPERATIVES, THREE FINANCIAL STATEMENTS

Without a doubt, managers should understand the external financial statements of their business that are reported to shareowners and lenders, whether the managers own shares in the business or not. Financial statements are the basic touchstone of every business. A separate, distinct financial statement is prepared for each of the three financial imperatives of every business:

- *Make profit.* The *income statement* (also called the *profit and loss statement*) summarizes the revenue and expenses of the business and the profit or loss result for a period of time such as one year.

- *Generate cash flows.* The *statement of cash flows* summarizes the various sources and uses of cash of the business for the same period as the income statement.

- *Control financial condition.* The *balance sheet* (also called the *statement of financial condition*) summarizes the various assets and liabilities of the business at the end of the income statement period, as well as how much of the excess of assets over liabilities was invested by the shareowners in the business and how much is attributable to the cumulative profit over the life of the business that was not distributed to its shareowners.

A business is profit-motivated, so its income statement (the financial statement that reports the profit or loss of the business for the period) occupies center stage. The market value of the ownership shares in the business depends heavily on the profit performance of the business. A business has to earn enough operating profit to pay the interest on its debt, so its lenders also keep sharp eye on profit performance.

A Business Example

I use a realistic business example to illustrate and explain the three external financial statements. This business manufactures and sells products to other businesses. It sells products from stock; in other words, the business carries an inventory of products from which it makes immediate delivery to customers. The business sells and buys on credit. It has invested in many long-life operating resources—buildings, machines, equipment, tools, vehicles, and computers. The business was started many years ago when several persons invested the initial ownership capital in the venture.

The business borrows money from banks on the basis of

short-term notes (having maturity dates less than one year) and long-term notes (having maturity dates three years or longer). The business has made a profit most years, but suffered losses in several years. To grow the business the shareowners invested additional capital from time to time. But the main reason for the increase in owners' equity is that the business has retained most of its annual profits in order to build up the capital base of the company instead of distributing 100 percent of its annual profits to shareowners.

For the year just ended, the business recorded $26 million sales revenue; this amount is net of discounts given customers from list or billed prices. The company's bottom-line profit after deducting all expenses for the year from sales revenue is $2.2 million. Bottom-line profit is called variously *net income, net earnings,* or just *earnings.* (The example assumes that the business did not have any nonrecurring, unusual, or extraordinary gains or losses during the year.) Profit equals 8.5 percent of sales revenue, which is typical for this industry ($2.2 million profit ÷ $26 million sales revenue = 8.5%).

KEY CONCEPT The business uses *accrual-basis accounting* to measure profit and to prepare its balance sheet (statement of financial condition). All businesses of any size that sell products and have inventories and that own long-lived operating resources use accrual-basis accounting. Accrual-basis accounting is required by financial reporting standards and by the federal income tax law (with some exceptions for smaller businesses). Business managers should have a good grip on accrual-basis accounting, and they should understand how accrual-basis accounting differs from cash flows.

ACCRUAL-BASIS ACCOUNTING

Before introducing the financial statements for the business example, I present Figure 2.1, in which cash flows are separated from the accrual-basis components for sales and expenses. (I culled this information from the accounts of the business.) Figure 2.1 is *not* a financial statement. Rather, I present this information to lay the groundwork for the business's financial statements. This figure presents the basic building blocks for sales revenue and expenses and for cash flows

Note: Amounts are in millions of dollars.

Revenue and expense cash flows

Note: Cash flows include amounts related to last year's and next year's revenue and expenses.

Accrual-basis sales revenue and expenses

Note: Revenue and expenses are of this and only this year; only one year is involved.

$3.2	$22.5	$3.5
Cash collections during the year from sales made last year or for sales to be made next year.	Cash collections during year from sales made during the year.	Sales made during the year but no cash collected during the year; cash will be collected next year or was already collected last year.

$25.7 $26.0

less   less

$7.5	$14.9	$8.9
Cash payments during the year for expenses of last year or next year.	Cash payments during the year for expenses of the year.	Expenses recorded during the year but not paid during the year; cash was paid either in previous year or will be paid next year.

$22.4 $23.8

$3.3 $2.2

Net cash flow during year from operating, or profit-making activities.	Net profit for year according to accrual-basis profit accounting methods.

FIGURE 2.1 *Cash flow and accrual components of sales revenue and expenses for the year just ended for the business example.*

during the year. This information also is very helpful to under-stand the balance sheet, which is explained later in the chapter.

Sales Revenue and Cash Flow from Sales Revenue

The revenue from most of the sales during the year was col-lected during the year—neither before the year started nor after the year ended. In Figure 2.1, observe that the company collected $22.5 million cash during the year from sales made during the year.* To complete the accrual-basis sales revenue picture for the year you have to consider sales made during the year for which cash was not collected during the year. To complete the cash flow picture you have to consider other sales-driven cash flows during the year, which are either from sales made last year or from sales that will be made next year. In summary (see Figure 2.1 for data):

- *Accrual-basis sales revenue for year:* $22.5 million cash collections during the year from sales made during the year + $3.5 million sales made during the year but cash not col-lected during year = $26 million sales revenue for year

- *Sales revenue–driven cash flows during year:* $22.5 mil-lion cash collections during the year from sales made dur-ing the year + $3.2 million cash collections during year from last year's sales or for next year's sales = $25.7 million cash flow from sales revenue

Expenses and Cash Flow for Expenses

Many expenses recorded in the year were paid in cash during the year—neither before the year started nor after the year ended. In Figure 2.1, note that the company recorded $14.9 million total expenses during the year for which it paid out $14.9 million cash during the year. Many expenses are paid weeks after the expense is originally recorded; the business first records a liability on its books for the expense, and the liability account is decreased when it is paid. To complete the

---

*The business makes many sales on credit, so cash collections from sales occur a few weeks after the sales are recorded. In contrast, some customers pay in advance of taking delivery of products, so cash collections occur before the sales are recorded at the time products are delivered to the cus-tomers.

cash flow picture you have to consider other cash flows during the year for expenses recorded last year or for expenses that won't be recorded until next year. To complete the accrual-basis expenses picture for the year you have to consider expenses recorded during the year for which cash was not paid during the year. In summary (see Figure 2.1 for data):

- *Accrual-basis expenses for year:* $14.9 million expenses recorded and paid in cash during year + $8.9 million expenses recorded but cash was not paid during year = $23.8 million expenses

- *Expense-driven cash flows during year:* $14.9 million expenses recorded and paid in cash during year + $7.5 million paid during year for last year's expenses or for next year's expenses = $22.4 million cash flow for expenses

Net Profit and Net Cash Flow for Year

K E Y CONCEPT Net profit for the year is $2.2 million, equal to $26 million sales revenue less $23.8 million expenses. In contrast, the net cash flow of revenue and expenses is $3.3 million for the year. *Both figures are correct.* The $2.2 million figure is the correct measure of profit for the year according to proper accounting methods for recording sales revenue and expenses to the year. The $3.3 million net cash flow figure is correct, but keep in mind that cash flows related to revenue and expenses of the previous year and the following year are intermingled with the cash flows of revenue and expenses of the year just ended.

THE INCOME STATEMENT

Figure 2.2 presents the basic format of the business's income statement for the year just ended. The income statement starts with sales revenue for the year and ends with the net income for the year. Between the top line and the bottom line a business reports several expenses and subtotals for intermediate measures of profit. A company that sell products discloses the amount of its cost-of-goods-sold expense immediately below sales revenue, which is deducted to get the first profit line, called *gross margin*. The word *gross* implies that

Note: Amounts are in millions of dollars.

Sales revenue	$26.0
Cost-of-goods-sold expense	XX.X
Gross margin	XX.X
Operating expenses	XX.X
Earnings before interest and income tax	X.X
Interest expense	.X
Earnings before income tax	X.X
Income tax expense	X.X
Net income	$ 2.2

FIGURE 2.2 *Format of external income statement for year.*

other expenses have to be deducted from sales revenue to arrive at the final, or bottom-line profit.

One or more classes of operating expenses are disclosed in external financial statements. How many and which specific types of operating expenses? The disclosure of operating expenses varies from business to business; financial reporting rules are lax in this regard. Few businesses disclose the amounts of advertising expenses, for example, or the amounts of top-management compensation. Many businesses lump a variety of different operating expenses into a conglomerate account called *sales, administrative, and general expenses.* In most external income statements, total operating expenses are deducted from gross margin to arrive at the profit figure labeled *earnings before interest and income tax expenses* (see Figure 2.2).

I'm sure you've noticed that instead of dollar amounts for expenses and the intermediate profit lines between the top line and the bottom line in Figure 2.2 I show only placeholders (e.g., XX.X). Showing the dollar amounts for these items would serve no particular purpose here. I wish to emphasize the basic format of the externally reported income statement, not the data in this financial statement. In Chapter 3 I develop an internal profit report for managers that is a much different format than the external income statement, which is more useful for decision-making analysis.

THE BALANCE SHEET

The usual explanation of the balance sheet is that it is the financial statement that summarizes a business's assets and liabilities. Well, yes and no. If you have in mind a complete reckoning of all the assets of the business at their current market or replacement values you are off the mark. The balance sheet does not list all assets at current values. On the other hand, the balance sheet comes close to listing all the liabilities of a business. You may find these opening comments about the balance sheet rather unusual, and I don't blame you if you think so.

The accounts, or basic elements presented in a balance sheet are the result of accrual-basis accounting methods for recording the revenue and expenses of the business. A balance sheet in large part consists of the remains of the profit accounting process. A balance sheet is not based on a complete survey of all the tangible and intangible assets of the business at their current values. For example, a business may have developed a well known and trusted brand name and have a well trained and dedicated workforce. But these two "assets" are not reported in its balance sheet. Having these two assets should be reflected in above-average profit performance, which is reported in the income statement of the business. The chief executive can brag about these two assets in the company's financial reports to shareowners and lenders, but don't look for them in the company's balance sheet.

The balance sheet at the start and end of the year for the business is presented in Figure 2.3. Cash usually is shown first in a balance sheet, as you see in Figure 2.3. Cash includes coin and currency on hand, balances in demand deposit checking accounts with banks, and often cash equivalents such as short-term, marketable securities that can be liquidated at a moment's notice. The dollar amounts reported in the balance sheet for assets other than cash and for liabilities and owners' equity accounts are called *book values,* because these are the amounts recorded in the books, or accounts, kept by the business.

Generally, the book values of the liabilities of a business are the amounts of cash owed to creditors and lenders that will be paid later. The book value of the asset *accounts receivable* is the amount of cash that should be received from customers,

Note: Amounts are in millions of dollars.

Assets

	Beginning of Year		End of Year	
Cash	$ 1.6		$ 2.0	
Accounts receivable	$ 2.0		$ 2.5	
Inventories	$ 3.9		$ 4.7	
Prepaid expenses	$ 0.5		$ 0.6	
Subtotal of current assets		$ 8.0		$ 9.8
Property, plant, and equipment	$15.5		$19.1	
Accumulated depreciation	($ 6.5)	$ 9.0	($ 8.2)	$10.9
Total assets		$17.0		$20.7

Liabilities and Owners' Equity

Advance payments from customers	$1.0		$1.2	
Accounts payable	$1.6		$2.0	
Accrued expenses payable	$0.6		$0.8	
Short-term notes payable	$1.5		$2.0	
Subtotal of current liabilities		$ 4.7		$ 6.0
Long-term notes payable		$ 3.5		$ 4.0
Owners' equity—invested capital	$4.0		$4.2	
Owners' equity—retained earnings	$4.8	$ 8.8	$6.5	$10.7
Total liabilities and owners' equity		$17.0		$20.7

Note: The amounts reported at the beginning of the year are the carryover balances at the end of the preceding year; the amounts continue seamlessly from the end of the preceding year to the start of the following year.

FIGURE 2.3 *Format of external balance sheet.*

usually within a month or so. The book value of *inventories* (products held for sale) and *property, plant, and equipment* are the costs of the assets. The cost of inventories is relatively recent under one method of accounting or, alternatively, relatively old under another. (Accountants can't agree on just one method for this particular asset.)

The total cost of property, plant, and equipment is relatively old unless most of these long-lived operating resources were recently acquired by the business. Their cost is spread over the estimated years of their use; the amount of cost that is recorded as depreciation expense is recorded in the accumulated depreciation offset account, which is deducted from the original cost of the assets (see Figure 2.3)

When the shareowners invest capital in the business, the appropriate owners' equity account is increased. At the end of the year the amount of profit for the year less the amount of profit distributed to the shareowners is recorded as an increase in the second owners' equity account, which is called *retained earnings* (see Figure 2.3).

The balance sheet assets and liabilities that are directly connected with the sales revenue and expenses of the business are summarized as follows:

- *Accounts receivable.* Receivables from sales made on credit to customers.
- *Inventories.* Products manufactured or purchased that have not yet been sold.
- *Prepaid expenses.* Costs paid ahead for next year's expenses.
- *Property, plant, and equipment less accumulated depreciation.* The original cost of long-term operating resources less the cumulative amount of the cost that has been recorded as depreciation expense so far.
- *Advance payments from customers.* Just what the account title implies—cash received in advance from customers for future delivery of products, so sales revenue has not yet been recorded.
- *Accounts payable.* Amounts owed to creditors for purchases on credit and for expenses that had not yet been paid to vendors and suppliers at balance sheet date.
- *Accrued expenses payable.* Cumulative amounts owed for certain expenses of period that had not been paid at balance sheet date.

These are called *operating* assets and liabilities because they are generated in the operations of making sales and incurring expenses. Operating liabilities are non-interest-bearing, which sets them apart from the interest-bearing notes owed by the business. Notes payable arise from borrowing money, not from the revenue and expense operations of the business. The operating assets and liabilities of a business constitute a good part of its balance sheet, as illustrated in Figure 2.3. This is typical for most businesses.

The beginning and ending balances in the balance sheet shown in Figure 2.3 are the sources of the data in Figure 2.1 for the cash flow and accrual-basis amounts of revenue and expenses. The derivation of the amounts are summarized as follows (amounts in millions of dollars):

$2.00	beginning balance of accounts receivable
$1.20	ending balance of advance payments from customers
$3.20	cash flow from last year's sales or for next year's sales
$2.50	ending balance of accounts receivable
$1.00	beginning balance of advance payments from customers
$3.50	sales made during the year but cash not collected during the year
$1.60	beginning balance of accounts payable
$0.60	beginning balance of accrued expenses payable
$4.70	ending balance of inventories
$0.60	ending balance of prepaid expenses
$7.50	cash payments during year of last year's or for next year's expenses
$1.70	depreciation expense for year (increase in accumulated depreciation)
$2.00	ending balance of accounts payable
$0.80	ending balance of accrued expenses payable
$3.90	beginning balance of inventories
$0.50	beginning balance of prepaid expenses
$8.90	Expenses recorded during year but not paid during year

THE STATEMENT OF CASH FLOWS

The third primary financial statement in the external financial reports of a business to its shareowners and lenders is the *statement of cash flows*. This financial statement summarizes the cash inflows and outflows of a business during the same period as the income statement. Figure 2.4 presents this financial statement for the business example. The second and third sections of the statement of cash flows are relatively straightforward. In the *investing activities* section, note that the business invested $3.6 million in new long-term operating assets during the year to replace old ones that reached the end of their useful lives and to expand the production and

Note: Amounts are in millions of dollars.

Cash flow from operating activities

Cash collections from revenue	$25.7	
Cash payments for expenses	($22.4)	$3.3

Cash flow from investing activities

Investments in new long-term operating assets	($3.6)

Cash flow from financing activities

Increase in short-term notes payable	$ 0.5	
Increase in long-term notes payable	$ 0.5	
Issuance of additional capital stock shares	$ 0.2	
Cash distributions from profit to shareowners	($ 0.5)	$0.7

Net increase of cash during year	$0.4
Beginning cash balance	$1.6
Ending cash balance	$2.0

Note: Cash flow from operating activities is presented according to the direct method, and cash outflows for expenses are condensed into one amount.

FIGURE 2.4 *Format of external statement of cash flows for year.*

warehouse capacity of the business. (Proceeds from disposals of long-term operating assets would have been reported as a cash inflow in this section.)

The *financing activities* section in the statement of cash flows summarizes cash flows of borrowing and payments on short-term and long-term debt and investment of additional capital by shareowners during the year as well as return of capital (if any) to them. Usually, the dealings with debt sources of capital are reported net (i.e., only the net increase or increase is disclosed). Reporting practices are not completely uniform in this regard however. It is acceptable to report borrowings separate from payments on debt instead of just the net increase or decrease. Generally, the issuance of new ownership shares should be reported separately from the return of capital to shareowners.

The first section of the statement of cash flows, called *cash flow from operating activities* (which is not the best designation in the world, in my opinion), reports the cash increase or decrease during the year from sales revenue and expense activities. This key figure also is called *operating cash flow* or *cash flow from profit.* To be frank, this is not an easy number to understand. In Figure 2.4, I present cash flow from operating activities about as briefly and simply as you can. Cash inflow from sales revenue was $25.7 million during the year, and cash outflow for expenses was $22.4 million during the year, which yields the $3.3 million cash flow from profit operating activities. This manner of presentation is referred to as the *direct method.*

Instead of the direct method, a business has the option of using an alternative method for presenting cash flow from operating activities, which is called the *indirect method.* The large majority of businesses elect the indirect method as a matter of fact—even though the financial reporting rule-making body of the accounting profession has expressed a preference for the direct method. The indirect method is explained next.

Indirect Method of Reporting Cash Flow from Operating Activities

Based on changes in the operating assets and liabilities from the beginning of the year to the end of the year, Figure 2.5 shows how the business's cash flow from operating activities would be presented in its statement of cash flows for the year.

The indirect method starts with net income for the year, then "adjusts" net income for the cash flow effects due to changes in the assets and liabilities that are directly connected with recording sales revenue and expenses (called *operating* assets and liabilities). Of course, the $3.3 million cash flow from operating activities for the year is the same whether the direct or the indirect method of presentation is used in the statement of cash flows. To follow the indirect method of presentation, keep in mind the following basic points:

- An increase in operating assets causes a negative effect on cash flow from profit, and a decrease causes a positive effect.

Net income	$2.2
Accounts receivable increase	(0.5)
Inventories increase	(0.8)
Prepaid expenses increase	(0.1)
Depreciation expense	1.7
Advance payments from customers increase	0.2
Accounts payable increase	0.4
Accrued expenses payable increase	0.2
Cash flow from operating activities	$3.3

FIGURE 2.5 *Indirect method of reporting cash flow from operating activities.*

- An increase in operating liabilities causes a positive effect on cash flow from profit, and a decrease causes a negative effect.

In most situations, the largest decrease in an operating asset is the depreciation expense recorded for the year. Depreciation expense is recorded in order to allocate a portion of the total cost of a business's long-term operating assets to the year. Recording depreciation expense is not a cash outlay; rather, it is the write-down of the long-term operating assets of the business that were bought and paid for in previous years. Note in Figure 2.5 that depreciation expense is by far the largest single factor in cash flow from operating activities.

END POINT

A business makes regular financial reports to its shareowners and lenders. Because they supply capital to the business, they are entitled to receive regular reports about what the business has done with their money. The hard core of these reports consists of three primary financial statements. They are called *external* financial statements because the information is released outside the business.

The income statement reports the revenue, expenses, and profit or loss of the business for the period. Recording revenue and expenses is based on *accrual-basis* accounting methods. The chapter begins by explaining the key differences between cash flows and accrual-basis profit accounting. Then the format and content of each of the three primary financial statements is illustrated and explained for a typical business.

The external financial statements are oriented to the outside sharcowners and lenders of the business who are not involved in managing the business. The development of the standards and conventions for presenting external financial statements has been guided by this basic orientation. For their decision-making and control functions, business managers need more useful internal profit reports, which I develop in the next chapter.

Reporting Profit to Managers

Managers have to keep on top of the unending stream of changes in today's business environment. Few factors remain constant very long. Managers need to quickly assess the profit and other financial impacts of these changes. Deciding on the best response to changes is never easy, but one thing is clear: Managers need all relevant information for their profit-making decision analysis.

USING THE EXTERNAL INCOME STATEMENT FOR DECISION-MAKING ANALYSIS

The external income statement (see Figure 2.2) is useful up to a point for decision-making analysis, but it does not present all the information about operating expenses that is needed by managers. To demonstrate this important point, consider the following situation. Suppose you have done extensive market research and you're convinced that reducing sales prices across the board next year by just 5 percent would result in a 25 percent increase in sales volume across the board. In order to concentrate on this basic decision, assume zero cost inflation next year (don't you wish!). Would this be a good move?

Of course, your prediction of a 25 percent sales volume increase is critical. This big jump in sales volume may or may not materialize. Such a large response to shaving sales prices implies that sales demand is very sensitive to sales

DANGER!

prices. In other words, you face a very elastic demand curve, as economists say. Does the external income statement provide *all* the information needed to analyze this decision? No, not entirely. The external profit report (income statement) doesn't include enough information about how operating expenses would react to the sales volume increase and the sales revenue increase.

External Income Statement for New Example

Figure 3.1 presents the external income statement for the most recent year for a new business example. This external profit performance report has been prepared according to *generally accepted accounting principles* (GAAP) regarding the format and disclosure standards for this key financial statement. Be warned, however, that every business is a little different when it comes to details in their income statements.

 Terminology differs somewhat from business to business. For instance, some companies prefer the term *gross profit* instead of *gross margin* in their external income statements (sales revenue minus cost-of-goods-sold expense). Many businesses report two or more classes of operating expenses below the gross margin line instead of just one amount for all selling and administrative expenses as shown in Figure 3.1. For instance, a business may disclose the amount of its research and development expense for the year as separate from all its other operating expenses. Nevertheless, the example shown in

Sales revenue	$39,661,250
Cost-of-goods-sold expense	$24,960,750
Gross margin	$14,700,500
Selling and administrative expenses	$11,466,135
Earnings before interest and income tax	$ 3,234,365
Interest expense	$ 795,000
Earnings before income tax	$ 2,439,365
Income tax expense	$ 853,778
Net income	$ 1,585,587

FIGURE 3.1 *External income statement for most recent year.*

Figure 3.1 is an archetype external income statement in essential respects. I should quickly mention that external financial statements are supplemented with footnotes (which are not shown for the example).

Analyzing Gross Margin

The first step in making a bottom-line profit for the year is to make enough *gross margin* to cover your operating expenses for the year and to cover your interest expense and income tax expense as well. The cost-of-goods-sold expense is deducted from sales revenue to arrive at this extremely important first-line measure of profit (see Figure 3.1).

As its name implies, cost-of-goods-sold expense is the cost of the products sold to customers. Cost of goods sold is usually the largest expense for a business that sells products, typically 50 to 60 percent or more of sales revenue (and as much as 80 to 85 percent for some high-volume retailers).

The gross margin ratio on sales varies from industry to industry, as you probably know. The cosmetics industry has very high gross profit margins, and Coca-Cola's gross profit traditionally has been over 60 percent. A full-service restaurant, as a rough rule of thumb, should keep its food costs at one-third of its sales revenue, leaving a two-thirds gross margin to cover all its other expenses and to yield a satisfactory bottom-line profit. In the past, Apple Computer made very high gross margins until it adopted a much more aggressive sales price strategy on its personal computers to protect its market share. This cut deeply into its historically high profit margins.

 A general rule is that the lower the gross margin ratio, the higher the *inventory turnover.* The interval of time from acquisition of the product to the sale of the product equals one inventory turnover. High turnover generally is five or more *turns* a year, or maybe six or seven turns a year depending on whom you talk with. Food supermarkets, for example, have extremely high inventory turnover—their products do not stay on the shelves very long. Even taking into account the holding period in their warehouses before the products get to the shelves in the stores, their inventory turnover is very high, and thus supermarkets can work on fairly thin gross margin percents of 20 percent, give or take a little.

In contrast, a retail furniture store may hold an item in inventory for more than six months on average before it is sold, so they need fairly high gross margin percents. In this business example, the company's gross margin is 37.1 percent of its sales revenue ($14,700,500 gross margin ÷ $39,661,250 sales revenue = 37.1% gross margin ratio). This is in the ball-park for many businesses.

K E Y CONCEPT Cost of goods sold is a *variable* expense; it moves more or less in lockstep with changes in sales volume (total number of units sold). If sales volume were to increase 10 percent, then this expense should increase 10 percent, too, assuming unit product costs remained constant over time. But unit product costs—whether the company is a retailer that pur-chases the products its sells or a producer that manufactures the products it sells—do not remain constant over time. Unit product costs may drift steadily upward over time with infla-tion. Or unit product costs can take sharp nosedives because of technological improvements or competitive pressures.

Returning to the decision situation introduced previously, the manager can use the information in the external income statement to do the gross margin analysis presented in Figure 3.2, which compares sales revenue, cost-of-goods-sold expense, and gross margin for the year just ended and for the contem-plated scenario in which sales prices are 5 percent lower and sales volume is 25 percent higher. Before looking at Figure 3.2, you might make an intuitive guess regarding what would happen to gross margin in this scenario, then compare your guess with what the numbers show. I'd bet that you are some-what surprised by the outcome shown in Figure 3.2. But num-bers don't lie.

Sales revenue would increase 18.75 percent: Although sales volume would increase 25.0 percent, the sales price of every unit sold would be only 95 percent of what it sold for during the year just ended. (Note that $1.25 \times 0.95 = 1.1875$, or an 18.75 percent increase in sales revenue.) Cost-of-goods-sold expense would increase 25.0 percent because sales volume, or the total number of units sold, would increase 25.0 percent. Still, gross margin would increase 8.14 percent, although this is far less than the percent increase in sales volume.

What about operating expenses? Would the total of these

	For Year Just Ended (Figure 3.1)	For New Scenario	Change	Percent Change
Sales revenue	$39,661,250	$47,097,734	$7,436,484	18.75%
Cost-of-goods-sold expense	$24,960,750	$31,200,938	$6,240,188	25.00%
Gross margin	$14,700,500	$15,896,796	$1,196,296	8.14%

FIGURE 3.2 *Gross margin analysis of sales price cut proposal.*

expenses (excluding interest and income tax expenses) increase more than the increase in gross margin? Without more information about the business's operating expenses there's no way to answer this question. You need information about how the operating expenses would react to the relatively large increase in sales volume and sales revenue. The internal management profit report presents this key information.

MANAGEMENT PROFIT REPORT

KEY CONCEPT
Figure 3.3 presents the *management profit report* for the business example. (In this internal financial statement I show expenses with parentheses to emphasize that they are deductions from profit.) Instead of one amount for selling and administrative expenses as presented in the external income statement, note that operating expenses are classified according to how they behave relative to changes in sales volume and sales revenue (see the shaded area in Figure 3.3). *Variable* operating expenses are separated from *fixed* operating expenses, and the variable expenses are divided into *revenue-driven* versus *unit-driven*. This three-way classification of operating expenses is the key difference between the external and internal profit reports.

KEY CONCEPT
Also note that a new profit line is included, labeled *contribution margin,* which equals gross margin minus variable operating expenses. It is called this because this profit *contributes* toward coverage of fixed operating expenses and toward interest expense, which to a large degree is also fixed in amount for the year.

Sales revenue	$39,661,250
Cost-of-goods-sold expense	($24,960,750)
Gross margin	$14,700,500
Variable revenue-driven operating expenses	($ 3,049,010)
Variable unit-driven operating expenses	($ 2,677,875)
Contribution margin	$ 8,973,615
Fixed operating expenses	($ 5,739,250)
Earnings before interest and income tax (EBIT)	$ 3,234,365
Interest expense	($ 795,000)
Earnings before income tax	$ 2,439,365
Income tax expense	($ 853,778)
Net income	$ 1,585,587

FIGURE 3.3 *Management profit report for business example.*

Bottom-line profit (net income) is exactly the same amount as in the external income statement (Figure 3.1). Contrary to what seems to be a popular misconception, businesses do not keep two sets of books. Profit is measured and recorded by one set of methods, which are the same for both internal and external financial reports. Managers may ask their accounting staff to calculate profit using alternative accounting methods, such as a different inventory and cost-of-goods-sold expense method or a different depreciation expense method, but only one set of numbers is recorded and booked. There is not a "real" profit figure secreted away someplace that only managers know, although this seems to be a misconception held by many.

The additional information about operating expenses provided in the management profit report (see Figure 3.3) allows the manager to complete his or her analysis and reach a decision. Before walking through the analysis of the proposal to cut sales prices by 5 percent to gain a 25 percent increase in sales volume, it is important to thoroughly understand the behavior of operating expenses.

Variable Operating Expenses

In the management profit report (Figure 3.3), variable operating expenses are divided into two types: those that vary with sales *volume* and those that vary with total sales *dollars*. In general, variable means that an expense varies with sales activity—either sales volume (the number of units sold) or sales revenue (the number of dollars generated by sales). Delivery expense, for example, varies with the quantity of units sold and shipped. On the other hand, commissions paid to salespersons normally are a percentage of sales revenue or the number of dollars involved.

Contribution margin, which equals sales revenue minus cost-of-goods-sold and variable operating expenses, has to be large enough to cover the company's fixed operating expenses, its interest expense, and its income tax expense and still leave a residual amount of final, bottom-line profit (net income). In short, there are a lot of further demands on the stepping-stone measure of profit called contribution margin. Even if a business earns a reasonably good total contribution margin, it still isn't necessarily out of the woods because it has fixed operating expenses as well as interest and income tax.

 In this business example, contribution margin equals 22.6 percent of sales revenue ($8,973,615 contribution margin ÷ $39,661,250 sales revenue = 22.6%). For most management profit-making purposes, the contribution margin ratio is the most critical factor to watch closely and keep under control. Gross margin is important, to be sure, but the contribution margin ratio is even more important. The contribution margin is an important line of demarcation between the variable profit factors above the line and fixed expenses below the line.

Fixed Expenses

Virtually every business has fixed operating expenses as well as fixed depreciation expense. The company's fixed operating expenses were $5,739,250 for the year, which includes depreciation expense because it is a fixed amount recorded to the year regardless of whether the long-term operating assets of the business were used heavily or lightly during the period. Depreciation depends on the choice of accounting methods adopted to measure this expense—whether it be the level, straight-line method or a quicker accelerated method. Other fixed operating expenses are not so heavily dependent on the choice of accounting methods compared with depreciation.

Fixed means that these operating costs, for all practical purposes, remain the same for the year over a fairly broad range of sales activity—even if sales rise or fall by 20 or 30 percent. Examples of such fixed costs are employees on fixed salaries, office rent, annual property taxes, many types of insurance, and the CPA audit fee. Once-spent advertising is a fixed cost. Generally speaking, these cost commitments are decided in advance and cannot be changed over the short run. The longer the time horizon, on the other hand, the more these costs can be adjusted up or down.

For instance, persons on fixed salaries can be laid off, but they may be entitled to several months or perhaps one or more years of severance pay. Leases may not be renewed, but you have to wait to the end of the existing lease. Most fixed operating expenses are cash-based, which means that cash is paid out at or near the time the expense is recorded—though it must be mentioned that some of these costs have to be pre-paid (such as insurance) and many are paid after being recorded (such as the CPA audit fee).

 In passing, it should be noted that other assets are occasionally written down, though not according to any predetermined schedule as for depreciation. For example, inventory may have to be written down or marked down if the products cannot be sold or will have to be sold below cost. Inventory also has to be written down to recognize shrinkage due to shoplifting and employee theft. Accounts receivables may have to be written down if they are not fully collectible. (Inventory loss and bad debts are discussed again in later chapters.)

Managers definitely should know where such write-downs are being reported in the profit report. For instance, are inventory knockdowns included in cost-of-goods-sold expense? Are receivable write-offs in fixed operating expenses? Managers have to know what all is included in the basic accounts in their internal profit report (Figure 3.3). Such write-downs are generally fixed in amount and would not be reported as a variable expense—although if a certain percent of inventory shrinkage is normal then it should be included with the variable cost-of-goods-sold expense. The theory of putting it here is that to sell 100 units of product, the business may have to buy, say, 105 units because 5 units are stolen, damaged, or otherwise unsalable.

CONTRIBUTION MARGIN ANALYSIS

The next step in the decision analysis, based on the information in the management profit report (Figure 3.3), is to determine how much the business's variable operating expenses would increase based on the sales revenue increase and the sales volume increase. Figure 3.4 presents this analysis, and the results are not encouraging. The variable revenue-driven operating expenses would increase by the same percent as sales revenue, and the variable unit-driven expenses would increase by the same percent as sales volume. The result is that contribution margin would *decrease* $44,863 (see Figure 3.4). This is before taking into account what would happen to fixed operating expenses at the higher sales volume level.

Fixed operating expenses are those that are not sensitive to incremental changes in actual sales volume. However, a business can increase sales volume only so much before some of its fixed operating expenses have to be increased. For example, one fixed operating expense is the cost of warehouse space (rent, insurance, utilities, etc.). A 25 percent increase in sales volume may require the business to rent more warehouse

	For Year Just Ended	New Scenario	Change	Percent Change
Sales revenue	$39,661,250	$47,097,734	$7,436,484	18.75%
Cost-of-goods-sold expense	($24,960,750)	($31,200,938)	($6,240,188)	25.00%
Gross margin	$14,700,500	$15,896,796	$1,196,296	8.14%
Variable revenue-driven operating expenses	($ 3,049,010)	($ 3,620,700)	($ 571,690)	18.75%
Variable unit-driven operating expenses	($ 2,677,875)	($ 3,347,344)	($ 669,469)	25.00%
Contribution margin	$ 8,973,615	$ 8,928,752	($ 44,863)	−0.50%
Fixed operating expenses	($ 5,739,250)			
Earnings before interest and income tax (EBIT)	$ 3,234,365			
Interest expense	($ 795,000)			
Earnings before income tax	$ 2,439,365			
Income tax expense	($ 853,778)			
Net income	$ 1,585,587			

FIGURE 3.4 *Contribution margin analysis of sales price cut proposal.*

space. In any case, you may decide to break off the analysis at this point since contribution margin would decrease under the sales price cut proposal.

You might be tempted to pursue the sales price reduction plan in order to gain market share. Well, perhaps this would be a good move in the long run, even though it would not increase profit immediately. The point about market share reminds me of a line in a recent article in the *Wall Street Journal:* "Stop buying market share and start boosting profits." The sales price reduction proposal takes too big a bite out of profit margins, even though sales prices would be reduced only 5 percent. Even given a 25 percent sales volume spurt, you would see a decline in contribution margin even before taking into account any increases in fixed operating expenses.

END POINT

The external income statement is useful for management decision-making analysis, but only up to a point. It does not provide enough information about operating expense behavior. The internal profit report to managers adds this important information for decision-making analysis. In management profit reports, operating expenses are separated into variable and fixed, and variable expenses are further separated into those that vary with sales volume and those that vary with sales revenue dollars. The central importance of the proper classification of operating expenses cannot be overstated.

This chapter walks through the analysis of a proposal to reduce sales prices in order to stimulate a sizable increase in sales volume. Using information from the external income statement, the impact of the proposal on gross margin is analyzed. To complete the analysis, managers need the information about operating expenses that is reported in the internal profit report. After analyzing the changes in variable operating expenses, it is discovered that contribution margin (profit before fixed operating expenses are deducted) would actually decrease if the sales price reduction were implemented. Furthermore, the sizable increase in sales volume raises the possibility that fixed operating expenses might have to be increased to accommodate such a large jump in sales volume.

Future chapters look beyond just the profit impact and consider other financial effects of changes in sales volume, sales revenue, and expenses—in particular, the impacts on cash flow from profit. A basic profit model and basic cash flow from profit model are developed in future chapters and applied to a variety of decision situations facing business managers. The discussion in this chapter is for the company as a whole (i.e., assuming all sales prices would be reduced). Of course, in actual business situations sales price changes are more narrowly focused on particular products or product lines. The profit model developed in later chapters can be applied to any segment or profit module of the business.

Interpreting Financial Statements

F Financial statements are the main and often the only source
of information to the lenders and the outside investors regarding a business's financial performance and condition. In addition to reading through the financial statements, they use
certain *ratios* calculated from the figures in the financial
statements to evaluate the profit performance and financial
position of the business. These key ratios are very important
to managers as well, to say the least. The ratios are part of the
language of business. It would be embarrassing to a manager
to display his or her ignorance of any of these financial specifications for a business.

A FEW OBSERVATIONS AND CAUTIONS

This chapter focuses on the financial statements included in
external financial reports to investors. These financial reports
circulate outside the business; once released by a business, its
financial statements can end up in the hands of almost anyone, even its competitors. The amounts reported in external
financial statements are at a *summary level;* the detailed
information used by managers is not disclosed in external
financial statements. External financial statements disclose a
good deal of information to its investors and lenders that they
need to know, but no more. There are definite limits on the
information divulged in external financial statements. For

instance, a business does not present a list of its major customers or stockholders in its external financial statements.

External financial statements are *general purpose* in nature and *comprehensive* of the entire business. The amounts reported for some assets—in particular, inventories and fixed assets—may be fairly old costs, going back several years. As mentioned in Chapter 2, assets are not marked up to current market values. The current replacement values of assets are not reported in external financial statements.

Profit accounting depends on many good faith *estimates*. Managers have to predict the useful lives of its fixed assets for recording annual depreciation expense. They have to estimate how much of its accounts receivable may not be collectible, which is charged off to bad debts expense. Managers have to estimate how much to write down its inventories and charge to expense for products that cannot be sold or will have to be sold at prices below cost. For products already sold, they have to forecast the future costs of warranty and guarantee work, which is charged to expense in the period of recording the sales. Managers have to predict several key variables that determine the cost of its employees' retirement plan. The amount of retirement benefit cost that is recorded to expense in the current year depends heavily on these estimates.

Because so many estimates have to be made in recording expenses, the net income amount in an income statement should be taken with a grain of salt. This bottom-line profit number could have been considerably higher or lower. Much depends on the estimates made by the managers in recording its sales and expenses—as well as which particular accounting methods are selected (more on this later).

I don't like to say it, but in many cases the managers of a business manipulate its external financial statements to one degree or another. Managers influence or actually dictate which estimates are used in recording expenses (just mentioned). Managers also decide on the timing of recording sales revenue and certain expenses. Managers massage sales revenue and expenses numbers in order to achieve preestablished targets for net income and to smooth the year-to-year fluctuations of net income. Managers should be careful, however. It's one thing to iron out the wrinkles and fluff up the pillows in the financial statements, but if managers go too far, they may cross the line and commit financial fraud for which they are legally liable.

Financial statements of public corporations are required to have annual audits by an independent CPA firm; many private companies also opt to have annual CPA audits. However, CPA auditors don't necessarily catch all errors and fraud. With or without audits, there's a risk that the financial statements are in error or that the business has deliberately prepared false and misleading financial statements. During the past decade, an alarming number of public corporations have had to go back and restate their profit reports following the discovery of fraud and grossly misleading accounting. This is most disturbing. Investors and lenders depend on the reliability of the information in financial statements. They do not have an alternative source for this information—only the financial statements.

PREMISES AND PRINCIPLES OF FINANCIAL STATEMENTS

The shareowners of a business are entitled to receive on a regular basis financial statements and other financial information about the business. Financial statements are the main means of communication by which the management of a business renders an accounting, or a summing-up, of their stewardship of the business entrusted to them by the investors in the business. The quarterly and annual financial reports of a business to its owners contain other information. However, the main purpose of a financial report is to submit financial statements to shareowners.

Generally accepted accounting principles (GAAP) and financial reporting standards have been extensively developed over the last half century. These guidelines rest on one key premise— the separation of management of a business from the outside investors in the business. In the formulation of GAAP it is assumed that financial statements are for those who have supplied the ownership capital to a business but who are not directly involved in managing the business. Financial statements are prepared for the "absentee owners" of a business, in other words. GAAP and financial reporting standards do not ignore the need for information by the lenders to a business.

But the shareowners of the business are the main constituency for whom financial statements are prepared.

Federal law governs the communication of financial information by businesses whose capital stock shares are traded on public markets. The federal securities laws are enforced mainly by the Securities and Exchange Commission (SEC), which was established in 1934. Also, the New York Stock Exchange, Nasdaq, and other securities markets enforce many rules and regulations regarding the release and communication of financial information by companies whose securities are traded on their markets. For instance, a business cannot selectively leak information to some stockholders or lenders and not to others, nor can a business tip off some of them before informing others later. The laws and requirements of financial reporting are designed to ensure that all stockholders and lenders have equal access to a company's financial information and financial statements.

A business's financial statements may not be the first news about its profit performance. Public corporations put out press releases concerning their earnings for the period just ended before the company releases its actual financial statements. Privately owned businesses do not usually send out letters about profit performance in advance of releasing their financial statements—although they *could* do this.

Financial Statements Example

Chapter 3 introduced the external income statement for a business, followed by the internal management profit report for the business. Now the *complete set* of financial statements for the business is presented, which consists of the following:

- Income statement for the year just ended (Figure 4.1)
- Statement of financial condition at the close of the year just ended and at the close of the preceding year (Figure 4.2)
- Statement of cash flows for the year just ended (Figure 4.3)
- Statement of changes in stockholders' equity for the year just ended (Figure 4.4)

 The income statement ranks first in terms of readability and intuitive understandability. Most people understand that profit equals revenue less expenses, although the technical jargon in

Sales revenue	$39,661,250
Cost-of-goods-sold expense	$24,960,750
Gross margin	$14,700,500
Selling and administrative expenses	$11,466,135
Earnings before interest and income tax	$ 3,234,365
Interest expense	$ 795,000
Earnings before income tax	$ 2,439,365
Income tax expense	$ 853,778
Net income	$ 1,585,587
Earnings per share*	$ 3.75

*Privately owned business corporations do not have to report earnings per share; publicly owned corporations are required to disclose this key ratio in their income statements.

FIGURE 4.1 *Income statement for the year just ended.*

income statements is a barrier to many readers. The balance sheet (or statement of financial condition) ranks second. Assets and liabilities are familiar to most people—although the values reported in this financial statement are not immediately obvious to many readers. The statement of cash flows is presented in a very technical format that makes the statement very difficult to read, even for sophisticated investors.

The *footnotes* that accompany the company's financial statements are not presented here for the business. Footnotes often run several pages. Footnotes, although difficult and time-consuming to read through, contain very important information. Stock analysts and investment managers scour the footnotes in financial reports, digging for important information about the business. The footnotes are not needed for explaining financial statement ratios. (For a discussion of footnotes, see Chapter 16 in my book *How to Read a Financial Report,* 5th ed., John Wiley & Sons, 1999.)

Publicly owned businesses present their financial statements in a format that compares the most recent three years (as required by SEC rules). The three-year comparative format makes it easier to follow trends, of course. Many privately

Assets

	At Close of Year Just Ended	At Close of Preceding Year
Cash	$ 2,345,675	$ 2,098,538
Accounts receivable	$ 3,813,582	$ 3,467,332
Inventories	$ 5,760,173	$ 4,661,423
Prepaid expenses	$ 822,899	$ 770,024
Total current assets	$12,742,329	$10,997,317
Property, plant, and equipment	$20,857,500	$18,804,030
Accumulated depreciation	($ 6,785,250)	($ 6,884,100)
Cost less accumulated depreciation	$14,072,250	$11,919,930
Total assets	$26,814,579	$22,917,247

Liabilities and Owners' Equity

Accounts payable	$ 2,537,232	$ 2,180,682
Accrued expenses payable	$ 1,280,214	$ 1,136,369
Income tax payable	$ 58,650	$ 117,300
Short-term debt	$ 2,250,000	$ 1,765,000
Total current liabilities	$ 6,126,096	$ 5,199,351
Long-term debt	$ 7,500,000	$ 5,850,000
Total liabilities	$13,626,096	$11,049,351
Capital stock (422,823 and 420,208 shares)	$ 4,587,500	$ 4,402,500
Retained earnings	$ 8,600,983	$ 7,465,396
Total owners' equity	$13,188,483	$11,867,896
Total liabilities and owners' equity	$26,814,579	$22,917,247

FIGURE 4.2 *Statement of financial condition at close of the year just ended and at close of the preceding year.*

owned businesses present their financial statements for two or three years, although practice is not uniform in this respect.

The company's income statement (Figure 4.1) and statement of cash flows (Figure 4.3) are presented for the most recent year only. The statement of financial condition (Figure 4.2) is presented at the close of its two most recent two years. Financial statement ratios are calculated for each year. The ratios are calculated the same way for all years for which financial

Cash Flows from Operating Activities

Net income	$1,585,587
Changes in operating assets and liabilities:	
Accounts receivable	($ 346,250)
Inventories	($1,098,750)
Prepaid expenses	($ 52,875)
Depreciation expense	$ 768,450
Accounts payable	$ 356,550
Accrued expenses payable	$ 143,845
Income tax payable	($ 58,650)
Cash flow from operating activities	$1,297,907

Cash Flows from Investing Activities

Investment in property, plant, and equipment	($3,186,250)
Proceeds from disposals of property, plant, and equipment	$ 265,480
Cash used in investing activities	($2,920,770)

Cash Flows from Financing Activities

Net increase in short-term debt	$ 485,000
Increase in long-term debt	$1,650,000
Issuance of capital stock shares	$ 185,000
Cash dividends to stockholders	($ 450,000)
Cash from financing activities	$1,870,000
Cash increase during year	$ 247,137
Cash balance at beginning of year	$2,098,538
Cash balance at end of year	$2,345,675

FIGURE 4.3 *Statement of cash flows for the year just ended.*

statements are presented. As a general rule, only a few ratios are presented in most financial reports. Thus investors and lenders have to calculate ratios or look in financial information sources that report the financial statement ratios for businesses.

The business in this example is a corporation that is owned by a relatively small number of persons who invested the capital to start the business some years ago. The business has over $39 million annual sales (see Figure 4.1). Many publicly owned corporations are much larger than this, and most privately owned businesses are smaller. Size is not the point, however.

	Capital Stock	Retained Earnings
Beginning balances (420,208 shares)	$4,402,500	$7,465,396
Net income for year		$1,585,587
Shares issued during year (2,615 shares)	$ 185,000	
Dividends paid during year		($ 450,000)
Ending balances (422,823 shares)	$4,587,500	$8,600,983

FIGURE 4.4 *Statement of changes in stockholders' equity for the year just ended.*

The techniques of financial analysis and the ratios discussed in the chapter are appropriate for any size of business.

LIMITS OF DISCUSSION

The chapter does not pretend to cover the broad field of *securities analysis* (i.e., the analysis of stocks and debt securities issued by public corporations that are traded in public marketplaces). This broad field includes the analysis of the competitive advantages and disadvantages of a business, domestic and international economic developments affecting a business, business combination possibilities, political developments, court decisions, technological advances, demographics, investor psychology, and much more. The key ratios explained in this chapter are the basic building blocks used in securities analysis.

The chapter does not discuss *trend analysis,* which involves comparing a company's latest financial statements with its previous years' statements to identify important year-to-year changes. For example, investors and lenders are very interested in the sales growth or decline of a business and the resulting impact on profit performance, cash flows, and financial condition. The chapter has a more modest objective—to explain the basic ratios used in financial statement analysis. Only a handful of ratios are discussed in the chapter, but they are extremely important and widely used.

The business example does not include any *extraordinary gains or losses* for the year. *Extraordinary* means onetime, nonrecurring events. For example, a business may sell off or abandon a major segment of its operations and record a large loss or gain. A business may record a substantial loss caused by a major restructuring or downsizing of the organization to recognize the cost of terminating employees who will receive severance packages or early-retirement bonuses. A business may lose a major lawsuit and have to pay a huge fine or damage award. A business may write off most of its inventories due to a sudden fall in demand for its products. The list goes on and on. These nonordinary, unusual gains and losses are reported separately from the ongoing, continuing operations of a company.

DANGER!

Extraordinary gains and losses are very frustrating in analyzing profit performance for investors, creditors, and managers alike. Making matters worse is that many businesses record huge amounts of extraordinary losses in one fell swoop in order to clear the decks of these costs and losses in future years. This is called "taking a big bath." Quite clearly, many managers prefer this practice. In public discussions, the investment community wrings their hands and lambastes this practice, as you see in many articles and editorials in the financial press. However, I think many investors would admit in private that they prefer that a business take a big bath in one year and thereby escape losses and expenses in future years. The thinking is that taking a big bath allows a business to start over by putting bad news behind it, wiping the slate clean so that future years escape these charges.

PROFIT RATIOS

Owners take the risk of whether their business can earn a profit and sustain its profit performance over the years. How much would you be willing to pay for a business that reports a loss year after year? The value of the owners' investment depends first and foremost on the profit performance of the business. Making sales and controlling expenses is how a business makes profit, of course. The profit residual from sales revenue is measured by a *return-on-sales ratio,* which equals a particular measure of profit divided by sales revenue for the period. An income statement reports several profit lines, beginning with *gross margin* down to bottom-line *net income.*

Figure 4.5 shows four profit ratios for the business example; each ratio equals the profit on that line divided by sales revenue. These return-on-sales profit ratios are *not* required to be disclosed in the income statement. Generally speaking, businesses do not report profit ratios with their external income statements, although many companies comment on one or more of their profit ratios elsewhere in their financial reports. Managers should pay very close attention to the profit ratios of their business of course.

The company's net income return on sales ratio is 4.0 percent ($1,585,587 net income ÷ $39,661,250 sales revenue = 4.0%). From each $100.00 of its sales revenue, the business earned $4.00 net income and had expenses of $96.00. The net income profit ratio varies quite markedly from one industry to another. Some businesses do well with only a 1 or 2 percent return on sales; others need more than 10 percent to justify the large amount of capital invested in their assets.

A popular misconception of many people is that most businesses rip off the public because they keep 20, 30, or more percent of their sales revenue as bottom-line profit. In fact, very few businesses earn more than a 10 percent bottom-line profit on sales. If you don't believe me, scan a sample of 50 or 100 earnings reports in the *Wall Street Journal* or the *New York Times*. The 4.0 percent net income profit ratio in the

Income Statement		Profit Ratios
Sales revenue	$39,661,250	
Cost-of-goods-sold expense	$24,960,750	
Gross margin	$14,700,500	37.1%
Selling and administrative expenses	$11,466,135	
Earnings before interest and income tax	$ 3,234,365	8.2%
Interest expense	$ 795,000	
Earnings before income tax	$ 2,439,365	6.2%
Income tax expense	$ 853,778	
Net income	$ 1,585,587	4.0%

FIGURE 4.5 *Return-on-sales profit ratios.*

example is not untypical, although 4.0 percent is a little low compared with most businesses.

Serious investors watch all the profit ratios shown in Figure 4.5. The first ratio—the gross margin return-on-sales ratio—is the starting point for the other profit ratios. Gross margin (also called *gross profit*) equals sales revenue minus only cost-of-goods-sold expense. The company's gross margin equals 37.1 percent of sales revenue (see Figure 4.5). If its gross margin ratio is too low, a business typically cannot compensate for this serious deficiency in gross margin by cutting other operating expenses, so its bottom line suffers. An inadequate gross margin cascades down to the bottom line, in other words. Therefore investors keep a close watch for any slippage in a company's gross margin profit ratio. Investors and stock analysts keep a close eye on year-to-year trends in profit ratios to test whether a business is able to maintain its profit margins over time. Slippage in profit ratios is viewed with some alarm. A business's profit ratios are compared with its main competitors' profit ratios as a way to test of the comparative marketing strength of the business. Higher than average profit ratios are often evidence that a business has developed very strong brand names for its products or has nurtured other competitive advantages.

BOOK VALUE PER SHARE

Suppose I tell you that the market price of a stock is $60.00 per share and ask you whether this value is too high, too low, or just about right. You could compare the $60.00 market price with the stockholders' equity per share reported in its most recent balance sheet—which is called the *book value per share*. The book value per share in the business example (see Figure 4.2) equals $31.19 ($13,188,483 total owners' equity ÷ 422,823 capital stock shares = $31.19). Book value per share has a respectable history in securities analysis. The classic book, *Security Analysis*, by Benjamin Graham and David Dodd, puts a fair amount of weight on the book value behind a share of stock.

 Just the other day I read an article in the business section of the *New York Times* that was very critical of a business. Among several cogent points discussed in the article was the fact that the current market price of its stock was 29 percent below its book value. Generally speaking, the market value of stocks is higher than their book values. The reason for the comment in the article is that when a stock trades below its book value, the investors trading in the stock are of the opinion that the stock is not worth even its book value. But book value is backed up by the assets of the business.

To illustrate this point, suppose the business in the example were to liquate all its assets at the amounts reported in its balance sheet, then pay off all its liabilities, and finally distribute the money left over to its stockholders. Each share of stock would receive cash equal to the book value per share, or $31.19 per share. So book value is a theoretical liquidation value per share. From this point of view, the market value of the shares should not fall below $31.19. But the profit prospects of the business may be very dim; the stockholders may not see much chance of improving profit performance in the near future. They may think that the business could not sell off its assets at their book values and that no one would pay book value for the business as a whole.

Of course, most businesses do not plan to liquidate their assets and go out of business in the foreseeable future. They plan to continue as a going concern and make a profit, at least for as far ahead as they can see. Therefore the dominant factor in determining the market value of capital stock shares is the *earnings potential* of the business, not the book value of its ownership shares. The best place to start in assessing the earning potential of a business is its most recent earnings performance.

Suppose I owned 10,000 capital stock shares of the business in the example and you were interested in buying my shares. What price would you offer for my shares? You've studied the financial statements of the business, and you predict that the business will probably improve its profit performance in the future. So you might be willing to pay $40, $50, or higher per share for my stock, which is based on your assessment of the future earnings potential of the business. Private corporations have no readily available market value information for their capital stock shares. So you're on your own regarding what price to pay for my stock shares.

Stockholders in public corporations have market value information at their fingertips, which is reported in the *Wall*

Street Journal, the *New York Times, Barron's, Investor's Business Daily,* and many other sources of financial market information. They know the prices at which buyers and sellers are trading stocks. The main factor driving the market price of a stock is its *earnings per share.*

EARNINGS PER SHARE

The income statement presented in Figure 4.1 includes *earnings per share* (EPS), which is $3.75 for the year just ended. Privately owned businesses whose capital stock shares are not traded in public markets do not have to report their earnings per share, and most don't. I include it in Figure 4.1 because publicly owned businesses whose capital stock shares are traded in a public marketplace (such as the New York Stock Exchange or Nasdaq) are required to report EPS.

Earnings per share (EPS) is calculated as follows for the business (see Figures 4.1 and 4.2 for data):

$$\frac{\$1{,}585{,}587 \text{ net income available for stockholders}}{422{,}823 \text{ total number of outstanding capital stock shares}}$$

$$= \$3.75 \text{ basic EPS}$$

For greater accuracy, the *weighted average* number of shares outstanding during the year should be used to calculate EPS—which takes into account that some shares may have been issued and outstanding only part of the year. Also, a business may have reduced the number of its outstanding shares during part of the year. I use the ending number of shares to make it easier to follow the computation of EPS.

KEY CONCEPT The numerator (top number) in the EPS ratio is *net income available for common stockholders,* which equals bottom-line net income minus dividends paid to preferred stockholders of the business. Many business corporations issue preferred stock shares that require a fixed amount of dividends to be paid each year. The total of annual dividends to the preferred stockholders is deducted from net income to determine net income available for the common stockholders. The business in the example has issued only one class of capital stock shares. It has not issued any preferred stock, so all its net income is available for its common stock shares.

Basic and Diluted EPS

Please notice the word *basic* in the preceding EPS calculation. Basic means that the *actual number* of common stock shares in the hands of stockholders is used as the denominator (bottom number) for calculating EPS. If a business were to issue more shares, the denominator would become larger and EPS would decrease. The larger number of shares would dilute EPS. In fact many business corporations have entered into contracts that oblige them to issue additional stock shares in the future. These shares have not yet been issued, but the business is legally committed to issue more shares in the future. In other words, there is the potential that the number of capital stock shares will be inflated and net income will have to be divided over a larger number of stock shares.

Many public businesses award their high-level managers *stock options* that give them the right to buy stock shares at fixed prices. These fixed purchase prices generally are set equal to the market price at the time the stock options are granted. The idea is to give the managers an incentive to improve the profit performance of the business, which should drive up the market price of its stock shares. When (and if) the market value of the stock shares rises, the managers exercise their rights and buy stock shares at the lower prices fixed in their option contracts. Managers can make millions of dollars by exercising their stock options. There is a wealth transfer from the nonmanagement stockholders to some of the management stockholders because the market price per share is lower than it would have been if shares had not been issued to the managers.

The calculation of basic EPS does *not* recognize the additional shares that may be issued when management stock options are exercised in the future. Also, some businesses issue convertible bonds and convertible preferred stock that at the option of the security holders can be traded in for common stock shares based on predetermined exchange rates. Conversions of senior securities into shares of common stock also cause dilution of EPS.

To alert investors to the potential effects of management stock options and convertible securities, a *second* EPS is calculated by public corporations, which is called the *diluted EPS*. This lower EPS takes into account the effects on EPS that would be caused by the issue of additional common stock shares under terms of management stock option plans and convertible securities (plus any other commitments a business has entered into that requires it to issue additional stock shares in the future). Both basic EPS and diluted EPS (if applicable) are reported in the income statements of publicly owned business corporations. The diluted EPS is a more conservative figure on which to base market value.

MARKET VALUE RATIOS

The capital stock shares of more than 10,000 business corporations are traded on public markets—the New York Stock Exchange, Nasdaq, and other stock exchanges. The day-to-day market price changes of these shares receive a great deal of attention, to say the least. More than any other factor, the market value of capital stock shares depends on the earnings per share performance of a business—its past performance and its future profit potential. It's difficult to prove whether basic EPS or diluted EPS is the driver of market value. In many cases the two are very close and the gap is not significant. In some cases, however, the spread between the two EPS figures is fairly large.

 In addition to earnings per share (EPS) investors in stock shares of publicly owned companies closely follow two other ratios: (1) the *dividend yield ratio* and (2) the *price/earnings ratio* (P/E). The dividend yield and P/E ratios are reported in the stock trading tables published in the *Wall Street Journal,* which demonstrates the importance of these two market value ratios for stock shares.

Dividend Yield Ratio

The dividend yield ratio equals the amount of cash dividends per share during the most recent, or trailing, 12 months divided by the current market price of a stock share. The dividend yield ratio is the measure of cash income from a share of stock based on its current market price. The annual return on an investment in stock shares includes both the cash dividends received during the period and the gain or loss in market value of the stock shares over the period. The calculation of the historical rate of return for a stock investment over two or more years and for a stock index such as the Dow Jones 30 Industrial or the Standard & Poor's 500 assumes that cash dividends have been reinvested in additional shares of stock. Of course, individual investors may decide not to reinvest their dividends. They may spend their dividend income or put the cash flow into other investments.

Price/Earnings Ratio

The market price of stock shares of a public business is divided by its most recent annual EPS to determine the *price/earnings ratio:*

$$\frac{\text{Current market price of stock share}}{\text{Earnings per share (either basic or diluted EPS)}}$$

$$= \text{price/earning ratio, or P/E}$$

Suppose a company's stock shares are trading at $60.00 per share and its EPS for the most recent year (called the *trailing* 12 months) is $3.00. Thus, its P/E ratio is 20. By the way, the *Wall Street Journal* uses diluted EPS to report P/E ratios in its stock trading tables. Like the other ratios discussed in this chapter, the P/E ratio is compared with industrywide and marketwide averages to judge whether it's too high or too low. I remember when a P/E ratio of 8 was typical. Today P/E ratios of 20 or higher are common.

The stock shares of a privately owned business are not actively traded, and thus the market value of its shares is difficult to ascertain. When shares do change hands occasionally, the price is usually kept private between the seller and buyer. Nevertheless, stockholders in these businesses are interested in what their shares are worth. To estimate the value of their stock shares, a P/E multiple can be used. In the example, the company's EPS is $3.75 for the most recent year (see Figure 4.1). Suppose you own some of the capital stock shares and someone offers to buy your shares. You could establish an offer price at, say, 12 times basic EPS, which is $45 per share. The potential buyer may not be willing to pay this price, of course. Or he or she might be willing to pay 15 or even 18 times EPS.

DEBT-PAYING-ABILITY RATIOS

If a business cannot pay its liabilities on time, bad things can happen. *Solvency* refers to the ability of a business to pay its liabilities when they come due. Maintaining solvency (debt-paying ability) is essential for every business. If a business defaults on its debt obligations it becomes vulnerable to legal proceedings by its lenders that could stop the company in its tracks, or at least seriously interfere with its normal operations.

Therefore, investors and lenders are very interested in the general solvency and debt-paying ability of a business. Bankers and other lenders, when deciding whether to make and renew loans to a business, direct their attention to certain solvency ratios. These ratios provide a useful profile of the business for assessing its creditworthiness and for judging the ability of the business to pay its loans and interest on time.

Short-Term Solvency Test: The Current Ratio

The *current ratio* is used to test the short-term liability-paying ability of a business. The current ratio is calculated by dividing total current assets by total current liabilities. From the data in the company's balance sheet (Figure 4.2), its current ratio is computed as follows:

$$\frac{\$12{,}742{,}329 \text{ current assets}}{\$6{,}126{,}096 \text{ current liabilities}} = 2.08 \text{ current ratio}$$

The current ratio is hardly ever expressed as a percent (which would be 208 percent in this case). The current ratio is stated as 2.08 to 1.00 for this company, or more simply just as 2.08. The general expectation is that the current ratio for a business should be 2 to 1 or higher. Most businesses find that their creditors expect them to maintain this minimum current ratio. In other words, short-term creditors generally prefer that a business limit its current liabilities to one-half or less of its current assets.

Why do short-term creditors put this limit on a business? The main reason is to provide a safety cushion for payment of its short-term liabilities. A current ratio of 2 to 1 means there is $2 of cash and assets that should be converted into cash during the near future to pay each $1 of current liabilities that come due in roughly the same time period. Each dollar of short-term liabilities is backed up with two dollars of cash on hand plus near-term cash inflows. The extra dollar of current assets provides a margin of safety.

In summary, short-term sources of credit generally demand that a company's current assets be double its current liabilities. After all, creditors are not owners—they don't share in the profit success of the business. The income on their loans is limited to the interest they charge. As creditors, they quite properly minimize their loan risks; they are not compensated to take on much risk.

Acid Test Ratio, or Quick Ratio

Inventory is many weeks away from conversion into cash. Products usually are held two, three, or four months before being sold. If sales are made on credit, which is normal when one business sells to another business, there's a second waiting period before accounts receivables are collected. In short, inventory is not nearly as liquid as accounts receivable; it takes a lot longer to convert inventory into cash. Furthermore, there's no guarantee that all the products in inventory will be sold, or sold above cost.

A more severe test of the short-term liability-paying ability of a business is the *acid test ratio,* which excludes inventory (and prepaid expenses also). Only cash, marketable securities investments (if the business has any), and accounts receivable are counted as sources available to pay the current liabilities of the business. This ratio is also called the *quick ratio* because only cash and assets quickly convertible into cash are included in the amount available for paying current liabilities.

The example company's acid test ratio is calculated as follows (the business has no investments in marketable securities):

$$\frac{\$2,345,675 \text{ cash} + \$3,813,582 \text{ accounts receivable}}{\$6,126,096 \text{ total current liabilities}}$$

$$= 1.01 \text{ acid test ratio}$$

 The general expectation is that a company's acid test ratio should be 1:1 or better, although you find many more exceptions to this rule than to the 2:1 current ratio standard.

Debt-to-Equity Ratio

Some debt is good, but too much is dangerous. The *debt-to-equity ratio* is an indicator of whether a company is using debt prudently or is overburdened with debt that could cause problems. The example company's debt-to-equity ratio is calculated as follows (see Figure 4.2 for data):

$$\frac{\$13{,}626{,}096 \text{ total liabilities}}{\$13{,}188{,}483 \text{ total stockholders' equity}}$$

$$= 1.03 \text{ debt-to-equity ratio}$$

This ratio reveals that the company is using $1.03 of liabilities for each $1.00 of stockholders' equity. Notice that *all* liabilities (non-interest-bearing as well as interest-bearing, and both short-term and long-term) are included in this ratio. Most industrial businesses stay below a 1 to 1 debt-to-equity ratio. They don't want to take on too much debt, or they cannot convince lenders to put up more than one-half of their assets. On the other hand, some businesses are much more aggressive and operate with large ratios of debt to equity. Public utilities and financial institutions have much higher debt-to-equity ratios than 1 to 1.

Times Interest Earned

To pay interest on its debt a business needs sufficient earnings before interest and income tax (EBIT). To test the ability to pay interest, the *times-interest-earned ratio* is calculated. For the example, annual earnings before interest and income tax is divided by interest expense as follows (see Figure 4.1 for data):

$$\frac{\$3{,}234{,}365 \text{ earnings before interest and income tax}}{\$795{,}000 \text{ interest expense}}$$

$$= 4.07 \text{ times interest earned}$$

There is no standard guideline for this particular ratio, although obviously the ratio should be higher than 1 to 1. In this example the company's earnings before interest and income tax is more than four times its annual interest expense, which is comforting from the lender's point of view. Lenders would be very alarmed if a business barely covered its annual interest expense. The company's management should be equally alarmed, of course.

ASSET TURNOVER RATIOS

A business has to keep its assets busy, both to remain solvent and to be efficient in making profit. Inactive assets are an albatross around the neck of the business. Slow-moving assets can cause serious trouble. Investors and lenders use certain *turnover ratios* as indicators of how well a business is using its assets and to test whether some assets are sluggish and might pose a serious problem.

Accounts Receivable Turnover Ratio

Accounts receivable should be collected on time and not allowed to accumulate beyond the normal credit term offered to customers. To get a sense of how well the business is controlling its accounts receivable, the *accounts receivable turnover ratio* is calculated as follows (see Figures 4.1 and 4.2 for data):

$$\frac{\$39,661,250 \text{ annual sales revenue}}{\$3,813,582 \text{ accounts receivable}} = 10.4 \text{ times}$$

The accounts receivable turnover ratio is one of the ratios published by business financial information services such as Dun & Bradstreet, Standard & Poor's, and Moody's. In this example, the business "turns" its customers' receivables a little more than 10 times a year, which indicates that it waits about a tenth of a year on average to collect its receivables from credit sales. This appears reasonable, assuming that the business extends one-month credit to its customers. (A turnover of 12 would be even better.)

Inventory Turnover Ratio

In the business example, the company sells products. Virtually every company that sells products carries an inventory, or stockpile of products, for a period of time before the products are sold and delivered to customers. The holding period depends on the nature of business. Supermarkets have short holding periods; retail furniture stores have fairly long inventory holding periods. Products should not be held in inventory longer than necessary. Holding inventory is subject to several risks and accrues several costs. Products may become obsolete, may be stolen, may be damaged, or may even be misplaced.

Products have to be stored, usually have to be insured, and may have to be guarded. And the capital invested in inventory has a cost, of course.

To get a feel for how long the business holds its inventory before sale, investors and lenders calculate the *inventory turnover ratio* as follows (see Figures 4.1 and 4.2 for data):

$$\frac{\$24,960,750 \text{ cost-of-goods sold expense}}{\$5,760,173 \text{ inventories}} = 4.3 \text{ times}$$

The inventory turnover ratio is another of the ratios published by business information service organizations. The company's 4.3 inventory turnover ratio indicates that it holds products about one-fourth of a year before selling them. The inventory turnover ratio is compared with the averages for the industry and with previous years of the business.

Asset Turnover Ratio

The *asset turnover ratio* is a test of how well a business is using its assets overall. This ratio is computed by dividing annual sales revenue by total assets (see Figures 4.1 and 4.2 for data):

$$\frac{\$39,661,250 \text{ annual sales revenue}}{\$26,814,579 \text{ total assets}} = 1.5 \text{ times}$$

This ratio reveals that the business made $1.50 in sales for every $1.00 of total assets. Conversely, the business needed $1.00 of assets to make $1.50 of sales during the year. The ratio tells us that business is relatively asset heavy. The asset turnover ratio is compared with the averages for the industry and with previous years of the business.

END POINT

Individual investors, investment managers, stock analysts, lenders, and credit rating services commonly use the financial statement and market value ratios explained in this chapter. Business managers use the ratios to keep watch on how their business is doing and whether there might be some trouble spots that need attention. Nevertheless, the ratios are not a panacea.

A financial statement ratio is like your body temperature. A normal temperature is good and means that probably nothing serious is wrong, though not necessarily. A very high or low temperature means something probably is wrong, but it takes an additional diagnosis to discover the problem. Financial statement ratios are like measures of vital signs such as your pulse rate, blood pressure, cholesterol level, body fat, and so on. Financial ratios are the vital signs of a business.

There's no end to the number of ratios than can be calculated from financial statements. The trick is to focus on a reasonable number of ratios that have the most interpretive value. Calculating the ratios takes time. Many investors and lenders do not actually calculate the ratios. They do "eyeball tests" instead of computing ratios. They visually compare the two numbers in the ratio and do rough arithmetic in their heads to see if anything appears to be out of whack. For example, they observe that current assets are more than twice current liabilities. They do not bother to calculate the exact measure of the current ratio. This is a practical and time-saving technique as opposed to calculating ratios. Many investors and lenders use the financial statement ratios published by information service providers who compile data and information on thousands of businesses.

PART 2

Assets and Sources of Capital

Building a Balance Sheet

This chapter identifies and explains the various assets and liabilities used by a business in making profit. A business invests in a portfolio of operating assets and takes on certain operating liabilities in the process of making sales and incurring expenses. The main theme of the chapter is that the profit making activities of a business (revenue and expenses) drive the assets and liabilities that make up its balance sheet.

SIZING UP TOTAL ASSETS

Figure 5.1 presents an abbreviated income statement for a business's most recent year. Previous chapters explain that income statements include more information about expenses and do not stop at the earnings before interest and income tax (EBIT) line of profit. Interest and income tax expenses are deducted to arrive at bottom-line net income. However, the condensed and truncated income statement shown in Figure 5.1 is just fine for the purpose at hand.

 This business example, like the examples in earlier chapters, is a hypothetical but realistic composite based on a variety of financial reports over the years. Any particular business you look at will differ in one or more respects from the example. Some businesses are smaller or larger than the one in the example; their annual sales revenue may be lower or higher.

Note: Amounts are in in millions of dollars.

Sales revenue	$52.0
Cost-of-goods-sold expense	$31.2
Gross margin	$20.8
Operating expenses	$16.9
Earnings before interest and income tax (EBIT)	$ 3.9

FIGURE 5.1 *Abbreviated income statement.*

The business in the example sells products, and therefore it has cost-of-goods sold expense. Many businesses sell services instead of products, and they don't have this expense. But the example serves as a good general-purpose template that has broad applicability across many lines of businesses.

A final comment about the example: I selected annual sales of $52 million as a convenient figure to work with (i.e., $1 million sales per week). This simplifies the computations in the following discussion and avoids diverting attention from the main points and spending too much time on number crunching.

Two Key Questions

Block by block this chapter builds the foundation of assets the business used to make sales of $52 million and to squeeze out $3.9 million profit (EBIT) from its sales revenue. Let me immediately put a question to you: What amount of total assets would you estimate that the business used in making annual sales of $52 million? Annual sales divided by total assets is called the *asset turnover ratio* (see Chapter 4). Indirectly, what I'm asking you is this: What do you think the asset turnover ratio might be for the business?

 The asset turnover ratios of businesses that manufacture and sell products tend to cluster in the range between 1.5 and 2.0. In other words, their annual sales revenue equals 1.5 to 2 times total assets for these kinds of businesses. To keep the arithmetic easy to follow in the discussion, assume that the total assets of the business in the example are $26 million. So its asset turnover ratio is 2.0: ($52 million annual sales revenue ÷ $26 million total assets = 2.0). An asset turnover ratio of 2.0 is on the high side, but I'll stick with it in the first part of the chapter.

KEY CONCEPT The second question is this: Where did the business get the $26 million invested in its assets? The money for investing in assets comes from two different sources—liabilities and owners' equity. This point is summarized in the well-known accounting equation:

$$\text{Assets} = \text{liabilities} + \text{owners' equity}$$

The accounting equation is the basis for double-entry book-keeping. The balance sheet takes its name from the balance between assets on one side of the equation and liabilities plus owners' equity on the other. The balance sheet is the financial statement that reports a business's assets, liabilities, and owners' equity accounts.

Return on Assets

The business used $26 million total assets to earn $3.9 million before interest and income tax, or EBIT. Dividing EBIT by total assets gives the rate of *return on assets* (ROA) earned by the business. In the example, the business earned a 15.0 percent ROA for the year ($3.9 million EBIT ÷ $26 million total assets = 15.0%). Is this ROA merely adequate, fairly good, or very good? Well, relative to what benchmark or point of reference?

The business has borrowed money for part of the total $26 million total capital invested in its assets. The average annual interest rate on its debt is 8.0 percent. Relative to this annual interest rate the company's 15.0 percent ROA is more than adequate. Indeed, the favorable spread between these two rates works to the advantage of the business owners. The business borrows money at 8.0 percent and manages to earn 15.0 percent on the money. Chapter 6 explores the very important issue regarding debt versus owners' equity as sources of capital to finance the assets of a business and discusses the advantages and risks of using debt capital.

 This chapter deals mainly with the types and the amounts of assets needed to make profit. The non-interest-bearing operating liabilities of businesses are also included in the discussion. These short-term payables occur spontaneously when a business buys inventory on credit, receives money in advance for future delivery of products or services to customers, and delays paying for expenses. Payables arising from these sources are called *spontaneous liabilities.* In contrast, borrowing money from lenders and raising money from shareholders are anything but sponta-neous. Persuading lenders to loan money to the business is a protracted process, as is getting people to invest money in the business as shareowners.

ASSETS AND SOURCES OF CAPITAL FOR ASSETS

Continuing the example introduced previously, the business has several different assets that at year-end add up to $26 million. One of its assets is inventories, which are products being held by the business for sale to customers. These prod-ucts haven't been sold yet, so the cost of the products is held in the asset account and will not be charged to expense until the products are sold. The cost of its inventories at year-end is $7.2 million. Of this amount, $2.4 million hadn't been paid for by the end of the year. The business has an excellent credit rating. Its suppliers give the business a month to pay for pur-chases from them.

In addition to the amounts it owes for inventory purchases, the business also has short-term liabilities of $2.6 million for unpaid operating expenses at year-end. Of its $16.9 operating expenses for the year (see Figure 5.1), $2.6 million had not been paid by the end of the year. Both types of liabilities—payables for purchases of inventory on credit and for unpaid operating expenses—are short-term, non-interest-bearing obli-gations of the business. These are called *operating liabilities,* or *spontaneous liabilities* (as mentioned). The total of these two short-term operating liabilities is $5 million in the example.

To summarize, the company's total assets, operating liabili-ties, and sources of capital for investing in its assets are shown in Figure 5.2.

In Figure 5.2 note that the $5 million of operating liabilities

Note: Amounts are in millions of dollars.

Total assets	$26.0	Short-term and long-term debt	$ 7.5
Less operating liabilities	$ 5.0	Owners' equity	$13.5
Capital needed for assets	$21.0	Capital from debt and owners' equity	$21.0

FIGURE 5.2 *Summary of assets, operating liabilities, and sources of capital.*

is deducted from total assets to determine the $21 million amount, which is the total capital needed for investing in its assets. I favor this layout for management analysis purposes because it deducts the amount of spontaneous liabilities from the total assets of the business. Recall that the normal operating liabilities from buying things on credit and delaying payment of expenses are called *spontaneous* because they arise in the normal process of carrying on the operations of the business, not from borrowing money at interest.

Operating liabilities do not bear interest (unless the business delays too long in paying these liabilities). If the business had paid all its operating liabilities by year-end, then its cash balance would have been $5 million lower and its total assets would have been $21 million. (I should mention that the business probably would not have had enough cash to pay all its operating liabilities before the end of the year.) A company's cash balance benefits from the float, which is the time period that goes by until the company pays its short-term operating liabilities. It's as if the business gets a $5 million interest-free loan from its creditors.

Debt versus Equity as Sources of Capital

KEY CONCEPT The $21 million of its assets ($26 million total assets minus the $5.0 million of its operating liabilities) is the amount of money that the business had to obtain from three general sources: (1) The business borrowed money; (2) the business raised money from shareowners; and (3) the business retained a good part of its annual earnings instead of distributing all of its annual profits to shareowners. These three sources of capital have provided the $21 million invested in its assets. Of this total capital, $7.5 million is from short-term and longer-term debt sources. The rest of the company's total capital is from owners' equity, which consists of the amounts invested by shareowners over the years plus the accumulated retained earnings of the business. Figure 5.2 does not differentiate between the cumulative amounts invested by shareowners and the retained earnings of the business—only the total $13.5 million for owners' equity is shown in Figure 5.2.

Interest is the cost of using debt capital, of course. In contrast, a business does not make a contractual promise to pay shareowners a predetermined amount or a percent of distribution from profit each year. Rather, the cost of equity capital is an imputed cost, equal to a sought-after amount of net income that the business should earn annually relative to the owners' equity employed in the business. The owners' equity is $13.5 million of the company's $21 million total capital. Shareowners expect the business to earn annual net income on owners' equity that is higher than the interest rate on its debt. Shareowners take more risk than lenders. Assume, therefore, that the business's objective is to earn a 15.0 percent or higher annual net income on owners' equity. In the example, therefore, net income should be at least $2,025,000 ($13.5 million owners' equity × 15.0% = $2,025,000 net income benchmark).

A company's actual earnings before interest and income tax (EBIT) for a year may not be enough to pay interest on its debt capital, pay income tax, and achieve its after-tax net income objective relative to owners' equity. What about this example, for instance? The business made $3.9 million EBIT, as reported in Figure 5.1. The annual interest rate on its debt was 8.0 percent, as mentioned earlier. So, its annual interest expense was $600,000 ($7.5 million total debt × 8.0% annual interest rate = $600,000).

So the business made $3.3 million earnings after interest and before income tax. Its income tax rate is 34 percent of this amount. Thus, its income tax is $1,122,000 and its net income, or earnings after interest and income tax, is $2,178,000. The business achieved its goal of earning 15.0 percent or better of net income on owners' equity ($2,178,000 net income ÷ $13,500,000 owners' equity = 16.1%). The shareowners may be satisfied with this 16.1 percent return on their capital, or they may insist that the business should do better.

Chapter 6 explores the strategy of using debt to enhance net income performance (as well as the risks of using debt capital, which a business may or may not be willing to take). The rest of this chapter focuses on the assets and operating liabilities that are driven by the profit-making activities of a business. A large chunk of a company's balance sheet (statement of financial condition) consists of these assets and operating liabilities.

CONNECTING SALES REVENUE AND EXPENSES WITH OPERATING ASSETS AND LIABILITIES

Figure 5.3 shows the lines of connection from sales revenue and expenses to the company's respective assets and operating liabilities. (The foregoing business example is continued in this section.) The assets and operating liabilities shown in Figure 5.3 are explained briefly as follows:

- Making sales on credit causes a business to record *accounts receivable*.

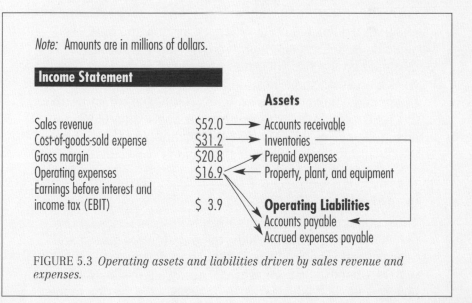

FIGURE 5.3 *Operating assets and liabilities driven by sales revenue and expenses.*

- Acquiring and holding products before they are sold to customers causes a business to record *inventories*.

- The costs of some operating expenses are paid before the cost is recorded as an expense, which causes a business to record *prepaid expenses*.

- Investments in long-term operating resources, called *property, plant, and equipment* (or, more informally, *fixed assets*), cause a business to record depreciation expense that is included in operating expenses.

- Inventory purchases on credit cause a business to record *accounts payable*.

- Many expenses are recorded before they are paid, which causes a business to record its unpaid expense amounts in either an *accounts payable* account or an *accrued expenses payable* account. These two payables are called *operating liabilities*.

Accounts Receivable

No dollar amounts (also called *balances*) are shown for the assets and operating liabilities in Figure 5.3. The amounts depend on the policies and practices of the business. The amount of the accounts receivable asset depends on the credit terms offered to the company's customers, whether most of the customers pay their bills on time, and how many customers are delinquent. For example, assume the business offers its customers one-month credit, which most take, but the company's actual collection experience is closer to five weeks, on average, because some customers pay late. In this situation the balance of its accounts receivable would be about five weeks of annual sales revenue, or approximately $5 million at the end of the year ($52 million annual sales revenue × 5/52 = approximately $5 million accounts receivable).

Inventories

The amount of the company's inventories asset depends on the company's holding period—the time from acquisition of products until the products are sold and delivered to customers. Suppose that, on average, across all products sold, the business holds products in inventory about 12 weeks. In this

situation the company's year-end inventory would be about
$7.2 million ($31.2 annual cost-of-goods-sold expense ×
12/52 = approximately $7.2 million). At the end of the year,
recent acquisitions of inventory had not been paid for because
the company buys on credit from the sources of products.

See the line of connection in Figure 5.3 from the inventories asset to accounts payable. Assume, for instance, that
about one-third of its ending inventories had not been paid
for. As a result, the year-end accounts payable would be about
$2.4 million from inventory purchases on credit. The total
amount of accounts payable also includes the amount of
unpaid expenses of the business at the end of the year for
which the business has been billed by its vendors.

Operating Liabilities

For most businesses, a sizable amount of operating expenses
recorded during the latter part of a year are not paid by the
end of the year. At the end of the year the business has unpaid
bills from its utility company for gas and electricity, from its
lawyers for work done during recent weeks, from the telephone company, from maintenance and repair vendors, and
so on. A business records the amounts it has been billed for
(received an invoice for) in the accounts payable operating liability account. A business also has a second and equally
important type of operating liability. A business has many
expenses that accumulate, or accrue over time, for which it
does not receive bills, and to record these "creeping" expenses
a business uses a second type of operating liability account
that is discussed next.

In my experience, business managers and investors do not
appreciate the rather large size of accruals for various operating expenses. Many operating expenses are not on a pay-as-
you-go basis. For example, accumulated vacation and sick
leave benefits are not paid until the employees actually take
their vacations and sick days. At year-end, the company calculates profit-sharing bonuses and other profit-sharing amounts,
which are recorded as expense in the period just ended, even
though they will not be paid until some time later. Product
warranty and guarantee costs should be accrued and charged
to expense so that these follow-up costs are recognized in the

same year that sales revenue is recorded—to get a correct matching of sales revenue and expenses to measure profit. In summary, a surprising number of expense accruals are recorded.

Expense accruals are recorded in a separate account, labeled *accrued expenses payable* in Figure 5.3, because they are quite different than accounts payable. For one thing, an account payable is based on an actual invoice received by the vendor, whereas accruals have no such hard copy that serves as evidence of the liability. Accruals depend much more on good faith estimates of the accountants and others making these calculations. Suppose the business in the example knows from experience that the balance of this operating liability tends to be about five weeks of its annual total operating expenses.

This ratio of accrued expenses payable to annual operating expenses is based on the types of accruals that the company records, such as accrued vacation and sick pay for employees, accrued property taxes, accrued warranty and guarantee costs on products, and so on. The five weeks reflects the average time between when these expenses are recorded and when they are actually paid, which can be quite a long time for some items but rather short for others. Thus, the year-end balance of the company's accrued expenses payable liability account is about $1.6 million ($16.9 million annual operating expenses × 5/52 = approximately $1.6 million).

Prepaid Expenses, Fixed Assets, and Depreciation Expense

Chapter 2 explains the accrual basis of profit accounting and cash flow from profit. One key point to keep in mind in comparing profit and cash flow is that a business has to prepay some of its operating expenses. I won't repeat that discussion here; I'll simply piggyback on the discussion and point out that a business has an asset account called *prepaid expenses,* which holds the prepaid cost amounts that have not been charged off to expense by the end of the year. Usually, the amount of the prepaid expenses asset account is relatively small—although, if the ending balance were large compared with a company's annual operating expenses, this strange state of affairs definitely should be investigated. A business manager should notice an unusually large balance in the pre- paid expenses and demand an explanation.

One of the operating expenses of a business is depreciation. This is a very unique expense, especially from the cash flow point of view (as Chapter 2 discusses at some length). I do not separate depreciation expense in Figure 5.3, although I do show a line of connection from the company's fixed assets account (property, plant, and equipment) to operating expenses. As I explain in Chapter 2, the original cost of fixed assets is spread over the years of their use according to an allocation method.

What about Cash?

A business has one other asset not shown in Figure 5.3 or mentioned so far—cash. Every business needs a working cash balance. Recall that in the example the company's annual sales revenue is $52 million, or $1 million per week on aver- age. But the actual cash collections in a given week could be considerably less or much more than the $1 million average. A business can't live hand to mouth and wait for actual cash collections to arrive before it writes checks. Employees have to be paid on time, of course, and a business can't ask its creditors to wait for payment until it collects enough money from its customers.

In short, a business maintains a minimum cash balance as a safety buffer. Many businesses keep rather large cash bal- ances, part of which usually is invested in safe, short-term marketable debt securities on which the business earns inter- est income. The average cash balance of a business relative to its annual sales revenue may be very low or fairly high. Cash balance policies vary widely from business to business. If I had to guess the cash balance of the business in the example, I would put it at around two or three weeks of annual sales revenue, or about $2 to $3 million. But I wouldn't be sur- prised if its cash balance were outside this range.

There's no doubt that every business needs to keep enough cash in its checking account (or on hand in currency and coin for cash-based businesses such as grocery stores and gambling casinos). But precisely how much? Every business manager would worry if cash were too low to meet the next payroll. Some liabilities can be put off for days or even weeks, but employees have to be paid on time. Beyond a minimum, rock-bottom cash balance amount to meet the payroll and to provide at least a bare-bones margin of safety, it is not clear how much additional cash balance a business should carry, just as some people may have only $5 or $10 in walking-around money and others could reach in their wallet and pull out $500.

 Unnecessary excess cash balances should be avoided. Excess cash is an unproductive asset that doesn't pay its way toward meeting the company's cost of capital (i.e., the interest on debt capital and the net income that should be earned on equity capital). For another thing, excess cash balances can cause managers to become lax in controlling expenses. Money in the bank, waiting only for a check to be written, is often an incentive to make unnecessary expenditures, not scrutinizing them as closely as needed. Also, excess cash balances can lead to greater opportunities for fraud and embezzlement.

Yet having a large cash balance is a tremendous advantage in some situations. The business may be able to drive a hard bargain with a major vendor by paying cash up front rather than asking for the normal credit terms. There are many such reasons for holding a cash balance over and above what's really needed to meet payroll and to provide for a safety buffer for the normal lags and leads in the cash receipts and cash disbursements of the company. Frankly, if this were my business I would want at least a three weeks' cash balance.

An executive of a leading company said he kept the company's cash balance "lean and mean" to keep its managers on their toes. There's probably a lot of truth in this. But if too much time and effort goes into managing day-to-day cash flow, then the more important strategic factors may not be managed well.

Figure 5.3 does not present a complete picture of the company's financial condition. Cash is missing, as just discussed, and the sources of the company's capital are not shown. It's time to fill in the remaining pieces of the statement of financial condition of the business, otherwise known as the *balance sheet*.

BALANCE SHEET TETHERED WITH INCOME STATEMENT

Figure 5.4 presents the income statement and balance sheet (statement of financial condition) for the business example. The income statement includes interest expense, income tax expense, and net income (which are discussed earlier in the chapter). The balance sheet includes the sources of capital that the business has tapped to invest in its assets—interest-bearing debt and owners' equity. The balance sheet is presented according to the discussion earlier in the chapter. In particular, note that the total amount of operating liabilities (the sum of accounts payable and accrued expenses payable) is deducted from total assets to determine the capital invested in assets.

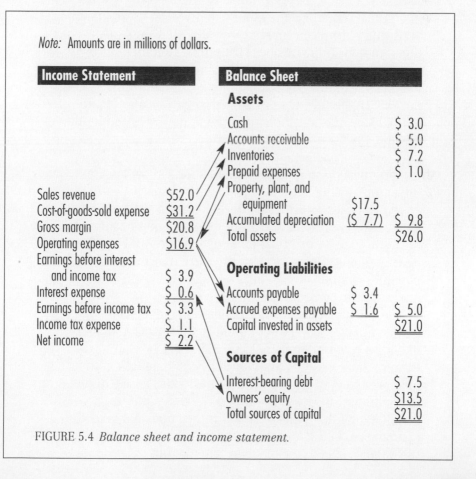

FIGURE 5.4 *Balance sheet and income statement.*

KEY CONCEPT   Figure 5.4 displays lines of connection, or tether lines, from sales revenue and expenses in the income statement to their corresponding assets and operating liabilities in the balance sheet. These lines are not actually shown in financial reports, of course. I include them in Figure 5.4 to stress that the profit-making activities of a business drive a good part of its balance sheet. Also, you might note the line from net income to owners' equity; net income increases the owners' equity. All or part of annual net income may be distributed in cash to its shareowners, which is recorded as a decrease in the business's owners' equity.

END POINT

A business needs assets to make profit. Therefore a business must raise capital for the money to invest in its assets. The seed capital comes from shareowners; they may invest additional money in the business from time to time after the business gets off the ground. Most businesses borrow money on the basis of interest-bearing debt instruments such as notes payable. Profitable businesses retain part or all of their annual earnings to supplement the money invested in the business by their shareowners.

The balance sheet, or statement of financial condition, reports the debt and equity capital sources of a business and the assets in which the business has invested. Several different types of assets are listed in the balance sheet. The balance sheet also reports the operating liabilities of a business that are generated by its profit-making activities and not from borrowing money. Operating liabilities are non-interest-bearing payables of a business, which are quite different from its interest-bearing debt obligations.

The relationships of sales revenue and expenses reported in a company's income statement to the assets and operating liabilities reported in its balance sheet are not haphazard. Far from it! Sales revenue and the different expenses in the income statement match up with particular assets and operating liabilities. Business managers, lenders, and investors should understand these critical connections between the components of the income statement and the components of the balance sheet. In particular, the amount of accounts receivable should be reasonable in comparison with annual sales revenue, and the amount of inventories should be reasonable in comparison with annual cost-of-goods-sold expense.

In short, the balance sheet of a business fits tongue and groove with its income statement. These two financial statements are presented separately in financial reports, but business managers, lenders, and investors should understand the interlocking nature of these two primary financial statements.

Business Capital Sources

This chapter explores the two basic sources of business capital: *debt* and *owners' equity*. Every business must make a fundamental decision regarding how to finance the business, which refers to the mix or relative proportions of debt and equity. By borrowing money, a business enlarges its equity capital, so the business has a bigger base of capital to carry on its profit-making activities. More capital generally means a business can make more sales, and more sales generally mean more profit.

KEY CONCEPT Using debt in addition to equity capital is referred to as *financial leverage*. If you visualize equity capital as the fulcrum, then debt may be seen as the lever that serves to expand the total capital of a business. The chapter explains the gain or loss resulting from financial leverage, which often is a major factor in bottom-line profit.

TIP It's possible, I suppose, to find a business that is so antidebt that the only liabilities it has are normal *operating liabilities* (i.e., accounts payable and accrued expenses payable).

These short-term liabilities arise *spontaneously* in making purchases on credit and from delaying the payment of certain expenses until sometime after the expenses have been recorded. A business can hardly avoid operating liabilities. But a business doesn't have to borrow money. A business could possibly raise all the capital it needs from shareowners and from retaining all or a good part of its annual earnings in the business. In short, a business theoretically could rely entirely on equity capital and have no debt at all—but this way of financing a business is very rare indeed.

BUSINESS EXAMPLE FOR THIS CHAPTER

Figure 6.1 presents a very condensed balance sheet and an abbreviated income statement for a new business example. The income statement is truncated at earnings before interest and income tax (EBIT). The two financial statements in Figure 6.1 are telescoped into a few lines. In this chapter we don't need all the details that are actually reported in these two financial statements. (See Figure 4.2 for the full format of a balance sheet and Figure 4.1 for a typical format of an external income statement.)

To support its $18.5 million annual sales, the business used $11.5 million total assets. Operating liabilities provided $1.5 million of its assets. In Figure 6.1 the company's operating liabilities are deducted from its total assets to get a very important figure—*capital invested in assets*. The business had to raise $10 million in capital from debt and owners' equity. The business borrows money on the basis of short-term and long-term notes payable. The business built up its owners' equity

Balance Sheet		Income Statement	
Assets used in making profit	$11,500,000	Sales revenue	$18,500,000
Operating liabilities (accounts payable and accrued expenses payable)	($ 1,500,000)	All operating expenses	($16,700,000)
Capital invested in assets	$10,000,000	Earnings before interest and income tax expenses (EBIT)	$ 1,800,000
Debt and equity sources of capital	$10,000,000		

FIGURE 6.1 *Condensed financial statements.*

from money invested by shareowners plus the cumulative amount of retained earnings over the years (undistributed net income year after year).

Once Again Quickly: Assets and Operating Liabilities

Chapter 5 explains that a business that sells products on credit needs four main assets in making profit: cash, accounts receivable, inventories, and long-lived resources such as land, buildings, machinery, and equipment that are referred to as *fixed assets* (or, more formally, as *property, plant, and equipment*). The chapter goes into the characteristics of each asset, explaining how sales revenue and expenses are connected with these assets. Chapter 5 also explains how expenses drive the *operating liabilities* of a business. In the process of making profit a business generates certain short-term, non-interest-bearing operating liabilities that are inseparable from its profit-making transactions. These payables of a business are called *spontaneous* liabilities because operating activities, not borrowing money, causes them. Operating liabilities are deducted from total assets to determine the amount of capital that has been raised by a business.

CAPITAL STRUCTURE OF BUSINESS

The capital a business needs for investing in its assets comes from two basic sources: *debt* and *equity*. Managers must convince lenders to loan money to the company and convince sources of equity capital to invest their money in the company. Both debt and equity sources demand to be compensated for the use of their capital. Interest is paid on debt and reported in the income statement as an expense, which like all expenses is deducted from sales revenue to determine bottom-line net income. In contrast, no charge or deduction for using equity capital is reported in the income statement.

Rather, net income is reported as the reward or payoff on equity capital. In other words, profit is defined from the shareowners point of view, not from the total capital point of view. Interest is treated not as a division of profit to one of the two sources of capital of the business but as an expense, and profit is defined to be the residual amount after deducting interest.

Sometimes the owners' equity of a business is referred to as its *net worth*. The fundamental idea of net worth is this:

$$\text{Net worth} = \text{assets} - \text{operating liabilities} - \text{debt}$$

Net income increases the net worth of a business. The business is better off earning net income, because its net worth increases by the net income amount. Suppose another group of investors stands ready to buy the business for a total price equal to its net worth. This offering price, or market value, of the business increases by the amount of net income. Cash distributions of net income to shareowners decrease the net worth of a business, because cash decreases with no corresponding decrease in the operating liabilities or debt of the business.

The amounts of cash distributions from net income are reported in the statement of cash flows, which is explained in Chapter 2. Dividends are also reported in a separate statement of changes in owners' equity accounts if this particular schedule is included in a financial report (see Figure 4.4 for an example).

The valuation of a business is not so simple as someone buying the business for an amount equal to its net worth. Business valuation usually takes into account the net worth reported in its balance sheet, but many other factors play a role in putting a value on a business. The amount a buyer is willing to offer for a business can be considerably higher than the company's net worth based on the figures reported in the company's most recent balance sheet. The valuation of a privately owned business is quite a broad topic, which is beyond the scope of this book. Likewise, the valuation of stock shares of publicly owned business corporations is a far-reaching topic beyond the confines of this book.

 At its most recent year-end, the business had $10 million invested in assets to carry on its profit-making operations (total assets less its operating liabilities). Suppose that debt has provided $4 million of the total capital invested in assets and owners' equity has supplied the other $6 million. Collectively, the mix of these two capital sources are referred to as the *capitalization* or the *capital structure* of the business. Be careful about the term capitalization: Similar terms mean something different. The terms *market capitalization, market cap,* or *cap* refer to the total market value of a publicly traded corporation, which is equal to the current market price per share of stock times the total number of stock shares outstanding (in the hands of stockholders).

A perpetual question that's not easy to answer concerns whether a business is using the optimal or best capital structure. Perhaps the business in the example should have carried more debt. Maybe the company could have gotten by on a smaller cash balance, say $500,000 less—which means that $500,000 less capital would have been needed. Perhaps the business should have kept its accounts receivable and inventory balances lower, which would have reduced the need for capital. Every business has to make tough choices regarding debt versus equity, asking shareowners for more money versus retaining earnings, and working with a lean working cash balance versus a larger and more comfortable cash balance. The answers to these questions are seldom easy and clear cut.

Basic Characteristics of Debt

Debt may be very short term, which generally means six months or less, or it may be long term, which generally means 10 years or longer—or for any period mutually agreed on between the business and its lender. The term *debt* means *interest-bearing* in all cases. Interest rates can be fixed over the life of the debt contract or subject to change, usually at the lender's option. On short-term debt, interest usually is paid at the end of the loan period. On long-term debt, interest usually is paid monthly or quarterly (sometimes semiannually).

KEY CONCEPT A key feature of debt is whether the principal of the loan (the amount borrowed) is *amortized* over the life of the loan instead of being paid at the end of the loan period. In addition to paying interest, the business (who is the borrower, or debtor) may be required to make payments periodically that reduce the principal balance of the debt instead of waiting until the final maturity date to pay off the entire principal amount at one time. For example, a loan may call for equal quarterly amounts over five years. Each quarterly payment is calculated to pay interest and to reduce a part of the principal balance so that at the end of the five years the loan principal will be paid off. Alternatively, the business may negotiate a *term* loan. Nothing is paid to reduce the principal balance during the life of a term loan; the entire amount borrowed (the principal) is paid at the maturity date of the loan.

The lender may demand that certain assets of the business be pledged as *collateral*. The lender would be granted the right to take control of the property in the event the business defaults on the loan. Real estate (land and buildings) is the most common type of collateral, and these types of loans are called *mortgages*. Inventory and other assets also serve as collateral on some business loans. Debt instruments such as bonds may have very restrictive *covenants* (conditions) or, conversely, may be quite liberal and nonbinding on the business. Some debt is convertible into equity stock shares, though generally this feature is limited to publicly held corporations whose stock shares are actively traded. The debt of a business may be a private loan, or debt securities may be issued to the public at large and be actively traded on a bond market.

Lenders look over the shoulders of the managers of the business. Lenders do not simply say, "Here's the money and call us if you need more." A business does not exactly have to bare its soul when applying for a loan, but the lender usually demands a lot of information from the business. If a business defaults on a loan (not making an interest payment on time or not being able to pay off the loan at maturity), the terms of the loan give the lender legally enforceable options that in the extreme could force the business into bankruptcy. If a business does not comply fully with the terms and provisions of its loans, it is more or less at the mercy of its lenders, which could cause serious disruptions or even force the business to terminate its operations.

Basic Characteristics of Equity

One person may operate a business as the sole proprietor and provide all the equity capital of the business. A *sole proprietorship* business is not a separate legal entity; it's an extension of the individual. Many businesses are legally organized as a *partnership* of two or more persons. A partnership is a separate entity or person in the eyes of the law. The general partners of the business can be held responsible for the liabilities of the partnership. Creditors can reach beyond the assets of the partnership to the personal assets of the individual partners to satisfy their claims against the business. The general partners have *unlimited liability* for the liabilities of the partnership. Some partnerships have two classes of partners—general and limited. Limited partners escape the unlimited liability of general partners but they have no voice in the management of the business.

Most businesses, even relatively small ones, favor the corporate form of organization. A *corporation* is a legal entity separate from its individual owners. A corporation is a legal entity that shields the personal assets of the owners (the stockholders, or shareowners) from the creditors of the business. A business may deliberately defraud its creditors and attempt to abuse the limited liability of corporate shareowners. In this case the law will "pierce the corporate veil" and hold the guilty individuals responsible for the debts of the business.

The corporate form is a practical way to collect a pool of equity capital from a large number of investors. There are literally millions of corporations in the American economy. In 1997 the Internal Revenue Service received over 4.7 million tax returns from business corporations. Most were small businesses. However, more than 860,000 businesses corporations had annual sales revenue over $1 million.

Other countries around the globe have the equivalent of corporations, although the names of these organizations as well as their legal and political features differ from country to country. A recent development in the United States is the creation of a new type of business legal entity called a *limited liability company* (LLC). This innovative business entity is a hybrid between a partnership and a corporation; it has characteristics of both. Most states have passed laws enabling the creation of LLCs.

Corporations issue *capital stock shares;* these are the units of equity ownership in the business. A corporation may issue only one class of stock shares, called *common stock* or *capital stock*. Or a corporation may issue both *preferred stock* and common stock shares. Preferred stock shares are promised an annual cash dividend per share. (The actual payment of the dividend is contingent on the corporation earning enough net income and having enough cash on hand to pay the dividend.) A corporation may issue both voting and nonvoting classes of stock shares. Some corporations issue two classes of voting shares that have different voting power per share (e.g., one class may have ten votes per share and the other only one vote per share).

Debt bears an explicit and legally contracted rate of interest. Equity capital does not. Nevertheless, equity capital has an imputed or implicit cost. Management must earn a satisfactory rate of earnings on the equity capital of the business to justify the use of this capital. Failure to do so reduces the value of the equity and makes it more difficult to attract additional equity capital (if and when needed). In extreme circumstances, the majority of stockholders could vote to dissolve the corporation and force the business to liquidate its assets, pay off its liabilities, and distribute the remainder to the stockholders.

DANGER! The equity shareholders in a business (the stockholders of a corporation) take the risk of business failure and poor performance. On the optimistic side, the shareowners have no limit on their participation in the success of the business. Continued growth can lead to continued growth in cash dividends. And the market value of the equity shares has no theoretical upper limit. The lower limit of market value is zero (the shares become worthless)—although corporate stock shares could be *assessable,* which means the corporation has the right to assess shareholders and make them contribute additional capital to the organization. Almost all corporate stock shares are issued as nonassessable shares, although equity investors in a business can't be too careful about this.

RETURN ON INVESTMENT

I was a stockholder in a privately owned business a few years ago. I owned 1,000 shares of common stock in the business and served on its board of directors. One thing really hit home. I came to appreciate firsthand that we (the stockholders) had a lot of money invested, and we expected the business to do well with our money. We could have invested our money elsewhere and received interest income or earned some other type of return on our alternative investment. Management was very much aware that their responsibility was to improve the value of our stock shares over time, which would require that the business earn a good return on our investment.

KEY CONCEPT The basic measure for evaluating the performance of capital investments is the *return on investment* (ROI), which always is expressed as a percent. To calculate ROI, the amount of return is divided by the amount of capital invested:

$$\text{ROI\%} = \frac{\text{return}}{\text{capital invested}}$$

ROI is always for a given period of time—one year unless clearly stated otherwise. *Return* is a generic term and means different things for different investments. For investments in marketable securities, return includes cash income received during the period and the increase or decrease in market value during the period. The ROI on an investment in marketable securities is negative if the decrease in market value is more than the cash income received during the period.

Market value is not a factor for some investments. One example is an investment in a certificate of deposit (CD) issued by a financial institution. Return equals just the interest earned. A CD is not traded in a public market place and has no market value. The value of a CD is the amount the financial institution will redeem it for at the maturity date, which is the face value on which interest is based. In the event that the financial institution doesn't redeem the CD at full value at maturity, the investor suffers a loss that could wipe out part or all of the interest earned on the CD. (CDs are guaranteed up to a certain limit by an agency of the federal government, but that's another matter.)

Real estate investments may or may not include market value appreciation in accounting for annual earnings, depending on whether market prices of the real estate properties can be reliably estimated or appraised at the end of each period. If market value changes are not booked, the return on a real estate investment venture is not known until the conclusion of the investment project.

Evaluating the investment performance of a business uses three different measures: (1) *return on assets* (ROA), (2) *interest rate,* and (3) *return on equity* (ROE). Figure 6.2 illustrates the calculations of these three key rates of return for the business introduced earlier. The example assumes that the business has $4 million debt capital and $6 million equity capital. (Different mixes of debt and equity capital are examined later.) The definitions for each rate of return are as follows:

- ROA = earnings before interest and income tax expenses, or EBIT ÷ (assets − operating liabilities)
- Interest rate = interest expense ÷ interest bearing debt
- ROE = net income ÷ owners' equity

Figure 6.2 is a *capital structure model* that can be used to analyze alternative scenarios such as a different debt-to-equity ratio, a higher or lower ROA performance, or a different interest rate. Figure 6.2 is the printout of a relatively simple personal computer worksheet. Different numbers can easily be plugged into the appropriate cell for one or more of the variables in the model in order to see how net income and the ROE would be affected. Alternative scenarios are examined later in the chapter using the capital structure model.

 Sales revenue less all operating expenses equals *earnings before interest and income tax* (EBIT). As shown in Figure 6.2, EBIT is divided three ways: (1) *interest* on debt capital, (2) *income tax,* keeping in mind that interest is deductible to

Earnings before interest and income tax (EBIT)	$1,800,000	÷	Assets less operating liabilities	$10,000,000	= 18.0%	Return on assets (ROA)
Interest expense	($ 300,000)	÷	Debt	$ 4,000,000	= 7.5%	Interest rate
Income tax expense @ 40% of taxable income	($ 600,000)		Government			
Net income	$ 900,000	÷	Owners' equity	$ 6,000,000	= 15.0%	Return on equity (ROE)

FIGURE 6.2 *Rates of return on assets, debt, and equity.*

determine taxable income, and (3) residual *net income.* In other words, the debt holders get a chunk of EBIT (interest), the federal and state governments get their chunks (income tax), and what's left over is profit for the shareowners of the business (net income). Note that the ROA rate and the interest rate are *before* income tax, whereas ROE is *after* income tax. The income tax factor is in the middle of things in more ways than one.

KEY CONCEPT — PIVOTAL ROLE OF INCOME TAX

In a world without income taxes, EBIT would be divided between the two capital sources—interest on debt and net income for the equity owners (the stockholders of a corporation). But in the real world income tax takes a big bite out of earnings after interest. In the example, the combined federal and state income tax rate is set at 40 percent of taxable income. As you probably know, interest expense is deducted from EBIT to determine taxable income ($1.8 million EBIT – $300,000 interest = $1.5 million taxable income; $1.5 million taxable income × 40% combined federal and state income tax rate = $600,000 income tax).

The following question might be asked: Should income tax be considered a return on government capital investment? The federal and state governments do not directly invest capital in a business, of course. In a broader sense, however, government provides what can be called *public capital.* Government provides public facilities (highways, parks, schools, etc.), political stability, the monetary system, the legal system, and police protection. In short, government provides the necessary infrastructure for carrying on business activity, and government funds this through income taxes and other taxes.

Under the federal income tax law (U.S. Internal Revenue Code), interest on debt is deductible in determining annual taxable income. Cash dividends paid to stockholders—which can be viewed as the equity equivalent of interest on debt— are *not* deductible in determining taxable income. This basic differentiation in the tax law has significant impact on the amount of EBIT needed to earn a satisfactory ROE on the equity capital of a business.

The business in the example needs to earn just $300,000 EBIT for its $300,000 interest. The $300,000 EBIT minus

$300,000 interest leaves zero taxable income and thus no income tax. In contrast, to earn $900,000 *after-tax* net income on equity, the business needs $1.5 million EBIT:

$$\frac{\$900,000 \text{ net income}}{1 - 40\% \text{ income tax rate}} = \frac{\$900,000}{0.60} = \$1,500,000 \text{ EBIT}$$

Income tax takes $600,000 of the $1,500,000 earnings after interest, leaving $900,000 net income after income tax.

Suppose for the moment that interest were not deductible to determine taxable income. In this imaginary income tax world the business would need $500,000 EBIT to cover its $300,000 interest. Income tax at the 40 percent rate would be $200,000 on this $500,000 EBIT, leaving $300,000 after tax to pay interest. The business would need $500,000 EBIT for interest and $1.5 million EBIT for net income, for a total of $2

Notes on Income Tax

The company example uses a 40 percent combined federal and state income tax rate, which is realistic. However, the taxation of business income varies considerably from state to state. Also, under the current federal income tax law, corporate taxable income from $335,000 to $10 million is taxed at a 34 percent rate. Annual taxable incomes below $335,000 are taxed at lower rates and above $10 million at a slightly higher rate. The example assumes that the business is a corporation and is taxed as a domestic C (or regular) corporation.

A corporation with 75 or fewer stockholders may elect to be treated as an S corporation. An S corporation pays no income tax itself; its annual taxable income is passed through to its individual stockholders in proportion to their ownership share. Sole proprietorships, partnerships, and limited liability companies are also tax conduits; they are not subject to income tax as separate entities but pass their taxable income through to their owner or owners who have to include their shares of the entity's taxable income in their personal income tax returns. Individual situations vary widely, as you know.

Corporations may have net loss carryforwards that reduce or eliminate taxable income in one year. There is also the alternative minimum tax (AMT) to consider, to say nothing of a myriad of other provisions and options (loopholes) in the tax law. It's very difficult to generalize. The main point is that in a given year in a given situation the taxable income of the business may not result in a normal amount of income tax.

million EBIT. The business would have to have earned a 20.0 percent ROA rate in this situation. But since interest is deductible, the business needed to earn only 18.0 percent ROA to pay interest and to generate 15.0 percent ROE for its shareowners.

RETURN ON EQUITY (ROE)

The example business is organized as a corporation. The company's shareowners invested money in the business for which they received shares of capital stock issued by the business. Keep in mind that the stockholders could have invested this money elsewhere. The business over the years retained a good amount of its annual net income instead of distributing all its annual net income as cash dividends to its stockholders. The total owners' equity capital of the business from both sources is $6.0 million. This amount includes the paid-in capital invested in the business by its stockholders and the cumulative amount of retained earnings.

DANGER! Stockholders' equity capital is at risk; the business may or may not be able to earn an adequate net income for its stockholders every year. For that matter, the company could go belly-up and into bankruptcy. In bankruptcy proceedings, stockholders are paid last, after all debts and liabilities are settled. There's no promise that cash dividends will be paid to stockholders even if the business earns net income. The ROE ratio does not consider what portion (if any) of the business's annual net income was distributed as cash dividends. The entire net income figure is used to compute the ROE ratio.

In the example (see Figure 6.2), the company's ROE was 15.0 percent for the year, which is not terrific but not too bad. This comment raises a larger question regarding which yardstick is most relevant. Theoretically, the $6 million owners' equity in the business could be pulled out and invested somewhere else to earn a return on the best alternative investment. Should the company's ROE be compared with the rate of return that could be earned on a riskless and highly liquid investment such as short-term U.S. government securities? Surely not. Everyone agrees that a company's ROE should be compared with *comparable* investment alternatives that have the same risk and liquidity characteristics as stockholders' equity.

K E Y CONCEPT The rate of return on the most relevant alternative (the next best investment alternative) is called the *opportunity cost of capital.* To avoid a prolonged discussion, simply assume that the stockholders want the business to improve on its 15.0 percent ROE performance. This implies that their opportunity cost of capital is higher than 15.0 percent, at least in the minds of the stockholders. Of course, the company should maintain its ROE and do even better if possible. One reason for the business's ROE being as good as it is that the company had a nice gain from financial leverage.

K E Y CONCEPT **FINANCIAL LEVERAGE**

Piling debt on top of equity capital is called *financial leverage.* As stated at the beginning of the chapter, if you visualize equity capital as the fulcrum, then debt may be seen as the lever that serves to expand the total capital of a business. For this reason, using debt is also called *trading on the equity.* The main advantage of debt is that a business has more capital to work with and is not limited to the amount of equity capital that a business can muster. The larger capital base can be used to crank out more sales, which should yield more profit. Of course, this assumes that the business can actually make profit from using its capital.

TIP Using debt also has another important potential advantage. If a business borrows money at an interest rate that is lower than its ROA rate, it makes a *financial leverage gain.* The idea is to borrow at a relatively low rate, earn a relatively high rate, and keep the difference. In Figure 6.2, note that the company earns 18.0 percent ROA but paid only 7.5 percent interest on its borrowed capital. (The business has several loans and pays different interest rates on each loan; the 7.5 percent is its composite average interest rate.) You don't have to be a rocket scientist to figure out that paying 7.5 percent for money and earning 18.0 percent on it is a good deal.

In the example, debt provides 40 percent of the capital invested in assets ($4 million of the total $10 million). Thus, 40 percent of the company's EBIT is attributable to its debt capital ($1.8 million EBIT × 40% = $720,000). But the business paid only $300,000 interest expense for the use of the debt capital. Therefore its gain is the excess, or $420,000 ($720,000 debt's share of EBIT – $300,000 interest = $420,000 financial leverage gain). Another way to compute the gain from financial leverage is to multiply the 10.5 percent *spread* between the 18.0 percent ROA earned by the business and its 7.5 percent interest rate times the amount of its debt (10.5% spread × $4 million debt = $420,000 financial leverage gain before income tax).

A financial leverage gain adds to the share of EBIT available for equity capital. Figure 6.3 illustrates the importance of the financial leverage gain in the company's profit performance for the year. Using debt provides additional earnings for the equity investors in the business. The shareowners earn EBIT on their capital in the business and also get the overflow of EBIT on debt capital after paying interest. In the example, financial leverage gain contributes a good share of the earnings for shareowners, as shown in Figure 6.3. The financial leverage gain adds 39 percent on top of EBIT earned on equity capital ($420,000 financial leverage gain ÷ $1,080,000 EBIT on equity capital = 39%).

 In analyzing profit performance, managers should separate two components of earnings before income tax: (1) the financial leverage gain and (2) the EBIT earned on owners' equity capital. As shown in Figure 6.3, the company's $1.5 million earnings before income tax consists of $420,000 financial

				debt percent			debt share
$1,800,000	EBIT	×	40%	of total capital	=	$ 720,000	of EBIT
						($ 300,000)	interest
						$ 420,000	financial leverage gain
				equity percent			equity share
$1,800,000	EBIT	×	60%	of total capital	=	$1,080,000	of EBIT
						$1,500,000	earnings for equity before income tax

FIGURE 6.3 *Components of earnings for equity.*

leverage gain plus the $1,080,000 pretax EBIT on equity capital. Therefore, a good part of the company's pretax profit is sensitive to the interest rate on its debt and its ratio of debt to equity. If its interest rate had been 18.0 percent (an unreasonably high interest rate these days) the financial leverage gain would have been zero.

The business, by using a moderate amount of debt capital, enhanced the earnings for its owners. Professor Ron Melicher, my longtime colleague at the University of Colorado, calls this the *earnings multiplier effect.* I very much like this term to describe the effects of financial leverage. The financial leverage multiplier effect cuts both ways, however. A percentage drop in the company's ROA causes earnings for equity to drop by a larger percentage.

Why not borrow to the hilt in order to maximize financial leverage gain? Well, for one thing, the amount of debt that can be borrowed is limited. Lenders will loan only so much money to a business, relative to its assets and its sales revenue and profit history. Once a business hits its borrowing capacity, more debt is either not available or interest rates and other lending terms become prohibitive. Furthermore, there are several disadvantages of debt.

DANGER! The deeper lenders are into the business the more restrictions they impose on the business, such as limiting cash dividends to shareowners and insisting that the business maintain minimum cash balances. Lenders may demand more collateral for their loans as the debt load of a business increases. Also, there is the threat that the lender may not renew the loans. Some businesses end up too top-heavy with debt and can't make their interest payments on time or pay their loans at maturity and the lender is not willing to renew the loan. These businesses may be forced into bankruptcy in an attempt to work out their debt problems.

In short, using debt capital has many risks. Interest rates change over time and the ROA rate earned by a business could plunge, even below its interest rate. Even relatively small changes in the ROA and interest rates can have a substantial impact on earnings. It's no surprise that many businesses are quite debt-averse, opting for low levels of debt even though they could carry more. The company in the example uses a fair amount of debt; using either more or less debt would have caused more or less financial leverage gain.

END POINT

Every business must decide on a blend of debt and equity capital to invest in the assets it needs to make a profit. The total capital invested in assets should be no more than necessary. Interest has to be paid on debt capital, and the business should earn at least a satisfactory return on equity capital in order to survive and thrive. The starting point is to earn an adequate return on assets (ROA), that is, an adequate amount of earnings before interest and income tax (EBIT) relative to the total capital invested in assets. Operating liabilities (mainly accounts payable and accrued expenses payable) are deducted from total assets to determine the amount of capital invested in assets.

Using debt enlarges the total capital base of a business, and with more capital a business can make more sales and generate more profit. Using debt for part of the total capital invested in assets offers the opportunity to benefit from financial leverage—as well as the risk of suffering a financial leverage loss if the business does not earn an ROA rate greater than the interest rate on its debt. Managers should measure the financial leverage gain or loss component of earnings for shareowners. The financial leverage gain or loss component of earnings is sensitive to changes in the interest rate, the debt level, and the ROA of the business.

Capital Needs
of Growth

In this chapter we return to the business example introduced in Chapter 3 and whose external financial statements are interpreted in Chapter 4. The business's financial performance for the year just ended was satisfactory at best. For instance, the business's profit ratio on sales (bottom-line net income divided by sales revenue) was just 4.0 percent. Its lackluster profit ratio resulted in a return on equity (ROE) of only 12.0 percent. Its shareowners have made it clear that the business should do better than this.

KEY
CONCEPT Later chapters explain analysis tools and strategies for improving profit. This chapter starts with the profit improvement plan for the coming year that has been developed by the business. The chapter focuses on the additional amount of capital that the business will need to carry out its profit improvement plan. The main theme of the chapter is this: *Profit planning also requires capital planning.* Managers cannot simply assume that the needed capital will become available like manna from heaven. They should determine how much additional capital would be needed to support profit growth and they should plan for the sources of the new capital.

PROFIT GROWTH PLAN

The business has developed an ambitious profit improvement plan for the coming year. Sales goals have been established for virtually every product the business sells. Sales pricing will be more aggressive. (The very important effects of changes in sales volume and sales price are examined in later chapters.) Advertising and sales promotion programs have been approved. Cost control will be a top priority in the coming year. To replace its old machines, equipment, tools, and vehicles the board of directors has approved a *capital expenditures* budget for the coming year. The business is optimistic that it can achieve its profit and return on equity goals for the coming year.

Figure 7.1 summarizes the company's profit plan for the coming year. Actual results for the year just ended are shown for comparison, as well as the percent increases over the year just ended. Note that interest expense has a question mark after it. At this point the exact amount of debt for the coming year is not known. The business will need to increase its assets to support the higher sales level next year, which means it will need more capital to invest in its assets.

Some of the additional capital may come from increasing its debt—by borrowing more money from its lenders. Clearly, the amount of the business's debt will not decrease given the planned increase in sales revenue. So the interest expense for the year just ended is carried forward for the coming year

	Year Just Ended	Coming Year	Change
Sales revenue	$39,661,250	$45,857,625	+15.6%
Cost-of-goods-sold expense	$24,960,750	$28,589,255	+14.5%
Gross margin	$14,700,500	$17,268,370	+17.5%
Variable and fixed operating expenses	$11,466,135	$12,675,896	+10.6%
Earnings before interest and income tax	$ 3,234,365	$ 4,592,474	+42.0%
Interest expense	$ 795,000	$ 795,000 **?**	+ 0.0%
Earnings before income tax	$ 2,439,365	$ 3,797,474	+55.7%
Income tax expense	$ 853,778	$ 1,329,116	+55.7%
Net income	$ 1,585,587	$ 2,468,358	+55.7%

FIGURE 7.1 *Profit improvement plan for coming year.*

until more is known about the amount of capital that the company will raise from external sources during the coming year. The final numbers below the earnings before interest and income tax (EBIT) line would be revised if the level of debt were increased. However, this last-minute adjustment shouldn't be very material.

As Figure 7.1 shows, the business has put together an overall plan for the coming year that would increase its bottom-line profit 55.7 percent over the year just ended, which is impressive. However, the profit plan, standing alone, does not reveal the amount of additional capital that will be needed for the increase in assets at the higher level of sales. Sales growth requires more assets to support the higher level of sales revenue and expenses. It would be very unusual to achieve sales growth without increasing assets. Sales growth needs to generate enough profit growth to cover the cost of the additional capital needed for the higher level of assets.

PLANNING ASSETS AND CAPITAL GROWTH

At the close of the business's most recent year, which is the starting point for the coming year of course, the capital invested in its assets and the sources of the capital are as follows (data is from the company's balance sheet presented in Figure 4.2):

Total assets	$26,814,579
Less operating liabilities	$ 3,876,096
Capital invested in assets	$22,938,483

Short-term and long-term debt	$ 9,750,000
Owners' equity	$13,188,483
Total sources of capital	$22,938,483

Remember Please recall that operating liabilities (mainly accounts payable and accrued expenses payable) are generated spontaneously from making purchases on credit and from unpaid expenses. These short-term liabilities are non-interest-bearing and are deducted from total assets to determine the amount of capital invested in assets. This capital has to be secured from borrowing and from owners' equity sources.

A Very Quick But Simplistic Method

According to the company's profit improvement plan for the coming year (Figure 7.1), sales revenue is scheduled to increase 15.6 percent. The business could simply assume that its total assets and operating liabilities would increase the same percent. This calculation yields about a $3.5 million increase in the capital invested in assets (total assets less operating liabilities). Based on this figure the business could anticipate, say, a $1 million increase in debt and a $2.5 million increase in owners' equity. (At an 8.0 percent annual interest rate the interest expense for the coming year would increase $80,000, and the interest and income tax expenses would be adjusted accordingly.)

This expedient but overly simplistic method for forecasting assets and capital growth has serious shortcomings:

- It assumes that sales revenue drives assets and operating liabilities when in fact only accounts receivable is driven directly by sales revenue; expenses drive the other short-term operating assets and short-term operating liabilities.

- It ignores the actual amount of capital expenditures planned for the coming year; the total investment in new long-term operating resources during a particular year does not move in lockstep with changes in sales revenue that year.

- It does not identify the amount of cash flow from profit during the coming year; in most situations this internal source of cash flow provides a sizable amount of the capital for increasing the assets of the business, which alleviates the need to go to external sources of capital.

The business should match up the increases in sales revenue and expenses with the particular operating assets and liabilities that are driven by the sales revenue and expenses. Then the amount of capital expenditures planned for the coming year should be factored into the analysis, as well as the planned increase or decrease in the company's working cash balance (more on this shortly).

K E Y CONCEPT Finally, the business should include the cash flow from profit (operating activities) during the coming year in planning the sources of its total capital needs during the coming year. Cash flow from profit during the coming year probably would not provide all the capital needed for growth, but usually provides a good share of it. Managers have to know the amount of internal capital that will be generated from profit so they know the additional amount of capital they will have to raise from external sources in order to fuel the growth of the business.

A Fairly Quick and Much More Sophisticated Method

One method for determining changes in assets and liabilities for the coming year and for planning where to get the additional capital for the higher level of assets in the coming year is to use a formal and comprehensive *budget system*. As you probably know, budgeting systems are time-consuming and somewhat costly—although for management planning and control purposes the time and money may be well spent. Many businesses, even some fairly large ones, do not use budgeting systems. But, they still have to plan for the impending capital needs to support the growth of the business.

This section demonstrates a method for planning assets and capital growth based on the profit improvement plan of the business, one that can be done fairly quickly and that avoids all the trappings of a detailed budgeting system approach. The first step is to forecast the changes in assets and operating liabilities during the coming year—see Figure 7.2. The balance sheet format is used, starting with the closing balances from the year just ended, which are the starting balances for the coming year.

Increases in sales revenue and expenses planned for the coming year drive many of the increases in assets and operating liabilities, as shown in Figure 7.2. The amounts of the increases in short-term operating assets and liabilities are computed based on the changes in sales revenue and expenses for the coming year in the profit improvement plan. The actual changes in each of these operating assets and liabilities in all likelihood would deviate from these estimates,

Assets

	Beginning Balances (from Figure 4.2)	Based on Profit Improvement Plan and Planning Decisions	Change
Cash	$ 2,345,675	Note 1	$ 200,000
Accounts receivable	$ 3,813,582	15.6%	$ 594,919
Inventories	$ 5,760,173	14.5%	$ 835,225
Prepaid expenses	$ 822,899	10.6%	$ 87,227
Total current assets	$12,742,329		
Property, plant, and equipment	$20,857,500	Note 2	$3,000,000
Accumulated depreciation	($ 6,785,250)	Note 3	($ 943,450)
Cost less accumulated depreciation	$14,072,250		
Total assets	$26,814,579		

Liabilities and Owners' Equity

Accounts payable	$ 2,537,232	Note 4	$ 325,108
Accrued expenses payable	$ 1,280,214	10.6%	$ 135,703
Income tax payable	$ 58,650	Note 5	$ 0
Short-term debt	$ 2,250,000		
Total current liabilities	$ 6,126,096		
Long-term debt	$ 7,500,000		
Total liabilities	$13,626,096		
Capital stock (422,823 and 420,208 shares)	$ 4,587,500		
Retained earnings	$ 8,600,983	Note 6	$1,868,358
Total owners' equity	$13,188,483		
Total liabilities and owners' equity	$26,814,579		

FIGURE 7.2 *Increases in assets, liabilities, and retained earnings.*

but probably not by too much—unless the business were to change its basic policies regarding credit terms it offers its customers, its average inventory holding periods, and so on.

To complete the picture the business has to make certain planning decisions for the coming year. These key planning decisions concern capital expenditures, whether to increase its working cash balance, and whether to pay out cash dividends to shareowners. Also the amount of depreciation that will be recorded in the coming year needs to be calculated. These key points are summarized as follows:

Planning Decisions for Coming Year

- **Note 1.** The business prefers to increase its working cash balance at least $200,000 to keep pace with the increase in sales growth. At the end of the most recent year its cash balance was about $2.3 million. I discuss in other chapters that there is no standard or generally agreed upon ratio of the working cash balance of a business relative to its annual sales or total assets or any other point of reference. This business plans to increase its sales revenue in the coming year to about $46 million (Figure 7.1). Whether a $2.3 million working cash balance is sufficient for $46 million annual sales is a matter of opinion. Many businesses would be comfortable with this balance, but many would not. This business believes that it should increase its working cash balance at least $200,000, which is shown in Figure 7.2.

- **Note 2.** Based on a thorough study of the condition, productivity, and capacity of its fixed assets, the business has adopted a $3 million budget for capital expenditures during the coming year. (Usually, the board of directors of a business must approve major capital outlays for investments in new long-term operating assets.) The decision regarding when to replace such items as old machines, equipment, vehicles, tools is seldom clear-cut and obvious. As a rough comparison, these business decisions are similar to deciding when to replace your old high-mileage auto with a new model. Many factors enter into the decisions regarding replacing old fixed assets of a business with newer models that may be more efficient and reliable, or that are needed to expand the capacity of the business.

- **Note 3.** Depreciation expense increases the accumulated depreciation account, which is a *contra,* or negative, account. Its balance is deducted from the fixed assets account in which the original cost of property, plant, and equipment is recorded. An increase in the accumulated depreciation account means that its negative balance becomes larger. The amount of depreciation expense for the coming year will be higher than last year because new fixed assets costing $3 million will be purchased during the year. The accounting department calculates the amount of depreciation expense that will be recorded during the coming year.

Recording depreciation expense does not require a cash outlay during the year—just the opposite in fact. The cash inflow from sales revenue includes recovery of part of the original cost of the business's long-term operating resources (recorded in the property, plant, and equipment account). Therefore the amount of depreciation expense recorded during a year is added to net income for calculating cash flow from profit for the coming year. (There are other cash flow adjustments to net income as well.)

- **Note 4.** Inventories will increase 14.5 percent, so accounts payable from inventory purchases on credit should increase this percent. Also, the accounts payable liability account includes expenses recorded in the period and that are still unpaid at the end of the period. This component should increase 10.6 percent, which is equal to the percent increase in operating expenses for the coming year. The increase in accounts payable includes both components.

- **Note 5.** Income tax payable may change during the coming year; in any case the increase or decrease is likely to be relatively minor, so a zero change is entered for this liability.

- **Note 6.** Net income planned for the coming year equals $2,468,358 according to the profit improvement plan (Figure 7.1). The board of directors would like to pay $600,000 cash dividends to shareowners during the coming year. Therefore retained earnings would increase $1,868,358 ($2,468,358 net income − $600,000 cash dividends to shareowners).

The forecast changes in operating assets, liabilities, and retained earnings that are presented in Figure 7.2 provide the essential information for determining the *internal* cash flow from profit for the coming year. Cash flow from profit may not be all the capital needed for growth, however. The business probably will have to go to its external sources for additional capital.

Cash flow from profit (operating activities) during the coming year is based on the profit improvement plan and the increases in operating assets and liabilities forecast for the coming year. The first section in Figure 7.3 calculates cash flow from profit, which is then compared with the demands for capital during the coming year. In this way the amount of additional capital from external sources is determined.

The business will have to raise almost $1.5 million in external capital during the coming year ($1,444,752, to be more exact). The business's chief executive working with the chief financial officer will have to decide whether to approach lenders to increase the debt load of the business and whether the business should turn to its shareowners and ask them to invest additional capital in the business. Of course, these are not easy decisions. The information in Figure 7.3 is the indispensable starting point.

END POINT

Growth is the central strategy of many businesses. Growth requires that additional capital be secured to provide money

Cash flow from profit (operating activities)		
Net income planned for coming year	$2,468,358	
Accounts receivable increase	($ 594,919)	
Inventories increase	($ 835,225)	
Prepaid expenses increase	($ 87,227)	
Depreciation expense	$ 943,450	
Accounts payable increase	$ 325,108	
Accrued expenses payable increase	$ 135,703	$2,355,248
Demands for capital		
Increase in working cash balance	$ 200,000	
Capital expenditures budget	$3,000,000	
Cash dividends to shareowners	$ 600,000	$3,800,000
External capital needed during coming year		$1,444,752

*Figures 7.1 and 7.2 are sources of above data.

FIGURE 7.3 *Cash flow from profit and external capital needed.*

for the increases in operating assets needed to support the higher sales level. Growth penalizes cash flow from profit to some extent. Generally speaking, a business cannot depend only on its internal cash flow from profit to supply all the capital needed for increasing its assets, and therefore it must go to outside sources of capital.

Based on the profit improvement plan for a business, the chapter demonstrates an efficient and practical method for forecasting the amount of capital needed to fuel the growth of the business and how much will have to come from its external capital sources in addition to its projected cash flow from profit for the coming year.

Profit and Cash Flow Analysis

Breaking Even and Making Profit

Successful companies are those who year in and year out earn
sufficient profit before interest and income tax from their
operations. Operating earnings is the litmus test of all successful businesses. How do they do it? Not just by making sales
but also by controlling their expenses so that they keep
enough of their sales revenue as operating profit. The long-
term sustainable success of a business rests on the ability of
its managers to earn operating profit consistently. Managers
must know well the pathways to operating profit and avoid
detours along the way.

ADDING INFORMATION IN THE MANAGEMENT PROFIT REPORT

The main business example used in previous chapters is continued in this chapter. Figure 8.1 presents the company's
management profit report for the year just ended—with
important new information presented here for the first time.
The design of this internal accounting profit report copies the
format introduced in Chapter 3. The new items of information
are as follows:

- Total *sales volume* (number of units) of all products sold
  during the period

- The *average sales revenue per unit* (average sales price per
  unit)

Sales Volume 578,500 Units

	Per Unit	Totals
Sales revenue	$68.56	$39,661,250
Cost-of-goods-sold expense	($43.15)	($24,960,750)
Gross margin	$25.41	$14,700,500
Variable revenue-driven operating expenses	($ 5.27)	($ 3,049,010)
Variable unit-driven operating expenses	($ 4.63)	($ 2,677,875)
Contribution margin	$15.51	$ 8,973,615
Fixed operating expenses		($ 5,739,250)
Operating profit		$ 3,234,365
Interest expense		($ 795,000)
Earnings before income tax		$ 2,439,365
Income tax expense		($ 853,778)
Net income		$ 1,585,587

FIGURE 8.1 *Management profit report for year just ended, including sales volume and per-unit values.*

- The *average product cost per unit* (average cost of goods sold per unit)
- The *average variable operating expenses per unit* (revenue-driven and unit-driven)

This additional information is needed for the profit analysis methods explained in this chapter.

The business has three major product lines and sells different products within each line. The business sells a fairly large number of different products, which is typical of most businesses. This chapter looks at the business as a whole, from the viewpoint of its top executives and board of directors. The chapter does not probe into profit margin differences between the business's product lines and separate products within each product line. These topics are discussed in later chapters.

 For measuring overall sales activity, businesses in many industries adopt a common denominator that cuts across all the products sold by the business. Examples are *barrels* for breweries, *tons* for steel mills, *passenger miles* for airlines, and *vehicles* for car and truck manufacturers.

The sales volume for the year reported in Figure 8.1 is the sum of all units sold during the year. Per-unit values in this management profit report are averages for all products. Of course, the averages depend on the *sales mix* of products during the year, which refers to the relative proportions of each product sold. Changes in a business's sales mix can cause significant changes in the average sales price and average costs, which can cause a major shift in profit.

These important points are explored in Chapter 17. In this chapter it does no harm to pretend that the company sells just one product. This one product serves as a stand-in, or proxy, for all the products sold by the company. The business sold 578,500 units at a $68.56 sales price; product cost was $43.15; and the company incurred $5.27 revenue-driven variable costs and $4.63 unit-driven variable costs for each unit sold. Therefore, the business earned $15.51 contribution margin per unit sold (Figure 8.1). This profit margin figure equals sales price minus product cost minus the two variable operating expenses.

The business sold 578,500 units at this margin per unit, so it earned $8,973,615 *contribution margin* ($15.51 contribution margin per unit × 578,500 units sales volume = $8,973,615 contribution margin). This measure of profit is before fixed operating expenses for the year and before interest and income tax expenses. Of course, contribution margin is not the bottom-line profit of a business. But it is an extremely important stepping-stone measure of profit that deserves close management attention.

Although not shown in Figure 8.1, contribution margin equals 22.6 percent of sales revenue ($8,973,615 contribution margin ÷ $39,661,250 sales revenue = 22.6%). Managers should compare this key ratio with prior years and against the company's profit objectives for the year just ended. Any slippage in this important ratio can have serious consequences, as later chapters demonstrate. This chapter focuses on how the business made the amount of profit that it did for the year. Later chapters focus on changes in sales volume, sales prices, cost changes, and other factors that improve or damage profit performance.

KEY CONCEPT — FIXED OPERATING EXPENSES

Fixed operating expenses are deducted from contribution margin to determine *operating profit,* which also is called *operating earnings,* or *earnings before interest and income tax* (EBIT). The general nature of fixed costs is explained in Chapter 3. A business has many operating expenses that vary either with sales volume or with sales revenue. In stark contrast, a business has many operating expenses that do not vary with sales activity. Instead these costs remain stuck in place over a range of sales activity levels.

Examples of typical fixed operating expenses are the following. A business signs annual or multiyear lease contracts for retail and warehouse space; the monthly rents are fixed in amount and do not depend on the sales of the business. Employees are hired and paid fixed salaries per month or are promised 40-hour weeks at certain hourly rates. Premiums are paid for six months to provide insurance coverage against casualty and liability losses. Utility and telephone bills are paid monthly and do not depend on sales levels. Property taxes and vehicle licenses are fixed amounts for the year. Many other examples of fixed operating costs could be listed.

In short, a business makes many commitments that incur certain operating costs for a period of time. These fixed costs cannot be avoided unless the business takes drastic action, such as breaking contracts, firing employees, or not paying property taxes. For all practical purposes, fixed operating expenses are pretty much locked in for the year. Fixed operating expenses often are called *overhead costs* because these costs hang over the head of the managers running the business like an albatross or millstone.

Why would any rational manager commit to overhead costs? Fixed operating expenses provide *capacity.* These costs make available the capacity to carry on sales activity and other operations of the business. Fixed expenses are incurred to provide the needed space, equipment, and personnel to sell products and to carry on the necessary operating activities of the business. By committing to these costs, the business acquires a certain amount of capacity, or ability to operate for the period.

Business managers should estimate the sales capacity of their business (i.e., the maximum sales volume that is feasible based on the fixed expenses of the business). Estimating sales capacity may not be all that precise, but a reasonable, ballpark estimate can be made. The manager could start by asking whether a 10 percent sales volume increase would require an increase in the business's fixed expenses. Managers should compare the business's sales capacity against actual sales volume. A business may have a large amount of unused sales capacity. Perhaps sales could grow 10, 20, or 30 percent before more space would have to be rented and more persons would have to be hired or more equipment would have to be installed. Having an estimate of the idle, unused sales capacity of the business is especially important in planning ahead and in analyzing the profit impact of changes in the key factors that drive profit, as the following discussion reveals.

 The term *fixed* should be used with caution. True, the fixed costs of a business for a period are largely unchanging and inflexible—but not down to the last penny. The main point about fixed operating expenses is that they are insensitive to the number of units sold during the period or the amount of sales revenue for the period—unless a business takes drastic action to scale down or expand its sales capacity. Many, if not most, fixed expenses can be adjusted if sales drop off precipitously or surge ahead rapidly. For example, suppose sales take a sudden and unexpected downturn. A business could sublet part of the space it rents, reduce insurance limits, or sell some of the property it owns. If on the other hand sales spurted up all of a sudden, a business could ask its employees who are guaranteed a 40-hour workweek at a fixed hourly rate to work overtime to handle the upsurge in sales. What the term *fixed* actually means is that these costs remain largely constant in the short run over a range of sales activity that might be 10 to 25 percent lower or higher than the actual sales volume of the business.

DEPRECIATION: A SPECIAL KIND OF FIXED COST

Depreciation expense accounting is unique; you could even say weird. The basic idea of allocating the cost of a long-term operating resource over its useful, productive life is sound and unimpeachable. (Ownership of land confers the right to occupy a certain space in perpetuity, so the cost of land is not depreciated.) The total cost of a company's long-term operating resources is reported in an asset account in its balance sheet, usually entitled *property, plant, and equipment.*

 The original costs of *fixed assets* are recorded in one account, and depreciation expense each period is recorded in a second account called *accumulated depreciation.* The balance in this contra, or offset, account is the cumulative amount of depreciation expense recorded to date. Its balance is deducted from the property, plant, and equipment asset account. In this way the balance sheet discloses both the cost of a company's fixed assets and how much of the cost has been depreciated so far.

For instance, at the close of its most recent year the business's fixed assets are reported as follows in its year-end balance sheet (from Figure 4.2):

Property, plant, and equipment	$20,857,500
Accumulated depreciation	($ 6,785,250)
Cost less accumulated depreciation	$14,072,250

In this example the business's fixed operating expenses for the year just ended include $768,450 depreciation expense. In other words, the business recorded a $768,450 write-off of its fixed assets in order to recognize the wear and tear on and the gradual loss of productivity of its long-term operating resources. In short, the year just ended was charged more than three-quarters of a million dollars for the use of fixed assets during the year. But, the amount of depreciation expense for the year should be taken with a grain of salt. Indeed, you need a saltshaker in the case of depreciation.

 Business managers should pay particular attention to the depreciation expense accounting methods used by their business for three main reasons:

1. Depreciation expense is not a cash outlay in the year it is recorded; the fixed assets being depreciated were bought and paid for in previous years (except for the new fixed assets acquired during the most recent year).

2. The computation of annual depreciation expense is based on an arbitrary time-based method of allocation—not on the actual level of use of fixed assets during the period.

3. For the vast majority of businesses, the amount of annual depreciation expense is determined by federal income tax—the useful lives permitted under the tax law are considerably shorter than realistic estimates for most fixed assets of most businesses; and the income tax law permits front-end loading of depreciation expense (except for buildings), which causes the expense to decline from year to year.

As a practical matter, most businesses use the useful lives for their fixed assets that are permitted by the federal income tax law, and they use one of the allocation methods allowed by the law. Most businesses abandon any attempt to base depreciation on realistic useful life estimates and actual patterns of use from year to year. One result is that a fixed asset, say a particular piece of machinery or equipment, could be fully depreciated on the books yet continue to be used for several additional years during which no depreciation expense is recorded. Business managers definitely should know whether certain of their operating fixed assets were used during the period for which no depreciation expense was recorded.

In times past there was an argument for the units-of-production depreciation method for manufacturers. The method, in brief, works as follows. The business estimates the total number of units expected to be manufactured using a particular machine or piece of equipment over its entire economic life. This number is divided into cost of the fixed asset to calculate depreciation per unit. The amount of depreciation recorded for the period depends on the number of units manufactured. Depreciation would be a *variable* cost if this method were used.

The units-of-production depreciation method is seldom if ever used—even though it has good theoretical support. Instead businesses' fixed assets are depreciated by either the straight-line method or an accelerated method. Both methods allocate a certain predetermined amount of a fixed asset's cost to each year of the estimated life of the asset regardless of how much or how little the asset actually might be used during the year. Therefore, depreciation is a fixed cost.

INTEREST EXPENSE

The business incurred $795,000 interest expense for the year just ended (Figure 8.1). Interest is not an operating expense—it's a *financial* expense. As you know, interest is the cost of using debt for part of the total capital invested in the assets of the business. Generally speaking, the total amount of capital invested in assets swings up and down with shifts in sales revenue—though certainly not in direct proportion to changes in sales revenue or sales volume (number of units sold). Thus the amount of debt tends to move in the same direction as changes in sales. However, the linkage between shifts in sales revenue and debt is not simple and cannot easily be put into a formula.

For relatively minor swings in its sales level a business probably would not adjust the amount of its debt in most situations, so its interest expense would remain fixed in amount. On the other hand, for major shifts in sales a business probably would adjust the amount of its debt, so its interest expense would change. In the following analysis assume that the business's annual interest expense is fixed—keeping in mind that a major change in sales volume probably would result in a corresponding change in debt and interest expense.

PATHWAYS TO PROFIT

The business's operating profit, earnings before income tax, and net income are presented in the management profit report (Figure 8.1). Reading a profit report is passive and reflective; computing profit is active and engaging. Managers don't get paid to know profit, but to make profit happen. Managers need a sure-handed analytical grip on the factors that drive profit. The following discussion explains methods of calculating profit, mainly for the purpose of demonstrating how profit is earned.

KEY CONCEPT Before calculating profit it's necessary to identify which particular profit definition is being used: *operating profit* (earnings before interest and income tax), *earnings before income tax* (earnings after interest expense), or bottom-line *net income* (earnings after income tax). Income tax is a contingent expense; basically it's a certain percent of taxable income. Taxable income, generally speaking, equals earnings before income tax because interest expense is deductible to determine taxable income. (Tax accountants will cringe when they read this sentence because there are many complexities in the federal income tax law; but to simplify I assume that taxable income equals the business's earnings before income tax.) In the example, the business's income tax rate is 35 percent of its earnings before income tax.

In the following analysis the business's fixed operating expenses and its fixed interest expense are combined into one total fixed cost for the year ($5,739,250 fixed operating expenses + $795,000 fixed interest expense = $6,534,250 total fixed costs). In other words, profit is defined as earnings before income tax. The business earned $2,439,365 profit for the year just ended (Figure 8.1).

There are three different ways to analyze how the business earned its profit for the year, and each offers valuable lessons for business managers.

Pathway to Profit #1: Margin Times Sales Volume

One pathway for calculating profit is as follows (data is from Figure 8.1):

> $15.51 contribution margin per unit
>
> × 578,500 total units sold (sales volume)
>
> = $8,973,615 total contribution margin
>
> − $6,534,250 fixed expenses
>
> = $2,439,365 profit

Technical note: Contribution margin per unit shown here is a rounded figure; the precise contribution margin per unit is used in calculating total contribution margin.

The linchpin in this computation is the multiplication of contribution margin per unit by sales volume to get total contribution margin. Sales volume needs a good contribution margin per unit to work with. Maybe you've heard the old joke: "A business loses a little on each sale but makes it up on volume." This isn't funny, you know.

The Breakeven Hurdle

KEY CONCEPT The business sold enough units to overcome its fixed expenses and earn a profit. Business managers worry a lot about their fixed costs—there's no profit unless the business's sales volume is large enough to cover its fixed expenses. The sales volume needed to cover fixed costs is called the *breakeven point,* or the *breakeven volume,* or more simply just *breakeven.* The breakeven point equals that exact sales volume at which total contribution margin equals total fixed expenses. The breakeven calculation tells a manager the sales volume that has to be achieved just to cover his or her fixed costs for the year.

Generally, businesses do not publicly divulge their breakeven volumes. Financial reporting standards do not require that this particular piece of information be disclosed in external financial reports. Some years ago, a series of articles in the financial press about Chrysler Corporation referred to the company's breakeven point. At that time Chrysler's breakeven point was 1.8 million vehicles a year. One article said that this breakeven point was reasonable because Chrysler had sold about 2.3 million vehicles in the previous year, but that the breakeven point was higher than Chrysler would like it to be heading into the trough of the industry's sales cycle. Although now out-of-date, these articles illustrate the importance of breakeven.

The breakeven point for the company example (i.e., the sales volume at which the company's profit would be zero) is computed as follows:

$$\frac{\$6,534,250 \text{ annual fixed expenses}}{\$15.51 \text{ unit contribution margin}} = 421,242 \text{ units}$$

Technical note: Contribution margin per unit shown here is a rounded figure; the precise contribution margin per unit is used in calculating breakeven volume.

If the business had sold only 421,242 units during the year it would have earned zero profit (earnings before income tax). The company's taxable income would have been zero and its income tax would have been zero. So net income would have been zero. Figure 8.2 illustrates the breakeven sales volume scenario.

The breakeven volume is a useful point of reference. It's a

Sales Volume 421,242 Units

	Per Unit	Totals
Sales revenue	$68.56	$28,879,837
Cost-of-goods-sold expense	($43.15)	($18,175,484)
Gross margin	$25.41	$10,704,353
Variable revenue-driven operating expenses	($ 5.27)	($ 2,220,175)
Variable unit-driven operating expenses	($ 4.63)	($ 1,949,928)
Contribution margin	$15.51	$ 6,534,250
Fixed operating expenses		($ 5,739,250)
Operating profit		$ 795,000
Interest expense		($ 795,000)
Earnings before income tax		$ 0
Income tax expense		$ 0
Net income		$ 0

Note: Pro forma means "as if," or based on certain conditions or circumstances.

FIGURE 8.2 *Pro forma profit report at hypothetical breakeven volume.*

good way to express the total fixed-costs commitment of a business (i.e., how many units have to be sold just to cover fixed costs). Also, sales volume can be compared against breakeven volume to measure a company's *margin of safety.* Furthermore, breakeven volume is very useful in analyzing profit behavior at different levels of sales volume.

Cash Flow Breakeven

As explained previously, depreciation is a fixed cost, but it is different in one very important respect from other fixed costs. Depreciation is not a cash outlay in the year the expense is recorded. The other fixed costs of a business are cash-based. Some of these fixed costs are prepaid (such as insurance premiums paid in advance for future coverage), and many are paid after the expense is recorded in either the accounts payable or the accrued expenses payable liability account. But the cash flows for these fixed costs take place mostly in the period in which the expenses are recorded. In contrast, there is no cash payment for depreciation expense.

Therefore, depreciation can be stripped out of the fixed costs for the period and the *cash flow breakeven volume* can be calculated as follows:

$6,534,250 annual total fixed expenses

– $768,450 depreciation expense for year

$$= \frac{\$5,765,800 \text{ cash-based fixed expenses for year}}{\$15.51 \text{ unit contribution margin}}$$

= 371,703 units

For cash flow analysis, this concept of breakeven is relevant. But managers are much more concerned about profit numbers that will be presented in the business's external income statement and its internal profit reports. So, the most used concept of breakeven includes all fixed costs.

Margin of Safety

One purpose of calculating breakeven is to compare it against actual sales volume. The excess of actual sales volume over breakeven sales volume provides the measure of a company's *margin of safety.* This excess over breakeven sales volume reveals how much the company's sales would have to drop before the business slips out of the black and into the red— from profit to loss. The company sold 578,500 units during the year just ended compared with its 421,242 units breakeven volume. So it sold 157,258 units over its breakeven, which is its margin of safety. The company's margin of safety equals 27 percent of its actual sales volume for the year (157,258 units excess over breakeven ÷ 578,500 units sold during the year = 27%). Of course this 27 percent margin of safety does not necessarily guarantee a profit next year. Sales could drop dramatically, or expenses could rise dramatically. Later chapters explore what would happen based on changes in the key factors that drive profit.

Pathway to Profit #2: Jumping the Breakeven Hurdle

A second way to calculate profit is to use the number of units sold in excess over breakeven as the source of profit, as follows:

578,500 total units sold (sales volume)

− <u>421,242</u> breakeven volume

= 157,258 units sold in excess of breakeven

× $15.51 contribution margin per unit

= $2,439,365 profit

Technical note: Contribution margin per unit shown here is a rounded figure; the precise contribution margin per unit is used in calculating profit.

This method assigns the first 421,242 units sold during the year to covering fixed expenses. In other words, the contribution margin from the first 421,242 units sold during the year is viewed as consumed by fixed expenses. The 157,258 units sold in excess of the breakeven volume are viewed as the source of profit. In other words, annual sales volume is divided into two piles: (1) the breakeven group and (2) the profit group.

Profit is the same amount as calculated by the first method, although the method of getting there is different. The difference is a little more complex than meets the eye. It's not just an exercise with numbers; it concerns how managers think about making profit in the first place. The first method of computing profit stresses the multiplication of unit contribution margin by sales volume to get total contribution margin for the period. Fixed expenses are not ignored, but are deducted from total contribution margin to work down to profit. In contrast, the excess over breakeven method puts fixed expenses first and profit second—the business first has to exceed its fixed expenses before it gets into the black.

Pathway to Profit #3: Average Profit Per Unit

The excess over breakeven profit method divides sales volume into two piles: (1) the breakeven quantity necessary to cover total fixed expenses and (2) the surplus over breakeven volume that provides profit. A third pathway to profit divides every unit sold into two parts: fixed expenses and profit.

The basic concept of the third method is that profit derives from spreading fixed expenses over a sufficiently large sales volume to ensure that the average fixed cost per unit is less than the contribution margin per unit. The fundamental thinking is that every unit sold has to do two things: (1) contribute its share to cover fixed expenses and (2) provide a profit residual. The computation of profit by this method is as follows:

$6,534,250 total fixed costs

÷ 578,500 units sales volume for year

= $11.29 average fixed cost per unit sold

versus $15.51 contribution margin per unit

= $ 4.22 average profit per unit

× 578,500 total units sold (sales volume)

= $2,439,365 profit

Technical note: The contribution margin per unit, average fixed cost per unit, and average profit per unit are rounded figures; the precise figures for each are used in calculating profit.

This method spreads fixed expenses for the year over the total number of units sold, which gives $11.29 as the average fixed cost per unit. Profit according to this method is viewed as the spread between the $11.29 average fixed cost per unit and the $15.51 contribution margin per unit, which is $4.22 average profit per unit. Of course, the amount of profit for the year (earnings before income tax) is the same as for the two computation methods explained previously.

Suppose the business had sold only 421,242 units (its breakeven volume). The average fixed expenses per unit sold would have been much higher. In fact, it would have been $15.51 per unit ($6,534,250 total fixed expenses ÷ 421,242 units breakeven volume = $15.51 average fixed cost per unit). In this hypothetical situation the average fixed cost per unit would equal the average contribution margin per unit. So the business would have made precisely zero profit per unit. In other words, profit would be zero.

END POINT

Because a business has fixed expenses, it has to worry about its breakeven point—which is determined by dividing its total fixed expenses for the period by its contribution profit margin per unit. The breakeven point is that precise sales volume at which the business's sales revenue would equal its total expenses and thus would experience exactly zero profit. The only advantage of breaking even is that the business would have no income tax to pay. At breakeven, the company's bottom-line net income is zero. Of course, a business does not deliberately try to earn zero profit.

This chapter examines the nature of fixed expenses, especially the depreciation expense component of fixed expenses, noting that fixed expenses are not really 100 percent fixed and unchangeable, but are treated as if they were over the short run for breakeven analysis and for examining the pathways to profit. The chapter demonstrates the three different ways to compute profit, each of which has unique advantages for management analysis. The manager may find one more useful than the others in a given situation or for explaining the profit strategy of his or her business to others.

Sales Volume Changes

Business managers face constant change in the pursuit of profit. All profit factors are subject to change—due to both external changes beyond the control of the business and changes initiated by the managers themselves. Many management decisions are triggered by change. Indeed, managers are often characterized as *change agents*.

Its suppliers may increase the purchase costs of the products sold by the business. Or the cost of manufacturing products may change, as may the productivity performance of its manufacturing operations. The company may raise wages for some or all of its employees, or wage rates might actually be reduced by employee givebacks or downsizing. The landlord may raise the rent; competitors may drop their sales prices and the business may have to follow suit. Managers may decide to raise sales prices. And so on.

One basic function of managers is to keep a close watch on all relevant changes and know how to deal with those changes. Changes set in motion a new round of profit-making decisions. This chapter is the first of four that analyze the impact of changes in the factors that drive profit. The basic factors are changed to determine the resulting change in profit. For example, if you sold 10 percent more units, would your profit be 10 percent higher? Nope, it's not as simple as this, and managers should know why.

THREE WAYS OF MAKING A $1 MILLION PROFIT

By and large, previous chapters take a macro, or business-as-a-whole, approach to profit analysis techniques that business managers need to understand. This chapter shifts gears and takes more of a micro and focused point of view. The typical business consists of many different profit pieces, or *profit modules,* as I prefer to call them. A profit module is a separate identifiable source of sales and profit of a business. A product line is a typical example of a profit module.

One product by itself could be a profit module if the product stands alone and generates a significant amount of sales revenue and profit. A separate store location or each branch of a business could be operated as a separate segment of the business and, accordingly, be accounted for as a profit module. Organizational units that have profit responsibility are also called *profit centers.*

A profit center may consist of two or more profit modules. A brand generally covers too broad a range of different products to be just one profit module, although in some cases a brand might be a profit module. Managers have to figure out the best way to organize their sales activities into separate and distinguishable profit modules, which are the constituent profit members of the whole business. For each one of these organizational slices of the total business, a meaningful measure of profit is adopted that is appropriate for that particular management unit of the organization. Certain designated managers plan and control each profit module, which is necessary to achieve the overall profit goals of the business.

Figure 9.1 presents management profit reports for three contrasting profit modules of a business. Each is a basic product line of the business. The generic product line is an example of high volume and low unit margin. The business's premier product line is at the opposite end of the how-to-make-profit spectrum—low volume and high unit margin. Its standard product line falls in the middle—moderate volume and moderate unit margin. Each product line generated a $1 million profit for the year just ended.

I designed these three examples so that profit is $1 million for each module. This makes it easier to compare the impacts caused by changes in profit factors between the three product

Standard Product Line

	100,000 units sold	
	Per Unit	**Totals**
Sales revenue	$100.00	$10,000,000
Cost of goods sold	$ 65.00	$ 6,500,000
Gross margin	$ 35.00	$ 3,500,000
Revenue-driven expenses @ 8.5%	$ 8.50	$ 850,000
Unit-driven expenses	$ 6.50	$ 650,000
Contribution margin	$ 20.00	$ 2,000,000
Fixed operating expenses	$ 10.00	$ 1,000,000
Profit	$ 10.00	$ 1,000,000

Generic Product Line

	150,000 units sold	
	Per Unit	**Totals**
Sales revenue	$ 75.00	$11,250,000
Cost of goods sold	$ 57.00	$ 8,550,000
Gross margin	$ 18.00	$ 2,700,000
Revenue-driven expenses @ 4.0%	$ 3.00	$ 450,000
Unit-driven expenses	$ 5.00	$ 750,000
Contribution margin	$ 10.00	$ 1,500,000
Fixed operating expenses	$ 3.33	$ 500,000
Profit	$ 6.67	$ 1,000,000

Premier Product Line

	50,000 units sold	
	Per Unit	**Totals**
Sales revenue	$150.00	$ 7,500,000
Cost of goods sold	$ 80.00	$ 4,000,000
Gross margin	$ 70.00	$ 3,500,000
Revenue-driven expenses @ 7.5%	$ 11.25	$ 562,500
Unit-driven expenses	$ 8.75	$ 437,500
Contribution margin	$ 50.00	$ 2,500,000
Fixed operating expenses	$ 30.00	$ 1,500,000
Profit	$ 20.00	$ 1,000,000

FIGURE 9.1 *Three contrasting profit modules of a business.*

lines. Profit is the same for all three modules, but the sales prices, unit margins, and fixed operating expenses are quite different for the three product lines. Note that the business had to sell three times as many units of its generic products (150,000 units) as its premier products (50,000 units) to earn the same profit.

Chapter 8 explains the different ways of analyzing profit, which I call *pathways to profit*. The three management profit reports presented in Figure 9.1 for the three profit modules follow the layout of the #1 pathway to profit, as follows:

Unit margin × sales volume = contribution margin

– fixed costs

= profit

The management profit reports in Figure 9.1 also include data for the #3 pathway to profit. For instance, for the premiere product line the business spread its $1.5 million fixed costs over 50,000 units, which gives a $30.00 average fixed cost per unit sold. On this product line, the business makes a $50.00 unit margin, so its profit is $20.00 per unit, which multiplied times the 50,000 units sales volume gives $1 million profit for the year. The #2 pathway to profit is brought into play later to explain why the percent change in profit is greater than the percent change in sales volume.

The three variable expenses per unit reported in Figure 9.1 for each profit module (i.e., product cost, revenue-driven, and unit-driven) are *incremental costs*. That is to say, if the business sells one more unit, then total cost increases by the per unit amounts shown in Figure 9.1. The total amount of each of these expenses for the period depends on the number of units sold (or sales volume). In contrast, the per-unit amount of fixed operating expenses for each product line is determined by dividing the total fixed costs for the period by the number of units sold. If the business had sold one unit more or one unit less than it did, the total amount of fixed costs for the period would be the same, but the average fixed cost per unit would be slightly different because this is a calculated amount that depends on the number of units sold.

Defining Profit and the Matter of Fixed Costs

Each profit module (product line) shown in Figure 9.1 is charged with its *direct* fixed operating expenses for the year. These include such costs as the salaries of the managers and other employees who work exclusively in this area of the business, advertising expenditures for the products (except for the generic product, which is not advertised), depreciation of various fixed assets used by each of these profit segments of the business, and so on. Several fixed costs of the business cannot be allocated directly to any of its profit modules (the general legal costs of the business, the compensation of companywide top-level executives, the cost of its annual independent audit, charitable contributions made by the business, the cost of institutional advertising in which the name of the company but no specific products are promoted, etc.). Every profit module is expected to earn a sufficient profit after deducting its direct fixed costs from its contribution margin.

Summing up, each of the three profit modules in the example (see Figure 9.1) earned $1 million for the year just ended. These are profit amounts prior to taking into account the indirect fixed expenses of the business and the interest expense and income tax expense of the business. The general manager of each product line is held accountable for its profit performance, of course.

SELLING MORE UNITS

Business managers, quite naturally, are sales oriented. No sales, no business; it's as simple as that. As they say in marketing—nothing happens until you sell it. Many businesses do not make it through their start-up phase because it's very difficult to build up and establish a sales base. Customers have to be won over. Once established, sales volume can never be taken for granted. Sales are vulnerable to competition, shifts in consumer preferences and spending decisions, and general economic conditions both domestically and globally.

Thinking more positively, sales volume growth is the most realistic way to increase profit. In most cases, sales price increases are met with some degree of customer resistance as well as a response from competitors. Indeed, demand may be extremely sensitive to sales prices. Cost containment and expense control are important, to be sure, but are more of a defensive tactic than a profit growth strategy as such.

Suppose that for all three product lines the business sold 10 percent more units during the year just ended. What amount of profit would have been earned from each product line? Of course, there's no such thing as a free lunch. An experienced manager would ask how the business could increase its sales volume. Would customers buy 10 percent more without any increase in advertising, without any sales price incentives, without some product improvements or other inducements? Not too likely. Increasing sales volume usually requires some stimulant such as more advertising.

 Another question an experienced manager might ask is whether the business has enough *capacity* to handle 10 percent additional sales. It's always a good idea to run a capacity check whenever looking at sales volume increases. Fixed expenses may have to be increased to enlarge the capacity needed to accommodate the additional sales volume. However, assume that the manager of each profit module had enough untapped capacity to take on 10 percent additional sales volume without having to increase any of his or her fixed operating expenses.

Figure 9.2 presents the profit results for the 10 percent higher sales scenario for each product line. Sales prices, unit product costs, and variable expenses per unit remain the same in each of the three profit modules. And, the direct fixed costs of each product line remain the same. Therefore, at the higher sales volume the average fixed cost per unit is lower. For instance, consider the standard product line. At the original 100,000 units sales volume, the $1 million in fixed costs average out to $10.00 per unit. At the higher 110,000 units sales volume, the average fixed costs per unit drop $.91 per unit, so the business makes $10.91 profit per unit. The driving force behind the $200,000 increase in profit is selling

Standard Product Line

| | Original Scenarios (see Figure 9.1) | | Changes | |
| | 100,000 units sold | | 10,000 additional units | |
	Per Unit	Totals	Per Unit	Totals	
Sales revenue	$100.00	$10,000,000		$1,000,000	
Cost of goods sold	$ 65.00	$ 6,500,000		$ 650,000	
Gross margin	$ 35.00	$ 3,500,000		$ 350,000	
Revenue-driven expenses @ 8.5%	$ 8.50	$ 850,000		$ 85,000	
Unit-driven expenses	$ 6.50	$ 650,000		$ 65,000	
Contribution margin	$ 20.00	$ 2,000,000		$ 200,000	10%
Fixed operating expenses	$ 10.00	$ 1,000,000	($0.91)	$ 0	
Profit	$ 10.00	$ 1,000,000	$0.91	$ 200,000	20%

Generic Product Line

| | 150,000 units sold | | 15,000 additional units | |
	Per Unit	Totals	Per Unit	Totals	
Sales revenue	$ 75.00	$11,250,000		$1,125,000	
Cost of goods sold	$ 57.00	$ 8,550,000		$ 855,000	
Gross margin	$ 18.00	$ 2,700,000		$ 270,000	
Revenue-driven expenses @ 4.0%	$ 3.00	$ 450,000		$ 45,000	
Unit-driven expenses	$ 5.00	$ 750,000		$ 75,000	
Contribution margin	$ 10.00	$ 1,500,000		$ 150,000	10%
Fixed operating expenses	$ 3.33	$ 500,000	($0.30)	$ 0	
Profit	$ 6.67	$ 1,000,000	$0.30	$ 150,000	15%

Premier Product Line

| | 50,000 units sold | | 5,000 additional units | |
	Per Unit	Totals	Per Unit	Totals	
Sales revenue	$150.00	$ 7,500,000		$ 750,000	
Cost of goods sold	$ 80.00	$ 4,000,000		$ 400,000	
Gross margin	$ 70.00	$ 3,500,000		$ 350,000	
Revenue-driven expenses @ 7.5%	$ 11.25	$ 562,500		$ 56,250	
Unit-driven expenses	$ 8.75	$ 437,500		$ 43,750	
Contribution margin	$ 50.00	$ 2,500,000		$ 250,000	10%
Fixed operating expenses	$ 30.00	$ 1,500,000	($2.73)	$ 0	
Profit	$ 20.00	$ 1,000,000	$2.73	$ 250,000	25%

FIGURE 9.2 *10 percent higher sales volumes.*

10,000 additional units at a $20.00 unit margin, not the decrease in average fixed cost per unit. This decrease is simply one result of the higher sales volume.

In all three cases, contribution margin improves exactly 10 percent, the same as the percent of sales volume increase. This is straightforward: Selling 10 percent more units with no change in unit margin drives up contribution margin exactly 10 percent. But please note the difference in the amounts of the contribution margin increases:

Contribution Margin Increases for Each Product Line

Premier   5,000 units increase × $50.00 unit margin = $250,000

Standard   10,000 units increase × $20.00 unit margin = $200,000

Generic   15,000 units increase × $10.00 unit margin = $150,000

Selling 10 percent more premier units would bring in a $50,000 higher contribution margin than would selling 10 percent more standard units. And selling 10 percent more standard units would make $50,000 more profit than selling 10 percent generic units.

Operating Leverage

CONCEPT   Note in Figure 9.2 that even though contribution margin increases 10 percent for each product line because of the 10 percent higher sales volume levels, the percent increases in profit are 1.5 to 2.5 times greater. For instance, profit on the standard product line would be 20 percent higher, or two times the 10 percent sales volume increase. The $200,000 increase in contribution margin equals 10 percent gain, but the $200,000 gain is 20 percent on the profit figure. In short, the 10 percent sales volume increase has a doubling effect on the percent increase in profit. The multiplier, or compounding effect is called *operating leverage*.

The additional 10,000 units sold equal 10 percent of the total units sold, but they equal 20 percent of the units sold in excess of the product line's breakeven point. The profit pile, or units sold in excess of breakeven, expands by 20 percent. This analysis is summarized as follows for the standard product line (data from Figure 9.2):

Analysis of Operating Leverage Effect

$1,000,000 fixed costs ÷ $20.00 unit margin = 50,000 units breakeven

100,000 units sales volume – 50,000 units breakeven = 50,000 units over breakeven

10,000 additional units sold ÷ 50,000 units over breakeven = 20% increase

So profit would increase 20 percent by increasing sales volume just 10 percent, as shown in Figure 9.2. In like manner, the percent of gain in profit (15 percent for generic products and 25 percent for premier products) can be calculated.

The nub of operating leverage is that the swing in profit is more than the sales volume swing. Operating leverage means that profit percent changes are a multiple of sales volume percent changes. There's hardly ever a 1:1 percent relationship. This rule is based on fixed expenses remaining constant at the higher sales level. If fixed expenses increase 10 percent right along with the sales volume increase (i.e., if fixed operating expenses increase 10 percent as well), then profit would go up only 10 percent.

 Operating leverage reflects the fact that the business has not been fully using the capacity provided by its fixed costs. When capacity is reached, and sooner or later it will be as sales volume grows, fixed expenses will have to be increased to provide more capacity. If the company had already been selling at its maximum capacity, then its fixed expenses would have had to be increased. This points out the importance of knowing where you are presently relative to the company's capacity.

SALES VOLUME SLIPPAGE

Suppose that the sales volumes had been 10 percent *lower* during the year just ended across the board for all three product lines. The effects of this downside scenario are presented in Figure 9.3, which is basically the negative mirror image of the 10 percent sales volume increase scenario. It's a good idea for the managers of each product line to keep this lower sales volume, or worst-case scenario, in mind so they know just how sensitive profit is to a falloff in sales volume.

The combined impact for all three product lines would have been a profit drop-off of $600,000, from $3 million in the original scenario to only $2.4 million profit in the 10 percent lower sales volume.

When faced with a falloff in sales volume, managers should be very concerned, of course, and they should probe into the reasons for the decrease. More competition? Are people switching to substitute products? Are hard times forcing customers to spend less? Is the location deteriorating? Has service to customers slipped? Are total quality management (TQM) techniques needed to correct the loss of sales?

Sales volume losses are one of the most serious problems confronting any business. Unless they are quickly reversed, the business has to make extremely wrenching decisions regarding how to downsize (laying off employees, selling off fixed assets, shutting down plants, etc.). The late economist Kenneth Boulding has called downsizing the management of decline, which hits the nail on the head, I think. It's an extremely unpleasant task, to say the very least.

The immediate (short-run) operating profit impact of a 10 percent sales volume decrease would depend heavily on whether the company could reduce its fixed expenses at the lower sales level. Assume not. In Figure 9.3, fixed operating expenses remain the same at the lower sales levels for each product line. In the sales decline scenario, operating leverage compounds the felony—profit decreases by a multiple of the 10 percent sales volume decrease in this scenario.

FIXED COSTS AND SALES VOLUME CHANGES

In analyzing the profit impacts of changes in sales volume, there is the question regarding what to do with fixed operating expenses. The simple expedient is to keep fixed costs the same at the higher or the lower sales volume. However, this is not an entirely satisfactory solution. For very small changes in sales volume, fixed costs do not change. In other words, fixed costs are insensitive to relatively small changes in sales volume.

In the typical situation, most fixed costs (e.g., depreciation expense recorded in the period, labor cost for employees paid monthly fixed salaries, and amounts paid for insurance pre-

Standard Product Line

| | Original Scenarios (see Figure 9.1) | | Changes | |
| | 100,000 units sold | | 10,000 additional units | |
	Per Unit	Totals	Per Unit	Totals
Sales revenue	$100.00	$10,000,000		($1,000,000)
Cost of goods sold	$ 65.00	$ 6,500,000		($ 650,000)
Gross margin	$ 35.00	$ 3,500,000		($ 350,000)
Revenue-driven expenses @ 8.5%	$ 8.50	$ 850,000		($ 85,000)
Unit-driven expenses	$ 6.50	$ 650,000		($ 65,000)
Contribution margin	$ 20.00	$ 2,000,000		($ 200,000) −10%
Fixed operating expenses	$ 10.00	$ 1,000,000	$1.11	$ 0
Profit	$ 10.00	$ 1,000,000	($1.11)	($ 200,000) −20%

Generic Product Line

| | 150,000 units sold | | 15,000 additional units | |
	Per Unit	Totals	Per Unit	Totals
Sales revenue	$ 75.00	$11,250,000		($1,125,000)
Cost of goods sold	$ 57.00	$ 8,550,000		($ 855,000)
Gross margin	$ 18.00	$ 2,700,000		($ 270,000)
Revenue-driven expenses @ 4.0%	$ 3.00	$ 450,000		($ 45,000)
Unit-driven expenses	$ 5.00	$ 750,000		($ 75,000)
Contribution margin	$ 10.00	$ 1,500,000		($ 150,000) −10%
Fixed operating expenses	$ 3.33	$ 500,000	$0.37	$ 0
Profit	$ 6.67	$ 1,000,000	($0.37)	($ 150,000) −15%

Premier Product Line

| | 50,000 units sold | | 5,000 additional units | |
	Per Unit	Totals	Per Unit	Totals
Sales revenue	$150.00	$ 7,500,000		($ 750,000)
Cost of goods sold	$ 80.00	$ 4,000,000		($ 400,000)
Gross margin	$ 70.00	$ 3,500,000		($ 350,000)
Revenue-driven expenses @ 7.5%	$ 11.25	$ 562,500		($ 56,250)
Unit-driven expenses	$ 8.75	$ 437,500		($ 43,750)
Contribution margin	$ 50.00	$ 2,500,000		($ 250,000) −10%
Fixed operating expenses	$ 30.00	$ 1,500,000	$3.33	$ 0
Profit	$ 20.00	$ 1,000,000	($3.33)	($ 250,000) −25%

FIGURE 9.3 *10 percent lower sales volumes.*

miums) would not be any different if sales volume had been 1 or 2 percent higher or lower, or even 5, 10, or 20 percent different in either direction. But at some point a business will have to increase its fixed costs to provide additional capacity on the upside or will have to cut fixed costs on the downside.

In the preceding analysis, the assumption is made that each product line has enough capacity to take on 10 percent additional sales volume without any increase in the direct fixed costs of the profit module. Keep in mind, however, that one or more fixed operating expenses might have to increase to support a higher sales volume. For instance, the business might have to rent more retail floor space, hire more salaried employees, or purchase additional equipment on which depreciation is recorded. For a moderate increase in sales volume, fixed expenses generally hold steady and don't increase, as a general rule, unless the business already is running at virtually 100 percent of its capacity.

Faced with moderate decreases in sales volume, businesses generally hold off and delay any serious reduction in capacity that would require laying off employees. Employees usually have been trained and have valuable experience to offer a business. It may be difficult to reduce many fixed expenses, at least in the short run. Some fixed expenses can be adjusted downward in short order. But if you had time to look at the typical fixed costs of a business, I think you would find that unwinding from many of the expenses would take time and would have serious consequences to the business.

Finally, I would mention that in dire circumstances, such as when a business goes into bankruptcy, all bets are off. A business may have to slash many fixed costs under pressures from creditors or by court order. Also, in takeover situations, in which one business buys out another business, often a key element of the takeover strategy is to drastically reduce the fixed costs of the acquired business. This often means laying off hundreds of thousands of employees and selling off assets.

END POINT

All profit factors are subject to change. Management neglect or ineptitude can lead to profit deterioration, sometimes very quickly. Increases in product cost as well as increases in variable and fixed expenses can do serious damage to profit performance. But managers may not be able to significantly improve certain factors. Fixed expenses may already be cut to the bone. One vendor may control product costs, or alternative vendors may offer virtually the same prices. Competition may put a fairly tight straitjacket on sales prices. Customers are sensitive to sales price increases. Sales volume is the key success factor for most businesses, which explains why managers are so concerned about market share. Market share is mentioned often in later chapters.

10

Sales Price and Cost Changes

Before we go any further, let me ask you a basic question. Suppose you could have one or the other, but not both, which would you prefer—a 10 percent sales volume increase or a 10 percent sales price increase? In most cases, there's a huge difference between the two. This chapter contrasts the difference between sales volume and sales price changes. You may be surprised. In any case, you should be very certain about the differences!

SALES PRICE CHANGES

Setting sales prices is one of the most perplexing decisions facing business managers. Competition normally dictates the basic range of sales prices. But usually there is some room for deviation from your competitors' prices because of product differentiation, brand loyalty, location advantages, and/or quality of service, to cite only a few of the many reasons that permit you to charge higher sales prices than your competition.

 Fixed operating expenses are insensitive to sales price increases. In contrast, sales volume increases may very well require increases in fixed operating expenses, especially when the company's capacity is crowded. Very few fixed expenses are directly affected by raising sales prices, even if the company is operating at full capacity. Advertising (a fixed cost once spent) might be stepped up to persuade customers that the hike in sales prices is necessary or beneficial. Other than this, it's hard to find many fixed operating expenses that are tied directly to sales price increases.

The same three profit module examples used in Chapter 9 for analyzing sales volume changes are used in this chapter to analyze sales price changes. This allows the comparison of the differences between the profit impacts of selling more or fewer units versus selling the same number of units but at higher or lower sales prices. With this in mind, consider the hypothetical scenario in which the business could have sold the same number units of each product line at 10 percent higher sales prices. Figure 10.1 presents this scenario for the three profit modules examples.

Profit more than doubles on the generic product line; and profit increases 92 percent and 69 percent on the standard and premier product lines, respectively (see Figure 10.1). Would this be realistic? Only to the extent that a 10 percent sales price increase would be realistic. Assume that the business could have sold all units during the year at the higher sales prices. The advantages of selling at 10 percent higher sales prices compared with selling 10 percent more sales volume are summarized in Figure 10.2.

In this scenario only one variable operating expense would increase—the one driven by sales revenue. Note that cost-of-goods-sold expense does not increase because the volume sold remains the same. In the sales volume increase situation (Chapter 9), the sales revenue increase is offset substantially by the increase in cost-of-goods-sold expense. In contrast, consider the standard product line here in the sales price increase case: $915,000 of the $1 million incremental sales revenue flows through to profit.

Chapter 3 introduces the format and logic of an internal management profit report. One key point is that expenses should be classified and reported according to their behavior, or what drives them.* Some operating expenses depend

---

Cost driver is a popular term these days. This refers to the specific factors that determine, or push, or drive a particular cost. Identifying cost drivers is the key step in the method of cost analysis and allocation called *activity-based costing* (ABC). Cost allocation is discussed in Chapter 18.

Standard Product Line

	Original Scenarios (see Figure 9.1)			Changes		
	100,000 units sold			No change		
	Per Unit	Totals		Per Unit	Totals	
Sales revenue	$100.00	$10,000,000		$10.00	$1,000,000	10%
Cost of goods sold	$ 65.00	$ 6,500,000				
Gross margin	$ 35.00	$ 3,500,000				
Revenue-driven expenses @ 8.5%	$ 8.50	$ 850,000		$ 0.85	$ 85,000	
Unit-driven expenses	$ 6.50	$ 650,000				
Contribution margin	$ 20.00	$ 2,000,000		$ 9.15	$ 915,000	46%
Fixed operating expenses	$ 10.00	$ 1,000,000				
Profit	$ 10.00	$ 1,000,000		$ 9.15	$ 915,000	92%

Generic Product Line

	150,000 units sold			No change		
	Per Unit	Totals		Per Unit	Totals	
Sales revenue	$ 75.00	$11,250,000		$ 7.50	$1,125,000	10%
Cost of goods sold	$ 57.00	$ 8,550,000				
Gross margin	$ 18.00	$ 2,700,000				
Revenue-driven expenses @ 4.0%	$ 3.00	$ 450,000		$ 0.30	$ 45,000	
Unit-driven expenses	$ 5.00	$ 750,000				
Contribution margin	$ 10.00	$ 1,500,000		$ 7.20	$1,080,000	72%
Fixed operating expenses	$ 3.33	$ 500,000				
Profit	$ 6.67	$ 1,000,000		$ 7.20	$1,080,000	108%

Premier Product Line

	50,000 units sold			No change		
	Per Unit	Totals		Per Unit	Totals	
Sales revenue	$150.00	$ 7,500,000		$15.00	$ 750,000	10%
Cost of goods sold	$ 80.00	$ 4,000,000				
Gross margin	$ 70.00	$ 3,500,000				
Revenue-driven expenses @ 7.5%	$ 11.25	$ 562,500		$ 1.12	$ 56,250	
Unit-driven expenses	$ 8.75	$ 437,500				
Contribution margin	$ 50.00	$ 2,500,000		$13.88	$ 693,750	28%
Fixed operating expenses	$ 30.00	$ 1,500,000				
Profit	$ 20.00	$ 1,000,000		$13.88	$ 693,750	69%

FIGURE 10.1 *10 percent higher sales prices.*

	10 Percent Sales Volume Increase (see Figure 9.2)		10 Percent Sales Price Increase (see Figure 10.1)	
Standard Product Line				
Contribution margin	$200,000	10%	$ 915,000	46%
Profit	$200,000	20%	$ 915,000	92%
Generic Product Line				
Contribution margin	$150,000	10%	$1,080,000	72%
Profit	$150,000	15%	$1,080,000	108%
Premier Product Line				
Contribution margin	$250,000	10%	$ 693,750	28%
Profit	$250,000	25%	$ 693,750	69%

FIGURE 10.2 *Comparison of 10 percent higher sales prices versus 10 percent higher sales volumes.*

directly on the dollar amounts of sales, not the quantity of products sold. As total sales revenue (dollars) increases, these expenses increase directly in proportion. In short, one more dollar of sales revenue causes these expenses to increase by a certain amount of cents on the dollar.

Most retailers accept national credit cards (Visa, Master-Card, Discover, American Express, Diners Club, etc.). The credit card charge slips are deposited daily with a local participating bank. The bank then discounts the total amount and credits the net balance in the business's checking account. Discount rates vary between 2 and 4 percent (sometimes lower or higher). In short, a business nets only $.98 or $.96 from each dollar of credit card sales. The credit card discount expense comes right off the top of the sales dollar.

Sales commissions are another common example of sales revenue-dependent expenses. As you probably know, many retailers and other businesses pay their sales representatives on a commission basis, usually a certain percent of the total sales amount such as 5 or 10 percent. The salespersons may also receive a base salary, which would be the fixed floor of the expense; only the commission over and above the fixed base would be variable. (This requires the separation of the fixed part and the variable part in the management profit report.)

Many businesses extend short-term credit to their customers, especially when selling to other businesses. No matter how carefully a business screens them before extending credit, a few customers never pay their accounts. Eventually, after making repeated collection efforts, the business ends up having to write off all or some of these receivables' balances as uncollectible. These losses are called *bad debts* and are a normal expense of doing business on credit. This expense depends on the sales amount, not sales volume (number of units sold).

Another example of an expense that varies with sales revenue is one you might not suspect—rent. Companies often sign lease agreements that call for rental amounts based on gross sales. There may be a base amount or fixed minimum monthly rent. In addition, there may be a variable amount equal to a percent of total sales revenue. This is common for retailers renting space in shopping centers. There are several other examples of expenses that vary with total sales revenue, such as franchise fees based on gross sales.

Summing up, sales revenue increases 10 percent for the three product lines (see Figure 10.1), but the incremental revenue is partially offset by the increase in the sales revenue-driven expenses. Thus the increases in contribution margins are less than the increases in sales revenue. In Figure 10.1 it is assumed that the fixed operating expenses of the profit modules do not change at the higher sales price levels. Thus, the contribution margin increases flow down to the profit lines.

Increasing sales volume 10 percent increases total contribution margin only 10 percent because the contribution margin per unit remains the same. And fixed operating expenses may have to be increased to support the higher sales volume. (In the examples, these fixed costs are held constant at the higher sales volume.) Increasing sales prices 10 percent improves contribution margin per unit much more than 10 percent, and total contribution margin rises accordingly. Note the standard product line, for instance (Figure 10.1). The contribution margin per unit increases $9.15, which is a 46 percent jump over the $20.00 figure before the sales price increase. Thus, total contribution margin increases $915,000, or 46 percent, at the higher sales price. And fixed operating expenses should not be affected by the higher sales price.

Frankly, a 10 percent increase in sales price with no increase in the product cost and no increase in the other expenses of the company is not too likely to happen. It is presented here to illustrate the powerful impact of a sales price increase and to contrast it with a 10 percent increase in sales volume (see Figure 10.2 again). Also, I should mention here that the cash flow impact of a 10 percent sales price increase differs from that of a sales volume increase like day from night (see Chapter 13).

WHEN SALES PRICES HEAD SOUTH

DANGER! Like it or not, business managers sometimes have to cut sales prices just to hang onto the present sales volume they have. They know that profit will suffer, but competitive pressures force them to cut sales prices, at least temporarily. Or they decide to cut prices to boost sales volume, but the number of units sold in fact remains the same, and later they have to nudge sales prices back up to previous levels. A 10 percent sales price cut would be the *negative* mirror image of the effects caused by the 10 percent sales price increase. Just put negative signs in front of the changes you see in Figure 10.1. If this happened, all the profit and then some would be wiped out on the generic product line, over 90 percent of the profit on the standard product line would evaporate, and the business would give up over 69 percent of its profit from the premier products.

To illustrate the serious profit damage from even a relatively small decrease in the average sales price of products over a period of time, assume that during the year just ended the business had to cut sales prices at times during the year such that, on average, the sales prices of the products sold in the three product lines suffered by 4 percent. This may not sound like too much of a catastrophe, but look at the results shown in Figure 10.3 for this scenario. Sales prices and sales revenue drop by 4 percent, but profit plunges from 28 to 43 percent, depending on the product line.

The reason for the lower drop in profit for the premier product line is that the unit margin of these products is a much larger percent of sales price, so a 4 percent cut in sales price doesn't take such a big bite out of the unit margin. For

Standard Product Line

Original Scenarios (see Figure 9.1)			Changes		
	100,000 units sold		No change		
	Per Unit	Totals	Per Unit	Totals	
Sales revenue	$100.00	$10,000,000	($4.00)	($400,000)	−4%
Cost of goods sold	$ 65.00	$ 6,500,000			
Gross margin	$ 35.00	$ 3,500,000			
Revenue-driven expenses @ 8.5%	$ 8.50	$ 850,000	($0.34)	($ 34,000)	
Unit-driven expenses	$ 6.50	$ 650,000			
Contribution margin	$ 20.00	$ 2,000,000	($3.66)	($366,000)	−18%
Fixed operating expenses	$ 10.00	$ 1,000,000			
Profit	$ 10.00	$ 1,000,000	($3.66)	($366,000)	−37%

Generic Product Line

	150,000 units sold		No change		
	Per Unit	Totals	Per Unit	Totals	
Sales revenue	$ 75.00	$11,250,000	($3.00)	($450,000)	−4%
Cost of goods sold	$ 57.00	$ 8,550,000			
Gross margin	$ 18.00	$ 2,700,000			
Revenue-driven expenses @ 4.0%	$ 3.00	$ 450,000	($0.12)	($ 18,000)	
Unit-driven expenses	$ 5.00	$ 750,000			
Contribution margin	$ 10.00	$ 1,500,000	($2.88)	($432,000)	−29%
Fixed operating expenses	$ 3.33	$ 500,000			
Profit	$ 6.67	$ 1,000,000	($2.88)	($432,000)	−43%

Premier Product Line

	50,000 units sold		No change		
	Per Unit	Totals	Per Unit	Totals	
Sales revenue	$150.00	$ 7,500,000	($6.00)	($300,000)	−4%
Cost of goods sold	$ 80.00	$ 4,000,000			
Gross margin	$ 70.00	$ 3,500,000			
Revenue-driven expenses @ 7.5%	$ 11.25	$ 562,500	($0.45)	($ 22,500)	
Unit-driven expenses	$ 8.75	$ 437,500			
Contribution margin	$ 50.00	$ 2,500,000	($5.55)	($277,500)	−11%
Fixed operating expenses	$ 30.00	$ 1,500,000			
Profit	$ 20.00	$ 1,000,000	($5.55)	($277,500)	−28%

FIGURE 10.3 *4 percent lower sales prices.*

comparison, the 4 percent (or $3.00) sales price cut for the generic products, net of the decrease in the revenue-driven expenses, represents a 29 percent reduction in the unit margin on these products. For the premier products, the 4 percent (or $6.00) price cut (net of the decrease in its revenue-driven expenses) is only an 11 percent reduction in the unit margin.

CHANGES IN PRODUCT COST AND OPERATING EXPENSES

In most cases, changes in sales volume and sales prices have the biggest impact on profit performance. Product cost probably would rank as the next most critical factor for most businesses (except for service businesses that do not sell products). A retailer needs smart, tough-nosed, sharp-pencil, aggressive purchasing tactics to control its product costs. On the other hand, it can be carried to an extreme.

I knew a purchasing agent (a neighbor when I lived in California some years ago) who was a real tiger. For instance, George would even return new calendars sent by vendors at the end of the year with a note saying, "Don't send me this calendar; give me a lower price." This may be overkill, though George eventually became general manager of the business.

DANGER!

Even with close monitoring and relentless control, both the variable and fixed operating expenses of a business may increase. Salaries, rent, insurance, utility bills, and audit and legal fees—virtually all operating expenses—are subject to inflation. To illustrate this situation, consider the scenario in which sales prices and sales volume remain the same but the company's product costs and its variable and fixed operating expenses increase. In particular, assume that the business's product costs and its unit-driven variable expenses increase 10 percent. Fixed costs increase only, say, 8 percent, because the depreciation expense component of total fixed expenses remains unchanged. Depreciation is based on the original cost of fixed assets and is not subject to the general inflationary pressures on operating expenses. Revenue-driven variable expenses, being a certain percent of sales revenue, do not change, because in this scenario sales revenue does not change (sales volumes and sales prices for each product line don't change).

Figure 10.4 presents the effects for this cost inflation

Standard Product Line

	Original Scenarios (see Figure 9.1)		Changes		
	100,000 units sold		No change		
	Per Unit	Totals	Per Unit	Totals	
Sales revenue	$100.00	$10,000,000			
Cost of goods sold	$ 65.00	$ 6,500,000	$6.50	$650,000	10%
Gross margin	$ 35.00	$ 3,500,000			
Revenue-driven expenses @ 8.5%	$ 8.50	$ 850,000			
Unit-driven expenses	$ 6.50	$ 650,000	$0.65	$ 65,000	10%
Contribution margin	$ 20.00	$ 2,000,000	($7.15)	($715,000)	−36%
Fixed operating expenses	$ 10.00	$ 1,000,000	$0.80	$ 80,000	8%
Profit	$ 10.00	$ 1,000,000	($7.95)	($795,000)	−80%

Generic Product Line

	150,000 units sold		No change		
	Per Unit	Totals	Per Unit	Totals	
Sales revenue	$ 75.00	$11,250,000			
Cost of goods sold	$ 57.00	$ 8,550,000	$5.70	$855,000	10%
Gross margin	$ 18.00	$ 2,700,000			
Revenue-driven expenses @ 4.0%	$ 3.00	$ 450,000			
Unit-driven expenses	$ 5.00	$ 750,000	$0.50	$ 75,000	10%
Contribution margin	$ 10.00	$ 1,500,000	($6.20)	($930,000)	−62%
Fixed operating expenses	$ 3.33	$ 500,000	$0.27	$ 40,000	8%
Profit	$ 6.67	$ 1,000,000	($6.47)	($970,000)	−97%

Premier Product Line

	50,000 units sold		No change		
	Per Unit	Totals	Per Unit	Totals	
Sales revenue	$150.00	$ 7,500,000			
Cost of goods sold	$ 80.00	$ 4,000,000	$8.00	$400,000	10%
Gross margin	$ 70.00	$ 3,500,000			
Revenue-driven expenses @ 7.5%	$ 11.25	$ 562,500			
Unit-driven expenses	$ 8.75	$ 437,500	$0.88	$ 43,750	10%
Contribution margin	$ 50.00	$ 2,500,000	($8.88)	($443,750)	−18%
Fixed operating expenses	$ 30.00	$ 1,500,000	$2.40	$120,000	8%
Profit	$ 20.00	$ 1,000,000	($11.28)	($563,750)	−56%

FIGURE 10.4 *Higher costs.*

scenario. As you can see, it's not a pretty picture. The company could ill afford to let its product costs and operating expenses get out of control. Virtually all (97 percent) of the profit on the generic product line would be eliminated in this case. The profit on the standard product line would plunge 80 percent, and the profit on the premier product line would suffer 56 percent. If the cost increases could not be avoided, then managers would have the unpleasant task of passing the cost increases along to their customers in the form of higher sales prices.

END POINT

If you had your choice, the best change is a sales price increase, assuming all other profit factors remain the same. A sales price increase yields a much better profit result than a sales volume increase of equal magnitude. Increasing sales volume ranks a distant second behind raising sales prices. Of course, customers are sensitive to sales price increases, and as a practical matter the only course of action to increase profit may be to sell more units at the established sales prices. Sales volume and sales prices are the two big factors driving profit. However, cost factors cannot be ignored, of course.

The unit costs of the products sold by the business and virtually all its operating costs—both variable and fixed—can change for the worse. Such unfavorable cost shifts would cause devastating profit impacts unless they are counterbalanced with prompt increases in sales prices. This and other topics are explored in the following chapters.

Price/Volume
Trade-Offs

Raising sales prices may very well cause sales volume to fall. Cutting sales prices may increase sales volume—unless competitors lower their prices also. Higher sales prices may be in response to higher product costs that are passed through to customers. Increasing product costs to improve product quality may jack up sales volume. Increasing sales commissions (a prime revenue-driven expense) may give the sales staff just the incentive needed to sell more units. Spending more on fixed operating expenses—such as bigger advertising budgets, higher rent for larger stores, or more expensive furnishings— may help sales volume.

None of this is news to experienced business managers. The business world is one of trade-offs among profit factors. In most cases, a change in one profit factor causes, or is in response to, a change in another factor.

Chapters 9 and 10 analyze profit factor changes one at a time; the other profit factors are held constant. (To be technically correct here, I should note that sales price changes cause revenue-driven expenses to change in proportion.) In the real world of business, seldom can you change just one thing at a time. This chapter analyzes the interaction of changes in two or more profit factors.

SHAVING SALES PRICES TO BOOST SALES VOLUME

The example of the three profit modules introduced in Chapter 9 and carried through in Chapter 10 continues in this chapter. Instead of the management profit report format used in the previous two chapters, however, this chapter uses a profit model for each product line. Figure 11.1 presents the profit models for each product line. A profit model is essentially a condensed version, or thumbnail sketch, of the profit reports.

Suppose the managers in charge of these three profit modules are seriously considering decreasing their sales prices 10 percent, which they predict would increase sales volume 10 percent. Of course, competitors may reduce their prices 10 percent, so the sales volume increase may not materialize. But the managers don't think their competitors will follow suit. The company's products are differentiated from the competition. (Brand names, customer service, and product specifications are types of differentiation.) There always has been some amount of sales price spread between the business's products and the competition. A 10 percent price cut should not trigger price reductions by competition, in the opinion of the managers.

One reason for reducing sales prices is that the business is not selling up to its full capacity. This is not unusual; many businesses have some slack or untapped sales capacity provided by their fixed expenses. In this example, assume that the fixed expenses of each product line provide enough space and personnel to handle a 20 to 25 percent larger sales volume. Spreading total fixed expenses over a larger number of units sold seems like a good idea. Rather than downsizing, which would require cutting fixed expenses, the first thought is to increase sales volume and thus take better advantage of the sales capacity provided by fixed expenses.

DANGER! Of course, the managers are very much aware that sales volume may not respond to the reduction in sales price as much as they predict. On the other hand, sales volume may increase more than 10 percent. In any case, they would closely monitor the reaction of customers. Obviously there is a serious risk here. Suppose sales volume doesn't increase; they may not be able to reverse directions quickly. The managers may not be able to roll back the sales price decrease without losing customers, who may forget the sales price decreases and see the reversal only as price increases.

Before the managers make a final decision, wouldn't it be a good idea to see what would happen to profit? Managers should run through a quick analysis of the consequences of the sales price decision before moving ahead. Otherwise they are operating in the dark and hoping for the best, which may

Standard Product Line

Sales price	$100.00
Product cost	$65.00
Revenue-driven expenses	$8.50
Unit-driven expenses	$6.50
Unit margin	$20.00
Sales volume	100,000
Contribution margin	$2,000,000
Fixed operating expenses	$1,000,000
Profit	$1,000,000

Generic Product Line

Sales price	$75.00
Product cost	$57.00
Revenue-driven expenses	$3.00
Unit-driven expenses	$5.00
Unit margin	$10.00
Sales volume	150,000
Contribution margin	$1,500,000
Fixed operating expenses	$500,000
Profit	$1,000,000

Premier Product Line

Sales price	$150.00
Product cost	$80.00
Revenue-driven expenses	$11.25
Unit-driven expenses	$8.75
Unit margin	$50.00
Sales volume	50,000
Contribution margin	$2,500,000
Fixed operating expenses	$1,500,000
Profit	$1,000,000

FIGURE 11.1 *Profit models for three product lines (data from Figure 9.1).*

actually turn out to be the worst. Figure 11.2 presents the analysis of the sales price reduction plan.

Whoops! Cutting sales prices would be nothing short of a disaster. Assuming the sales volume predictions turn out to be correct, the sales price reduction would push the generic product line into the red and cause substantial profit deterioration in the other two product lines. Why is there such a devastating impact on profit? Why would things turn out so badly? For each product line sales price, revenue-driven expenses and sales volume change 10 percent. But the key change is the percent decrease in unit margin for each product. For instance, the standard product unit margin would go down a huge 46 percent, from $20.00 to $10.85 (see Figure 11.2). Thus contribution margin drops 40 percent and profit drops 81 percent.

The puny 10 percent gain in sales volume is not nearly enough to overcome the 46 percent plunge in unit margin. You can't give up almost half your unit contribution margin and make it back with a 10 percent sales volume increase. In fact, any trade-off that lowers sales price on the one side with an equal percent increase in sales volume on the other side pulls the rug out from under profit.

Yet frequently we see sales price reductions of 10 percent or more. What's going on? First of all, many sales price reductions are from list prices that no one takes seriously as the final price—such as sticker prices on new cars. List prices are only a point of departure for getting to the real price. Everyone wants a discount. I'm sure you've heard people say, "I can get it for you wholesale."

The example is based on real prices, or the sales revenue per unit actually received by the business. Can a business cut its real sales price 10 percent and increase profit? Sales volume would have to increase much more than 10 percent, which I explain shortly. Would trading a 10 percent sales price cut for a 10 percent sales volume increase ever be a smart move? It would seem not; we have settled this point in the preceding analysis, haven't we? Well, there is one exception that brings out an important point.

A Special Case: Sunk Costs

Notice in Figure 11.1 that the unit costs for the products remain the same at the lower sales price; there are no

	Before	After	Change
Standard Product Line			
Sales price	$100.00	$90.00	−10%
Product cost	$65.00	$65.00	
Revenue-driven expenses	$8.50	$7.65	−10%
Unit-driven expenses	$6.50	$6.50	
Unit margin	$20.00	$10.85	−46% ←
Sales volume	100,000	110,000	10%
Contribution margin	$2,000,000	$1,193,500	−40%
Fixed operating expenses	$1,000,000	$1,000,000	
Profit	$1,000,000	$193,500	−81%
Generic Product Line			
Sales price	$75.00	$67.50	−10%
Product cost	$57.00	$57.00	
Revenue-driven expenses	$3.00	$2.70	−10%
Unit-driven expenses	$5.00	$5.00	
Unit margin	$10.00	$2.80	−72% ←
Sales volume	150,000	165,000	10%
Contribution margin	$1,500,000	$462,000	−69%
Fixed operating expenses	$500,000	$500,000	
Profit (Loss)	$1,000,000	($38,000)	−104%
Premier Product Line			
Sales price	$150.00	$135.00	−10%
Product cost	$80.00	$80.00	
Revenue-driven expenses	$11.25	$10.13	−10%
Unit-driven expenses	$8.75	$8.75	
Unit margin	$50.00	$36.12	−28% ←
Sales volume	50,000	55,000	10%
Contribution margin	$2,500,000	$1,986,875	−21%
Fixed operating expenses	$1,500,000	$1,500,000	
Profit	$1,000,000	$486,875	−51%

FIGURE 11.2 *10 percent lower sales prices and 10 percent higher sales volumes.*

changes in the product cost per unit for the product lines. This seems to be a reasonable assumption. To have products for sale, the business either has to buy (or make) them at this unit cost or, if already in inventory, has to incur this cost to replace units sold. This is the normal situation, of course. But it may not be true in certain unusual and nontypical cases.

A business may not replace the units sold; it may be at the end of the product's life cycle. For instance, the product may be in the process of being phased out and replaced with a newer model. In this situation the historical, original accounting cost of inventory becomes a *sunk cost,* which means that it's water over the dam; it can't be reversed.

 Suppose the units held in inventory will not be replaced, that the business is at the end of the line on these units and is selling off its remaining stock. In this situation the book value of the inventory (the recorded accounting cost) is not relevant. What the business paid in the past for the units should be disregarded.* For all practical purposes the unit product cost can be set to zero for the units held in stock. The manager should ignore the recorded product cost and find the highest sales price that would move all the units out of inventory.

VOLUME NEEDED TO OFFSET SALES PRICE CUT

In analyzing sales price reductions, managers should determine just how much sales volume increase would be needed to offset the 10 percent sales price cut. In other words, what level of sales volume would keep contribution margin the same? For the moment, assume that the fixed expenses would remain the same—that the additional sales volume could be taken on with no increase in fixed costs. The sales volumes needed to keep profit the same for each product line are computed by dividing the contribution margins of each product

*The original cost (book value) of products that will not be replaced when sold should be written down to a lower value (possibly zero) under the lower-of-cost-or-market (LCM) accounting rule. This write-down is based on the probable disposable value of the products. If such products have not yet been written down, the manager should make the accounting department aware of this situation so that the proper accounting adjusting entry can be recorded.

line at the original sales prices by the unit margins at the lower sales prices:

Product Contribution Margin ÷ Lower Unit Margin = Required Sales Volume

Standard $2,000,000 ÷ $10.85 = 184,332 units

Generic $1,500,000 ÷ $2.80 = 535,714 units

Premier $2,500,000 ÷ $36.12 = 69,204 units

Figure 11.3 summarizes the effects of these higher sales volumes and shows that the number of units sold would have to increase by rather large percents—from a 257 percent increase for the generic product line to a 38 percent increase for the premier product line. Would such large sales volume gains be possible? Doubtful, to say the least. And to achieve such large increases in sales volume, fixed expenses would have to be increased, probably by quite large amounts. Also, interest expense would increase because more debt would be used to finance the increase in operating assets needed to support the higher sales volume.

 The moral of the story, basically, is that a 10 percent sales price cut usually takes such a big bite out of unit contribution margin that it would take a huge increase in sales volume to stay even (i.e., to earn the same profit as before the price cut). Managers should think long and hard before making sales price reductions.

Short-Term and Limited Sales

The preceding analysis applies the sales price reduction to all sales for the entire year. However, many sales price reductions are limited to a relatively few items and are short-lived, perhaps for only a day or weekend. Furthermore, the sale may bring in customers who buy other items not on sale. Profit margin is sacrificed on selected items to make additional sales of other products at normal profit margins.

 Indeed, many retailers seem to have some products on sale virtually every day of the year. In this case the normal profit margin is hard to pin down, since almost every product takes its turn at being on sale. In short, every product may have two profit margins—one when not on sale and one when on sale.

	Before	After	Change
Standard Product Line			
Sales price	$100.00	$90.00	−10%
Product cost	$65.00	$65.00	
Revenue-driven expenses	$8.50	$7.65	−10%
Unit-driven expenses	$6.50	$6.50	
Unit margin	$20.00	$10.85	−46%
Sales volume	100,000	184,332	84% ←
Contribution margin	$2,000,000	$2,000,000	
Fixed operating expenses	$1,000,000	$1,000,000	
Profit	$1,000,000	$1,000,000	
Generic Product Line			
Sales price	$75.00	$67.50	−10%
Product cost	$57.00	$57.00	
Revenue-driven expenses	$3.00	$2.70	−10%
Unit-driven expenses	$5.00	$5.00	
Unit margin	$10.00	$2.80	−72%
Sales volume	150,000	535,714	257% ←
Contribution margin	$1,500,000	$1,500,000	
Fixed operating expenses	$500,000	$500,000	
Profit	$1,000,000	$1,000,000	
Premier Product Line			
Sales price	$150.00	$135.00	−10%
Product cost	$80.00	$80.00	
Revenue-driven expenses	$11.25	$10.13	−10%
Unit-driven expenses	$8.75	$8.75	
Unit margin	$50.00	$36.12	−28%
Sales volume	50,000	69,204	38% ←
Contribution margin	$2,500,000	$2,500,000	
Fixed operating expenses	$1,500,000	$1,500,000	
Profit	$1,000,000	$1,000,000	

FIGURE 11.3 *Sales volumes needed to offset 10 percent sales price cuts.*

The average profit margin for the year depends on how often the item goes on sale.

In any case, the same basic analysis also applies to limited, short-term sales price reductions. The manager should calculate, or at least estimate, how much additional sales volume would be needed on the sale items just to remain even with the profit that would have been earned at normal sales prices. Complicating the picture are sales of other products (not on sale) that would not have been made without the increase in sales traffic caused by the sale items. Clearly, the additional sales made at normal profit margins are a big factor to consider, though this may be very hard to estimate with any precision.

THINKING IN REVERSE: GIVING UP SALES VOLUME FOR HIGHER SALES PRICES

Suppose the general managers of the three product lines are thinking of a general 10 percent sales price increase, knowing that sales volume probably would decrease. In fact, they predict the number of units sold will drop at least 10 percent. Sales managers generally are very opposed to giving up any sales volume, especially a loss of market share that could be difficult to recapture later. Any move that decreases sales volume has to be considered very carefully. But for the moment let's put aside these warnings. Would a 10 percent sales price hike be a good move if sales volume dropped only 10 percent?

The profit analysis for this trade-off is shown in Figure 11.4. However, before you look at it, what would you expect? An increase in profit? Yes, but would you expect the profit increases to be as large as shown in Figure 11.4? The unit margins on each product line would increase substantially, from 28 percent on the premier products to 72 percent on the generic products. These explosions in unit margins would more than offset the drop in sales volumes and would make for dramatic increases in profit. Fixed expenses wouldn't go up with the decrease in sales volume. If anything, some of the fixed operating costs possibly could be reduced at the lower sales volume level.

The big jumps in profit reported in Figure 11.4 are based on the prediction that sales volume would drop only 10 percent. But actual sales might fall 15, 20, or even 25 percent.

	Before	After	Change
Standard Product Line			
Sales price	$100.00	$110.00	10%
Product cost	$65.00	$65.00	
Revenue-driven expenses	$8.50	$9.35	10%
Unit-driven expenses	$6.50	$6.50	
Unit margin	$20.00	$29.15	46% ←
Sales volume	100,000	90,000	−10%
Contribution margin	$2,000,000	$2,623,500	31%
Fixed operating expenses	$1,000,000	$1,000,000	
Profit	$1,000,000	$1,623,500	62%
Generic Product Line			
Sales price	$75.00	$82.50	10%
Product cost	$57.00	$57.00	
Revenue-driven expenses	$3.00	$3.30	10%
Unit-driven expenses	$5.00	$5.00	
Unit margin	$10.00	$17.20	72% ←
Sales volume	150,000	135,000	−10%
Contribution margin	$1,500,000	$2,322,000	55%
Fixed operating expenses	$500,000	$500,000	
Profit	$1,000,000	$1,822,000	82%
Premier Product Line			
Sales price	$150.00	$165.00	10%
Product cost	$80.00	$80.00	
Revenue-driven expenses	$11.25	$12.38	10%
Unit-driven expenses	$8.75	$8.75	
Unit margin	$50.00	$63.87	28% ←
Sales volume	50,000	45,000	−10%
Contribution margin	$2,500,000	$2,874,375	15%
Fixed operating expenses	$1,500,000	$1,500,000	
Profit	$1,000,000	$1,374,375	37%

FIGURE 11.4 *10 percent higher sales prices and 10 percent lower sales volumes.*

Profit can be calculated for any particular sales volume decrease prediction, of course. No one knows how sales volume might respond to a 10 percent sales price increase. Sales may not decrease at all. For instance, the higher prices might enhance the prestige or upscale image of the standard products and attract a more upscale clientele who are quite willing to pay the higher price. Or sales may drop more than 25 percent because customers search for better prices elsewhere.

How much could sales volume fall and keep total contribution margin the same? This sales volume is computed for the standard product line as follows:

$$\frac{\$2,000,000 \text{ contribution margin target}}{\$29.15 \text{ higher unit margin}} = 68,611 \text{ units}$$

Sales volume would have to drop more than 30 percent (from 100,000 units in the original scenario to less than 70,000 units at the higher sales prices). Sales may not drop off this much, at least in the short run. And fixed operating expenses probably could be reduced at the lower sales volume level.

Given a choice, my guess is that the large majority of business managers would prefer keeping their market share and not giving up any sales volume, even though profit could be maximized with higher sales prices and lower sales volumes. Protecting sales volume and market share is deeply ingrained in the thinking of most business managers.

Any loss of market share is taken very seriously. By and large, you'll find that successful companies have built their success on getting and keeping a significant market share so that they are a major player and dominant force in the marketplace.

True, some companies don't have a very large market share—they carve out a relatively small niche and build their business on low sales volume at premium prices. The preceding analysis for the premier product line demonstrates the profit potential of this niche strategy, which is built on higher unit margins that more than make up for smaller sales volume.

END POINT

Seldom does one profit factor change without changing or being changed by one or more other profit factors. The interaction effects of the changes should be carefully analyzed before making final decisions or locking into a course of action that might be difficult to reverse. Managers should keep their attention riveted on unit margin. Profit performance is most responsive to changes in the unit margin.

Basically, there are only two ways to improve unit margin: (1) increase sales price or (2) decrease product cost and/or other variable operating expenses per unit (see Chapter 12). The sales price is the most external or visible part of the business—the factor most exposed to customer reaction. In contrast, product cost and variable expenses are more internal and invisible. Customers may not be aware of decreased expenses unless such cost savings show up in lower product quality or worse service.

Last, the importance of protecting sales volume and market share is mentioned in the chapter. Marketing managers know what they're talking about on this point, that's for sure. Recapturing lost market share is not easy. Once gone, customers may never return.

12

Cost/Volume Trade-Offs and Survival Analysis

I It might seem simple enough. Suppose your unit product cost goes up. Then all you have to do is to raise sales price by the same amount to keep the contribution margin the same, true? Not exactly. Sales volume might be affected by the higher price, of course. Even if sales volume remained the same, the higher sales price causes revenue-driven expenses to increase. So it's more complicated than it might first appear.

PRODUCT COST INCREASES: WHICH KIND?

There are two quite different reasons for product cost increases. First is inflation, which can be of two sorts. General inflation is widespread and drives up costs throughout the economy, including those of the products sold by the business. Or inflation may be localized on particular products—for example, problems in the Middle East may drive up oil and other energy costs; floods in the Midwest may affect corn and soybean prices. In either situation, the product is the same but now costs more per unit.

The second reason for higher product costs is quite different than inflation. Increases in unit product costs may reflect either quality or size improvements. In this situation the product itself is changed for the better. Customers may be willing to pay more for the improved product, with the result that the company would not suffer a decrease in sales volume. Or, if the sales price remains the same on the improved product, then sales volume may increase.

Customers tend to accept higher sales prices if they perceive that the company is operating in a general inflationary market environment, when everything is going up. On a comparative basis, the product does not cost more relative to price increases of other products they purchase. Sales volume may not be affected by higher sales prices in a market dominated by the inflation mentality. On the other hand, if customers' incomes are not rising in proportion to sales price increases, demand would likely decrease at the higher sales prices.

If competitors face the same general inflation of product costs, the company's sales volume may not suffer from passing along product cost increases in the form of higher sales prices because the competition would be doing the same thing. The exact demand sensitivity to sales price increases cannot be known except in hindsight. Even then, it's difficult to know for sure, because many factors change simultaneously in the real world.

 Whenever sales prices are increased due to increases in product costs—whether because of general or specific inflation or product improvements—managers cannot simply tack on the product cost increase to sales price. They should carefully take into account variable expenses that are dependent on (driven by) sales revenue.

To illustrate this point, consider the standard product line example from previous chapters. The sales price and per-unit costs for the product are as follows (from Figure 9.1).

Standard Product	
Sales price	$100.00
Product cost	$ 65.00
Revenue-driven expenses @ 8.5%	$ 8.50
Unit-driven expenses	$ 6.50
Unit margin	$ 20.00

Suppose, for instance, that the company's unit product cost goes up $9.15, from $65.00 to $74.15 per unit. (This is a rather large jump in cost, of course.) The manager shouldn't simply raise the sales price by $9.15. In the example, the revenue-driven variable operating expenses are 8.5 percent of sales revenue. So the necessary increase in the sales price is determined as follows:

$$\frac{\$9.15 \text{ product cost increase}}{0.915} = \$10.00 \text{ sales price increase}$$

Dividing by 0.915 recognizes that only 91.5 cents of a sales dollar is left over after deducting revenue-driven variable expenses, which equal 8.5 cents of the sales dollar. Only 91.5 cents on the dollar is available to provide for the increase in the unit product cost. If the business raises its sales price exactly $10.00 (from $100.00 to $110.00), the unit margin for the standard product would remain exactly the same, which is shown as follows:

Standard Product Sales Price for Higher Product Cost	
Sales price	$110.00
Product cost	$ 74.15
Revenue-driven expenses @ 8.5%	$ 9.35
Unit-driven expenses	$ 6.50
Unit margin	$ 20.00

Therefore the company's total contribution margin would be the same at the $110.00 sales price, assuming sales volume remains the same, of course.

VARIABLE COST INCREASES AND SALES VOLUME

As just mentioned, one basic type of product cost increase occurs when the product itself is improved. These quality improvements may be part of the marketing strategy to stimulate demand by giving customers a better product at the same sales price. In addition to product cost, one or more of the specific variable operating expenses could be deliberately increased to improve the quality of the service to customers.

For example, faster delivery methods such as overnight Federal Express could be used, even though this would cost more than the traditional delivery methods. This would increase the volume-driven expense. The company could increase sales commissions to improve the personal time and effort the sales staff spends with each customer, which would increase the revenue-driven expense.

In our example, suppose the general manager of the standard product line is considering a new strategy for product and service quality improvements that would increase product cost and unit-driven operating expenses 4 percent. Revenue-driven variable expenses would be kept the same, or 8.5 percent of sales revenue. Tentatively, she has decided not to increase sales prices because in her opinion the improved products and service would stimulate demand for these products. It goes without saying that customers would have to be aware of and convinced that the product has improved. Before making a final decision, she asks the critical question: What increase in sales volume would be necessary just to keep profit the same?

Figure 12.1 presents this even-up, or standstill, scenario in which product cost and unit-driven variable expenses increase 4 percent but sales price remains the same. Fixed expenses are held constant, as is the variable revenue-driven operating expenses. Sales volume would have to increase 16,686 units, or 16.7 percent. By the way, the required sales

Standard Product Line			
	Before	**After**	**Change**
Sales price	$100.00	$100.00	
Product cost	$65.00	$67.60	4.0%
Revenue-driven expenses	$8.50	$8.50	
Unit-driven expenses	$6.50	$6.76	4.0%
Unit margin	$20.00	$17.14	−14.3% ←
Sales volume	100,000	116,686	16.7% ←
Contribution margin	$2,000,000	$2,000,000	
Fixed operating expenses	$1,000,000	$1,000,000	
Profit	$1,000,000	$1,000,000	

FIGURE 12.1 *Sales volume required for a 4 percent cost increase.*

volume for this scenario of higher cost and lower unit margin can be computed directly as follows:

Required Sales Volume at Higher Costs

$$\frac{\$2{,}000{,}000 \text{ contribution margin target}}{\$17.14 \text{ lower unit margin}}$$

$$= 116{,}686 \text{ sales volume}$$

The relatively large increase in sales volume needed to offset the relatively minor 4 percent cost increase is because the cost increase causes a 14.3 percent drop in unit margin. So a 16.7 percent jump in sales volume would be needed to keep profit at the same level. The key point is the drop in the unit margin caused by the cost increase. It takes a large increase in sales volume to make up for the drop in the unit margin.

There is more bad news. More capital would be needed at the higher sales volume level; the capital invested in assets would be higher due mainly to increases in accounts receivable and inventory. The impact on cash flow at the higher sales volume level is explained in Chapter 13.

BETTER PRODUCT AND SERVICE PERMITTING HIGHER SALES PRICE

The alternative to selling more units to overcome the cost increases is to sell the same number of units at a higher sales price. Figure 12.2 presents the higher sales price that would keep profit the same as before, given the 4 percent higher product cost and 4 percent higher unit-driven variable expenses. In this scenario the cost increase is loaded into the sales price and is not reflected in a sales volume increase.

Following this strategy, the sales price would be increased to $103.13 (rounded).* In this case the business improved the product and the service to its customers. There is no increase in profit. This product upgrade would be customer-driven—if

*The required sales price is computed as follows: ($67.60 product cost + $6.76 unit-driven cost + $20.00 unit margin) ÷ (1.000 − 0.085) = $103.13 sales price (rounded). In other words, the sales price, net of the revenue-driven cost per unit as a percent of sales price, must cover the product cost and the sales volume–driven expense per unit and provide the same unit margin as before.

Standard Product Line			
	Before	**After**	**Change**
Sales price	$100.00	$103.13	3.1%
Product cost	$65.00	$67.60	4.0%
Revenue-driven expenses	$8.50	$8.77	
Unit-driven expenses	$6.50	$6.76	4.0%
Unit margin	$20.00	$20.00	
Sales volume	100,000	100,000	
Contribution margin	$2,000,000	$2,000,000	
Fixed operating expenses	$1,000,000	$1,000,000	
Profit	$1,000,000	$1,000,000	

FIGURE 12.2 *Higher sales price required for a 4 percent cost increase*

the company failed to improve its product and/or service, then it might lose sales, because the customers want the improvements and are willing to pay. This may seem to be a strange state of affairs, but you see examples every day where the customer wants a better product and/or service and is willing to pay more for the improvements.

LOWER COSTS: THE GOOD AND BAD

Suppose a business were able to lower its unit product costs and its variable expenses per unit. On the one hand, such cost savings could be true efficiency or productivity gains. Sharper bargaining may reduce purchase costs, for example, or better manufacturing methods may reduce labor cost per unit produced. Wasteful fixed overhead costs could be eliminated or slashed. The key question is whether the company's products remain the same, whether the products' perceived quality remains the same, and whether the quality of service to customers remains the same.

Maybe not. Product cost decreases may represent quality degradations, or possibly reduced sizes such as smaller candy bars or fewer ounces in breakfast cereal boxes. Reducing variable operating expenses may adversely affect the quality of service to customers—for instance, by spreading fewer personnel over the same number of customers.

Lower Costs and Higher Unit Margin

If the company can lower its costs and still deliver the same product and the same quality of service, then sales volume should not be affected (everything else remaining the same, of course). Customers should see no differences in the products or service. In this case the cost savings would improve unit margins and profit would increase accordingly.

Improvements in the unit margins are very powerful; these increases have the same type of multiplier effect as the operating leverage of selling more units. For example, suppose that because of true efficiency gains the business is able to lower product costs and unit-driven expenses such that unit margin on its standard product line is improved, say, $1.00 per unit. Now this may not seem like much, but remember that the business sells 100,000 units during the year.

Therefore, the $1.00 improvement in unit margin would add $100,000 to the contribution margin line, which is a 5 percent gain on its original $2 million contribution margin. Lowering product cost and the unit-driven operating costs should not cause fixed costs to change, so all of the $100,000 contribution margin gain would fall to profit. The $100,000 gain in profit is a 10 percent increase on the $1 million original profit, or double the 5 percent gain in contribution margin.

Total quality management (TQM) is getting a lot of press today, indicated by the fact that it has been reduced to an acronym. Clearly, managers have always known that product quality and quality of service to customers are absolutely critical factors, though perhaps they lost sight of this in pursuit of short-term profits. Today, however, managers obviously have been made acutely aware of how quality conscious customers are (though I find it surprising that today's gurus are preaching this gospel as if it were just discovered).

Lower Costs Causing Lower Sales Volume

Cost savings may cause degradation in the quality of the product or service to customers. It would be no surprise, therefore, if sales volume would decrease. The unit margin would improve, but sales volume may drop as some customers abandon the business because of poorer product quality. Still, a business might adopt the strategy of deliberately knocking down the quality of its products (or some of its products) and the general level of service to its customers to boost unit margin, gambling that the higher unit margin will more than offset the loss of sales volume. (Of course, this brings up the loss-of-market-share problem again, which I won't go into here.)

To illustrate this scenario of lower cost and lower sales volume, suppose the business could lower the product costs in its standard product line from $65.00 to $60.00 per unit, but this cost savings results in lesser-grade materials, cheaper trim, and so forth. And the company could save on its shipping costs and reduce its unit-driven variable costs from $6.50 to $5.00 per unit, but in exchange delivery time to the customers would take longer. The combined $6.50 cost savings would increase unit margin by the same amount. The general manager of this profit module knows that many customers will be driven off by the changes in product quality and delivery times. She wants to know just how far sales volume would have to fall to offset the $6.50 gain in unit margin.

Figure 12.3 shows that if sales volume fell to 75,472 units, profit would be the same. In other words, selling 75,472 units at a $26.50 unit margin each would generate the same contribution margin as before. If sales fell by only 10,000 or 15,000 units, profit would be more than before. And, certainly, fixed costs would not go up at the lower sales volume. If anything, fixed costs probably could be reduced at the lower sales volume.

Standard Product Line			
	Before	**After**	**Change**
Sales price	$100.00	$100.00	
Product cost	$65.00	$60.00	−7.7%
Revenue-driven expenses	$8.50	$8.50	
Unit-driven expenses	$6.50	$5.00	−23.1%
Unit margin	$20.00	$26.50	32.5% ←
Sales volume	100,000	75,472	−24.5% ←
Contribution margin	$2,000,000	$2,000,000	
Fixed operating expenses	$1,000,000	$1,000,000	
Profit	$1,000,000	$1,000,000	

FIGURE 12.3 *Lower costs causing lower sales volume.*

This sort of profit strategy goes against the grain of many managers. Of course, the business could lose more than 25 percent of sales volume, in which case its profit would be lower than before. Once a product becomes identified as a low-cost/low-quality brand, it's virtually impossible to reverse this image in the minds of most customers. Thus, it's no surprise why many managers take a dim view of this profit strategy.

SUBTLE AND NOT-SO-SUBTLE CHANGES IN FIXED COSTS

Why do fixed operating expenses increase? The increase may be due to general inflationary trends. For instance, utility bills and insurance premiums seem to drift relentlessly upward; they hardly ever go down. In contrast, fixed operating expenses may be deliberately increased to expand capacity. The business could rent a larger space or hire more employees on fixed salaries.

And there's a third reason: Fixed expenses may be increased to improve the sales value of the present location. The business could invest in better furnishings and equipment (which would increase its annual depreciation expense). Fixed expenses could decrease for the opposite reasons, of course. But, we'll focus on increases in fixed expenses.

Suppose in the company example that total fixed operating expenses were to increase due to general inflationary trends. There were no changes in the capacity of the business or in the retail space or appearance (attractiveness) of the space. As far as customers can tell there have been no changes that would benefit them. The company could attempt to increase its sales price—the additional fixed expenses could be spread over its present sales volume.

However, this assumes sales volume would remain the same at the higher sales price. Sales volume might decrease at the higher sales price unless customers accept the increase as a general inflationary-driven increase. Sales volume might be sensitive to even small sales price increases. Many customers keep a sharp eye on prices, as you know. The business should probably allow for some decrease in sales volume when sales prices are raised.

SURVIVAL ANALYSIS

As I recall, many years ago there was a series in a magazine called "Can This Marriage Be Saved?" Which is not a bad way to introduce the situation in which any business can find itself from time to time—selling a product or product line that is losing money hand over fist. Perhaps the entire business is in dire straits and can't make money on any of its products. Before throwing in the towel, the manager in charge should at least do the sort of analysis explained in this chapter to determine what would have to be done to salvage the product or keep the business going.

Profile of a Loser

A successful formula for making profit can take a wrong turn anytime. Every step on the pathway to profit is slippery and requires constant attention. Managers have to keep a close watch on all profit factors, continuously looking for opportunities to improve profit. Nothing can be taken for granted. A popular term these days is *environmental scan,* which is a good term to use here. Managers should scan the profit radar to see if there are any blips on the screen that signal trouble.

Suppose you're the manager in charge of a product line, territory, division, or some other major organization unit of a large corporation. You are responsible for the profit performance of your unit, of course. A brief summary of your most recent annual profit report is presented in Figure 12.4, which is titled the Bad News Profit Report to emphasize the loss for the year. This report is shown in a condensed format to limit attention to absolutely essential profit factors. Only one variable operating expense is included (which is unit-driven). The examples in this and previous chapters also include revenue-driven variable operating expenses, but this distinction takes a backseat in the following analysis.

In addition to sales volume, note that the example also includes annual capacity and breakeven volume for the year just ended.

You have taken a lot of heat lately from headquarters for the $145,000 loss. Your job is to turn things around—and fairly fast. Your bonus next year, and perhaps even your job, depends on moving your unit into the black.

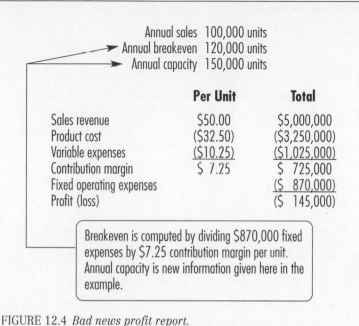

	Per Unit	Total
Annual sales	100,000 units	
Annual breakeven	120,000 units	
Annual capacity	150,000 units	
Sales revenue	$50.00	$5,000,000
Product cost	($32.50)	($3,250,000)
Variable expenses	($10.25)	($1,025,000)
Contribution margin	$ 7.25	$ 725,000
Fixed operating expenses		($ 870,000)
Profit (loss)		($ 145,000)

Breakeven is computed by dividing $870,000 fixed expenses by $7.25 contribution margin per unit. Annual capacity is new information given here in the example.

FIGURE 12.4 *Bad news profit report.*

First Some Questions about Fixed Expenses

One thing you might do first is to take a close look at your $870,000 fixed operating expenses. Your fixed expenses may include an allocated amount from a larger pool of fixed expenses generated by the organizational unit to which your profit module reports, or they may include a share of fixed expenses from corporate headquarters. Any basis of allocation is open to question; virtually every allocation method is somewhat arbitrary and can be challenged on one or more grounds.

For instance, consider the legal expenses of the corporation. Should these be allocated to each profit responsibility unit throughout the organization? On what basis? Relative sales revenue, frequency of litigation of each unit, or according to some other formula? Likewise, what about the costs of centralized data processing and accounting expenses of the business? Many fixed expenses are allocated on some arbitrary basis, which is open to question.

It's not unusual for many costs to be allocated across different organizational units; every manager should be aware of the methods, bases, or formulas that are used to allocate costs. It is a mistake to assume that there is some natural or objective basis for cost allocation. Most cost allocation schemes are arbitrary and therefore subject to manipulation. Chapter 17 discusses cost allocation schemes in more detail.

Questions about the proper method of allocation should be settled before the start of the year. Raising such questions after the fact—after the profit performance results are reported for the period—is too late. In any case, if you argue for a smaller allocation of fixed expenses to your unit, then you are also arguing that other units should be assessed a greater proportion of the organization's fixed expenses— which will initiate a counterargument from those units, of course. Also, it may appear that you're making excuses rather than fixing the problem.

Another question to consider is this: Is a significant amount of depreciation expense included in the fixed expenses total? Accountants treat depreciation as a fixed expense, based on generally accepted methods that allocate original cost over the estimated useful economic lives of the assets. For instance, under current income tax laws, buildings are depreciated over 39 years and cars and light trucks over 5 years. Just because accountants adopt such methods doesn't mean that depreciation is, in fact, a fixed expense.

Contrast depreciation with, for example, annual property taxes on buildings and land (real estate). Property tax is an actual cash outlay each year. Whether or not the business made full use of the building and land during the year, the entire amount of tax should be charged to the year as fixed expense. There can be no argument about this. On the other hand, depreciation raises entirely different issues.

Suppose your loss is due primarily to sales volume that is well below your normal volume of operations. You can argue that less depreciation expense should be charged to the year and more shifted to future years. The reasoning is that the assets were not used as much—the machines were not operated as many hours, the trucks were not driven as many miles, and so on. On the other hand, depreciation may be truly caused by the passage of time. For instance, depreciation of computers is based on their expected technological life.

Using the computers less probably doesn't delay the date of replacing the computers.

Generally speaking, arguing for less depreciation is not going to get you very far. Most businesses are not willing to make such a radical change in their depreciation policies (i.e., to slow down recorded depreciation when sales volume takes a dip). Also, this would look suspicious—the business would appear to be choosing expense methods to manipulate reported profit.

What's the Problem?

Your first thought might be that sales volume is the main problem since it is below your breakeven point (see Figure 12.4). To review briefly, the breakeven point is determined as follows:

$$\frac{\$870,000 \text{ fixed expenses}}{\$7.25 \text{ unit margin}} = 120,000 \text{ units breakeven volume}$$

To reach breakeven (the zero profit and zero loss point) you would have to sell an additional 20,000 units, which would add $145,000 additional contribution margin at a $7.25 unit margin. By the way, notice that breakeven is 80 percent of capacity (120,000 units sold ÷ 150,000 units capacity = 80%). By almost any standard, this is far too high. Anyway, just reaching the breakeven point is not your ultimate goal, though it would be better than being in the red.

Suppose you were able to increase sales volume beyond the breakeven point, all the way up to sales capacity of 150,000 units, an increase of 50,000 units from the actual sales level of 100,000 units. A 50 percent increase in sales volume may not be very realistic, to say the least. At any rate, your annual profit report would appear as shown in Figure 12.5.

Even if your sales volume could be increased to full capacity, profit would be only $217,500, which equals only 2.9 percent of sales revenue. For the large majority of businesses—the only exceptions being those with very high inventory turnover ratios—a meager 2.9 percent return on sales is seriously inadequate. Your return-on-sales profit goal probably should be in the range of 10 to 15 percent.

In short, increasing sales volume is not the entire answer. You have two other basic options: Reduce fixed expenses or improve unit margin.

Annual sales 150,000 units
Annual breakeven 120,000 units
Annual capacity 150,000 units

	Per Unit	Total
Sales revenue	$50.00	$7,500,000
Product cost	($32.50)	($4,875,000)
Variable expenses	($10.25)	($1,537,500)
Contribution margin	$ 7.25	$1,087,500
Fixed operating expenses		($ 870,000)
Profit (loss)		$ 217,500

Notice that even at full capacity, profit is only 2.9 percent of sales revenue, which in almost all industries is far too low.

FIGURE 12.5 *Sales at full capacity profit report.*

There may be flab in your fixed expenses. It goes without saying that you should cut the fat. The more serious question is whether to downsize (reduce fixed operating expenses and capacity). For instance, assume you could slash fixed expenses by one-third ($290,000) but that this would reduce capacity by one-third, down to 100,000 units. If no other factors change, your profit performance would be as shown in Figure 12.6.

Your profit would be $145,000, which is better than a loss. But profit would still be only 2.9 percent of sales revenue, which is much too low as already explained. Keep in mind that making profit requires a substantial amount of capital invested in the assets needed to carry on profit-making operations. The capital invested in assets is supplied by debt and equity sources and carries a cost (as discussed in Chapter 6).

Suppose, to illustrate this cost-of-capital point, that the $5 million sales revenue level requires investing $2 million in assets—one-half from debt at 8.0 percent annual interest and one-half from equity on which the annual ROE target is 15.0 percent. The interest expense is $80,000 ($1 million debt × 8.0%), leaving only $65,000 earnings before tax. Net income

Annual sales 100,000 units
Annual breakeven   80,000 units
Annual capacity 100,000 units

	Per Unit	Total
Sales revenue	$50.00	$5,000,000
Product cost	($32.50)	($3,250,000)
Variable expenses	($10.25)	($1,025,000)
Contribution margin	$ 7.25	$ 725,000
Fixed operating expenses		($ 580,000)
Profit (loss)		$ 145,000

Notice that even if fixed expenses are reduced by one-third, profit is only 2.9 percent of sales revenue, which in almost all industries is far too low.

FIGURE 12.6 *Profit at one-third less fixed costs and capacity.*

after income tax is not enough to meet the company's ROE goal, which would be the $1 million owners' equity capital times 15.0 percent, or $150,000 net income.

By cutting fixed operating expenses you have removed any room for growth, because sales volume would be at capacity. In summary, it's fairly clear that your main problem is a unit contribution margin that is too low.

Improving Unit Margin

Now for the tough question: How would you improve unit margin? Is sales price too low? Are product cost and variable expenses too high? Do all three need improving? Answering these questions strikes at the essence of the manager's function. Managers are paid for knowing what to do, what has to be changed, and how to make the changes. Analysis techniques don't provide the final answers to these questions. But the analysis methods certainly help the manager size up and quantify the impact of changes in factors that determine unit contribution margin.

One useful approach is to set a reasonably achievable profit goal—say $500,000—and load all the needed improvement on each factor to see how much change would be needed in each. To move from $145,000 loss to $500,000 profit is a $645,000 swing. If sales volume stays the same at 100,000 units, then achieving this improvement would require that the unit margin be increased $6.45 per unit, which is a tall order. You could compare the $6.45 unit margin increase to each profit factor; doing this shows that the following improvement percents would be needed:

Unit Margin Improvement as Percent of Each Profit Factor

$6.45 ÷ $50.00 sales price = 13 percent increase

$6.45 ÷ $32.50 product cost = 20 percent decrease

$6.45 ÷ $10.25 variable expenses = 63 percent decrease

Making changes of these magnitudes would be very tough, to say the least.

DANGER! Raising sales prices 13 percent would surely depress demand. Lowering product cost 20 percent is not realistic in most situations. And lowering variable expenses 63 percent may be just plain impossible. A combination of improvements would be needed instead of loading all the improvement on just one factor. Also, sales volume probably would have to be increased.

Suppose you develop the following plan: Sales prices will be increased 5 percent and sales volume will be increased 10 percent (based on better marketing and advertising strategies). Product cost will be reduced 4 percent by sharper purchasing, and variable expenses will be cut 8 percent by exercising tighter control over these expenses. Last, you think you can eliminate about 10 percent fat from fixed expenses (without reducing sales capacity). If you could actually achieve all these goals, your profit report would look as shown in Figure 12.7.

You would make your profit goal and then some, but only if all the improvements were actually achieved. Profit would be 9.1 percent of sales revenue ($522,700 profit ÷ $5,775,000 sales revenue = 9.1 percent). This plan may or may not be achievable. You may have to go back to the drawing board to figure out additional improvements.

Annual sales 110,000 units
Annual breakevenn 65,965 units
Annual capacity 150,000 units

	Per Unit	Total
Sales revenue	$52.50	$5,775,000
Product cost	($31.20)	($3,432,000)
Variable expenses	($ 9.43)	($1,037,300)
Contribution margin	$11.87	$1,305,700
Fixed operating expenses		($ 783,000)
Profit (loss)		$ 522,700

FIGURE 12.7 *Profit improvement plan.*

END POINT

Chapters 11 and 12 examine certain basic trade-offs; both chapters rest on the premise that seldom does one profit factor change without changing or being changed by one or more other profit factors. Mentioned earlier but worth repeating here is that managers must keep their attention riveted on unit contribution margin. Profit performance is very sensitive to changes in this key operating profit number, as demonstrated by several different situations in Chapters 11 and 12.

Chapter 11 examines the interplay between sales price and volume changes. Sales prices are the most external part of the business. In contrast, product cost and variable expenses (the subject of this chapter) are more internal to the business. Customers may not be aware of these expense decreases unless such cost savings show through in lower product quality or worse service. Frequently, cost savings are not cost savings at all, in the sense that customer demand is adversely affected.

Cost increases can be caused by inflation (general or specific), by product improvements in size or quality, or by the quality of service surrounding the product. To prevent profit deterioration, cost increases have to be recovered through higher sales volume or through higher sales prices. This chapter examines the critical differences between these two alternatives.

Depending on higher sales volume to compensate for cost increases may not be very realistic; sales volume would have to increase too much. This type of analysis does give managers a useful point of reference, however. Cost increases generally have to be recovered through higher sales prices. This chapter demonstrates the analysis tools for determining the higher sales prices.

Profit Gushes: Cash Flow Trickles?

You'd probably assume that if profit improved, say, $200,000 next year, then cash flow from profit would increase $200,000 during the year. Not true. In most cases the increase in cash flow from profit would be less. The cash flow shortfall may be rather insignificant and not worth worrying about too much. But the lag in cash flow from increasing profit often is quite significant.

This chapter demonstrates one basic point that business managers should have clear in their minds: Certain ways of improving profit have much better cash flow benefits than others. The preceding four chapters analyze and demonstrate the ways a business can improve its profit, which on the flip side are the ways a business can see profit slip away. Hardly anything has been mentioned about changes in cash flow caused by changes in profit. The moral of this chapter is, don't count your cash flow chickens until the eggs are hatched!

LESSONS FROM CHAPTER 2

Remember Chapter 2 explains accrual-basis accounting, necessary to measure profit, which is more complex than simply recording cash collections from sales and cash payments for expenses. Accrual-basis accounting entails the following:

- Recording revenue from credit sales *before* the cash is collected from customers at a later time
- Recording certain expenses *before* the costs are paid at a later time
- Recording certain expenses *after* the costs are paid at an earlier time
- Waiting to record the expense for cost of products sold to customers until the sale is recorded, even though the products are paid for *before* they are sold
- Recording depreciation expense for using long-term operating assets over the several years of their use, even though the assets are paid for *before* they are used

For the most part, cash flows in from sales and out for expenses occur at different times than when sales revenue and expenses are recorded. To correctly measure profit, a business cannot use cash-basis accounting and must use accrual-basis accounting. More work, but a truer profit measure.

The amounts reported in the external income statements of a business to its creditors and shareowners and in its internal profit reports to managers are all accrual-basis accounting numbers. These numbers do *not* equal the actual amounts of cash flows during the period. The actual cash flows during the period are higher or lower than the corresponding accrual-basis numbers. The bottom-line cash flow from profit during the period can be very different from bottom-line profit. Business managers need bifocal lenses when focusing on profit versus cash flow from profit.

CASH FLOW FROM BOOSTING SALES VOLUMES

The analysis of changes in profit over the preceding four chapters deals with changes in sales revenue and expenses. These changes are accrual-basis numbers, not cash flow numbers. Let's return to the first scenario from Chapter 9, in which sales volume (the number of units sold over the year) increases 10 percent. Figure 13.1 summarizes the *changes* in sales revenue and expenses for each of the three product lines in the example.

The amounts of changes presented in Figure 13.1 are *accrual-basis accounting numbers.* For instance, the $1 million sales revenue increase for the standard product is the

Standard Product Line

	Changes
Sales revenue	$1,000,000
Cost of goods sold	$ 650,000
Gross margin	$ 350,000
Revenue-driven expenses @ 8.5%	$ 85,000
Unit-driven expenses	$ 65,000
Contribution margin	$ 200,000
Fixed operating expenses	$ 0
Profit	$ 200,000

Generic Product Line

	Changes
Sales revenue	$1,125,000
Cost of goods sold	$ 855,000
Gross margin	$ 270,000
Revenue-driven expenses @ 4.0%	$ 45,000
Unit-driven expenses	$ 75,000
Contribution margin	$ 150,000
Fixed operating expenses	$ 0
Profit	$ 150,000

Premier Product Line

	Changes
Sales revenue	$ 750,000
Cost of goods sold	$ 400,000
Gross margin	$ 350,000
Revenue-driven expenses @ 7.5%	$ 56,250
Unit-driven expenses	$ 43,750
Contribution margin	$ 250,000
Fixed operating expenses	$ 0
Profit	$ 250,000

FIGURE 13.1 *Changes in sales revenue and expenses from higher sales volumes (data from Figure 9.2).*

amount of additional sales revenue that would be recorded if the business sells 10 percent more units. If the business made all sales for cash on the barrelhead and did not extend credit to its customers there would be a one-to-one correspondence between the amount of the accrual-basis sales revenue recorded during the period and the cash flow from sales revenue during the period.

Cash Inflow from Sales Revenue Increase

The business in the example extends credit to its customers. If next year the business sells 10 percent more units of the standard product line at the same sales prices, then sales revenue would increase $1 million. But this doesn't mean that the business will collect $1 million additional cash from its customers during the year. Cash inflow from the additional sales revenue would be less. Customers are offered one month of credit before they have to pay the business. Thus the actual cash inflow from the additional sales would be less than $1 million because sales made during the last month of the year would not be collected by the end of the year.

During the year the business would collect 11 months of the additional sales revenue, but not the final, twelfth month. Assuming sales are level during the year, the business would collect $^{11}/_{12}$ of the $1 million additional sales revenue ($1 million additional sales revenue × $^{11}/_{12}$ = $916,667 cash collections during the year). The remainder wouldn't be collected until the early part of the following year. In short, there is a one-month lag in collecting sales made on credit.

Cash Outflows for Expense Increases

Expenses are a little more complicated than sales revenue from the cash flow point of view. First is cost-of-goods-sold expense. In the 10 percent higher sales volume scenario, cost-of-goods-sold expense increases $650,000 for the standard product line (see Figure 13.1). You might assume that cash outlays would also increase $650,000. Actually, cash outflow would be more than this because the business would increase its inventory of standard products to support the higher sales level. In addition to paying for units sold, the business would build up its inventory, which requires additional cash outlay. As a general rule, selling more units means that a business must have more units on hand to sell. It's possible that a business could sell 10 percent more units without increasing its inventory. But generally speaking, inventory rises more or less proportionally with a rise in sales volume.

A business either manufactures the products it sells or it purchases the products it sells from other businesses. In either case, an increase in inventory usually involves a corresponding increase in accounts payable. Raw materials used in the production process are purchased on credit, and many other manufacturing costs are not paid for immediately. Products from other businesses are bought on credit. Instead of making immediate cash payment when inventory is increased, a business delays payment, perhaps by a month or so.

However, vendors and suppliers are not willing to extend credit and wait for payment until the buyer sells the products. They won't wait out the entire inventory-holding period; they want their money sooner than that. That is, the business's inventory-holding period is longer than the credit period of its accounts payable. In this example, the business holds products in inventory for two months on average before they are sold and delivered to customers. The average credit period of its inventory-driven accounts payable is only one month. The business has to make cash payment for the second month of holding inventory.

At the end of the year the business's inventory is two months higher for the additional layer of sales—one month unpaid (reflected in the increase of accounts payable) and one month paid. The business paid for the 12 months of products sold plus an additional month for the increase in inventory. In short, the cash outlay for inventory for the increase in sales volume of the standard product line is $704,167 ($650,000 additional cost of goods sold expense for the year $\times$ $^{13}/_{12}$ = $704,167 cash outlay for cost of goods sold and inventory buildup).

When sales volume increases, variable expenses also increase (see Figure 13.1). Both revenue-driven and unit-driven variable expenses increase for all three of the product lines. Of course, this is the very definition of variable expenses—costs that go up and down with increases and decreases in sales. Many variable operating expenses are not paid until a month or more *after* the expenses are recorded. The obligations for these unpaid expenses are recorded in two liability accounts—accounts payable and accrued expenses payable.

For most businesses, the amounts of their accounts payable for unpaid operating expenses and accrued expenses payable are fairly significant amounts. To expedite matters, assume that there is a one-month delay, or lag, in paying variable operating expenses. This is in the ballpark for many businesses. For each $12.00 of increase in variable operating expenses, assume the business pays only $11.00 during the year. The other dollar will be paid in the early part of the following year. For example, in the sales volume increase scenario, unit-driven variable operating expenses for the standard product line increase $65,000 (see Figure 13.1). Thus the cash outlay during the year for this increase is $59,583 ($65,000 additional expenses $\times$ $^{11}/_{12}$ = $59,583 cash outlay).

Summing Up the Cash Flow Effects

The differences between cash flows and the accrual-basis amounts of changes in sales revenue and expenses for the year caused by increasing sales volume are summarized as follows:

- There is a one-month lag in collecting sales revenue because the business sells on credit, so only $^{11}/_{12}$ of the increase in sales revenue is collected in cash through the end of the year.

- The sales volume increase requires a corresponding increase in inventories that is equal to two months, or $^{2}/_{12}$, of the cost-of-goods-sold increase; accounts payable for inventories also increase, equal to one month of the increase in inventories. So the cash outlay for the inventories increase is only $^{1}/_{12}$ of the cost of goods sold increase.

- There is a one-month lag in paying variable operating expenses, so only $^{11}/_{12}$ of the increase in operating expenses is paid in cash through the end of the year.

 Basically there is a one-month time differential between the accrual-basis changes in sales revenue and expenses and the cash flows in from sales and out for expenses. There is a one-month cash flow delay from the sales revenue increase, a one-month additional cash outlay for the cost of goods sold increase, and a one-month delay in paying the variable expenses increase. This one-month shift is fairly realistic for many businesses; it certainly moves the accrual-basis numbers much closer to when actual cash flows occur.

CASH FLOWS ACROSS DIFFERENT PRODUCT LINES

Figure 13.2 presents the cash flow effects from increasing sales volume 10 percent for the three product lines of the business. I'd wager that the cash flow effects, especially for the generic product line, surprise you. If not, you'd better take a closer look at Figure 13.2.

The best cash flow result is for the premier product line, but even here the cash flow increase for the year would be only $162,500 compared with the $250,000 profit increase. For the standard product line, the cash flow yield is only $75,000 for a $200,000 gain in profit, and cash flow actually decreases $5,000 for the generic product line, even though profit increases $150,000.

For each of the product lines, the delay in collecting the increase in sales revenue combined with the cash outlay for increasing inventories puts a double whammy on cash flow. The slim margin on the generic products means that the cost of goods sold is a relatively high proportion of sales revenue. So the increase in inventories puts a particularly large demand on cash to be invested in inventories at the higher sales volume level. The premier product is just the reverse. The high margin on these products means that the increase in inventories does not do as much damage to cash flow.

CASH FLOW FROM BUMPING UP SALES PRICES

Chapter 10 examines the profit effects from increasing sales prices, holding all other profit factors constant. The profit gains are much more favorable compared with increasing sales volume the same percent, as explained in Chapter 10. The cash flow effects of a 10 percent sales price increase are also much more favorable. Figure 13.3 presents the cash flow effects from increasing sales prices 10 percent for the three product lines. The one-month shift for cash flows explained

Standard Product Line

	Changes	Cash Flows
Sales revenue	$1,000,000	$ 916,667
Cost of goods sold	$ 650,000	$ 704,167
Gross margin	$ 350,000	$ 212,500
Revenue-driven expenses @ 8.5%	$ 85,000	$ 77,917
Unit-driven expenses	$ 65,000	$ 59,583
Contribution margin	$ 200,000	$ 75,000
Fixed operating expenses	$ 0	$ 0
Profit	$ 200,000	$ 75,000

Generic Product Line

	Changes	Cash Flows
Sales revenue	$1,125,000	$1,031,250
Cost of goods sold	$ 855,000	$ 926,250
Gross margin	$ 270,000	$ 105,000
Revenue-driven expenses @ 4.0%	$ 45,000	$ 41,250
Unit-driven expenses	$ 75,000	$ 68,750
Contribution margin	$ 150,000	($ 5,000)
Fixed operating expenses	$ 0	$ 0
Profit	$ 150,000	($ 5,000)

Premier Product Line

	Changes	Cash Flows
Sales revenue	$ 750,000	$ 687,500
Cost of goods sold	$ 400,000	$ 433,333
Gross margin	$ 350,000	$ 254,167
Revenue-driven expenses @ 7.5%	$ 56,250	$ 51,563
Unit-driven expenses	$ 43,750	$ 40,104
Contribution margin	$ 250,000	$ 162,500
Fixed operating expenses	$ 0	$ 0
Profit	$ 250,000	$ 162,500

FIGURE 13.2 *Changes in operating cash flow from increases in sales volume.*

Standard Product Line

	Changes	Cash Flows
Sales revenue	$1,000,000	$ 916,667
Cost of goods sold	$ 0	$ 0
Gross margin	$1,000,000	$ 916,667
Revenue-driven expenses @ 8.5%	$ 85,000	$ 77,917
Unit-driven expenses	$ 0	$ 0
Contribution margin	$ 915,000	$ 838,750
Fixed operating expenses	$ 0	$ 0
Profit	$ 915,000	$ 838,750

Generic Product Line

	Changes	Cash Flows
Sales revenue	$1,125,000	$1,031,250
Cost of goods sold	$ 0	$ 0
Gross margin	$1,125,000	$1,031,250
Revenue-driven expenses @ 4.0%	$ 45,000	$ 41,250
Unit-driven expenses	$ 0	$ 0
Contribution margin	$1,080,000	$ 990,000
Fixed operating expenses	$ 0	$ 0
Profit	$1,080,000	$ 990,000

Premier Product Line

	Changes	Cash Flows
Sales revenue	$ 750,000	$ 687,500
Cost of goods sold	$ 0	$ 0
Gross margin	$ 750,000	$ 687,500
Revenue-driven expenses @ 7 5%	$ 56,250	$ 51,563
Unit-driven expenses	$ 0	$ 0
Contribution margin	$ 693,750	$ 635,938
Fixed operating expenses	$ 0	$ 0
Profit	$ 693,750	$ 635,938

FIGURE 13.3 *Changes in operating cash flow from increases in sales prices (data from Figure 10.1).*

earlier for the sales volume scenario is adopted here for the sales price increase scenario.

The cash flow effects are much more favorable for the sales price increase scenario than the sales volume scenario. For each of the three product lines, the increase in cash flow from profit due to the higher sales prices is a very large percent of the increase in profit. This is much better than in the sales volume increase scenario. The much more favorable cash flow effect is due to the difference in the inventories factor. In the sales price increase scenarios, the business does not have to increase inventories of products and thus avoids the drag on cash flow that this causes.

A word of caution is in order. Raising sales prices 10 percent looks good on paper compared with increasing sales volume 10 percent. But bumping up sales prices 10 percent in a competitive market, or in most markets for that matter, may not be possible. Customers may flock to your competitors, of course, or demand may decrease at the higher prices. But, having said this, businesses can often sneak in minor increases without drawing attention to the higher sales prices. Even relatively small sales price increases can improve profit more effectively than much larger increases in sales volume. And profit increases from higher sales prices have much better cash flow effects.

END POINT

Improving profit performance is a relentless pressure on business managers. The preceding four chapters analyze the profit effects from changes in the key factors that drive profit—sales volume, sales price, variable operating expenses, and fixed expenses. This chapter shifts attention to changes in cash flow driven by changes in profit factors. Managers must keep in mind that profit is an accrual-basis accounting number and not a cash flow number. The actual cash flow increase during the period from improving profit can be, and usually is, significantly different than the gain in profit. Indeed, the chapter demonstrates that in certain situations the cash flow effect can be negative from increasing profit. Managers need a good handle on both the profit effect and the cash flow effect from changing profit factors.

PART 4

Capital Investment Analysis

CHAPTER

Determining Investment Returns Needed

This chapter explains how the cost of capital is factored into the analysis of business investments to determine the future returns needed from an investment. An investment has to pay its way. The future returns from an investment should recover the capital put into the investment and provide for the cost of capital during each period along the way. The future returns should do at least this much. If not, the investment will turn out to be a poor decision; the capital should have been invested elsewhere.

The analysis in this chapter is math-free. No mathematical equations or formulas are involved. I use a computer spreadsheet model to illustrate the analysis and to do the calculations. The main example in the chapter provides a general-purpose template that can be easily copied by anyone familiar with a spreadsheet program. However, you don't have to know anything about using spreadsheets to follow the analysis.

A BUSINESS AS AN ONGOING
Remember **INVESTMENT PROJECT**

Chapter 5 explains that a business needs a portfolio of assets to carry on its profit-making operations. For the capital needed to invest in its assets, a business raises money from its owners, retains all or part of its annual earnings, and borrows money. The combination of these three sources constitutes the capital structure, or capitalization, of a business. Taken together, the first two capital sources are called *owners' equity,* or just *equity* for short. Borrowed money is referred to as *debt.* Interest is paid on debt, as you know. Its shareowners expect a business to earn an annual return on their equity at least equal to, and preferably higher than, what they could earn on alternative investment opportunities for their capital.

KEY CONCEPT

COST OF CAPITAL

A business's earnings before interest and income tax (EBIT) for a period needs to be sufficient to do three things: (1) pay interest on its debt, (2) pay income tax, and (3) leave residual net income that satisfies the shareowners of the business. Based on the total amount of capital invested in its assets and its capital structure, a business determines its EBIT goal for the year. For instance, a business may establish an annual EBIT goal equal to 20 percent of the total capital invested in its assets. This rate is referred to as its *cost of capital.*

The annual cost-of-capital rate for most businesses is in the range of 15 to 25 percent, although there is no hard-and-fast standard that applies to all businesses. The cost-of-capital rate depends heavily on the target rate for net income on its owners' equity adopted by a business. The interest rate on a business's debt is definite, and its income tax rate is fairly definite. On the other hand, the rate of net income set by a business as its goal to earn on owners' equity is not definite. A business may adopt a rather modest or a more aggressive benchmark for earnings on its equity capital.

DANGER!

Of course, a business may fall short of its cost-of-capital goal. Its actual EBIT for the year may be enough to pay its interest and income tax, but its residual net income may be less than the business should earn on its owners' equity for the year. For that matter, a business may suffer an operating loss and not even cover its interest obligation for the year. One reason for reporting financial statements to outside shareowners and lenders is to provide them with information so they can determine how the business is performing as an investor, or user of capital.

A company's cost of capital depends on its capital structure. Assume the following facts for a business:

Capital Structure and Cost of Capital Factors

- 35 percent debt and 65 percent equity mix of capital sources
- 8.0 percent annual interest rate on debt
- 40 percent income tax rate (combined federal and state)
- 18.0 percent annual ROE objective

These assumptions are realistic for a broad range of businesses, but not for every business, of course. Some businesses use less than 35 percent debt capital and some more. Over time, interest rates fluctuate for all businesses. Furthermore, one could argue that an 18.0 percent ROE objective is too ambitious. The 40 percent combined federal and state income tax rate is based on the present rate for the federal taxable income brackets for midsized businesses plus a typical state income tax rate. In any case, the cost-of-capital factors can be easily adapted to fit the circumstances of a particular business once an investment spreadsheet model has been prepared.

Suppose the business with this capital structure has $10 million capital invested in its assets. What amount of annual earnings before interest and income tax (EBIT) should the business make? This question strikes at the core idea of the cost of capital—the minimum amount of operating profit needed to pay interest on its debt, to pay its income tax, and to produce residual net income that achieves the ROE goal of the business.

Figure 14.1 shows the answer to this question. Given its debt-to-equity ratio, the company's $10 million capital comes from $3.5 million debt and $6.5 million equity—see the condensed balance sheet in Figure 14.1. The annual interest cost of its debt is $280,000 ($3.5 million debt × 8.0% interest rate = $280,000 interest). The business needs to make $280,000 operating profit (or earnings before interest and income tax) to pay this amount of interest.

 Interest is deductible for income tax, as you probably know. This means that a business needs to make operating profit equal to but no more than, its interest to pay its interest. In other words, the $280,000 of operating profit is offset with an

Condensed Balance Sheet		Condensed Income Statement	
Assets less operating liabilities	$10,000,000	Earnings before interest and income tax (EBIT)	$2,230,000
		Interest	($ 280,000)
Sources of Capital		Taxable income	$1,950,000
Debt	$ 3,500,000	Income tax	($ 780,000)
Equity	$ 6,500,000	Net income	$1,170,000
Total	$10,000,000		

FIGURE 14.1 *Operating profit (EBIT) needed based on capital structure of the business.*

equal amount of interest deduction, so the business's taxable income is zero on this layer of operating profit.

The cost of equity capital is a much different matter. On its $6.5 million equity capital, the business needs to earn $1,170,000 net income ($6.5 million equity × 18.0% ROE = $1,170,000 net income). To earn $1,170,000 net income after income tax, the business needs to earn $1,950,000 operating earnings before income tax ($1,170,000 net income goal ÷ 0.6 = $1,950,000). The 0.6 is the after-tax keep; for every $1.00 of taxable income the company keeps only 60¢ because the income tax rate is 40 percent, or 40¢ on the dollar. On $1,950,000 earnings after interest and before income tax, the applicable income tax is $780,000 at the 40 percent income tax rate, which leaves $1,170,000 net income after tax.

Take note of one key difference between the net income needed to be earned on equity versus the interest needed to be earned on debt. From each $1.00 of operating profit (earnings before interest and income tax, or EBIT) a business can pay $1.00 of interest to its debt sources of capital. But from each $1.00 of operating profit a business makes only 60¢ net income for its equity owners after deducting the 40¢ income tax on the dollar. Put another way, on a before-tax basis a business needs to earn just $1.00 of operating profit to cover $1.00 of interest expense. But it needs to earn $1.67 (rounded) to end up with $1.00 net income because income tax takes 67¢.

In summary, based on its capital structure, the business should aim to earn at least $2,230,000 operating profit, or EBIT, for the year. If it falls short of this benchmark, its residual net income for the year will fall below its 18.0 percent annual ROE goal. If it does better, its ROE will be more than 18.0 percent, which should help increase the value of the equity shares of the business.

SHORT-TERM AND LONG-TERM ASSET INVESTMENTS

Looking down the asset side of a business's balance sheet, you find a mix of short-term and long-term asset investments. One major short-term asset investment is inventories. The inventories asset represents the cost of products held for sale. These products will be sold during the coming two or three months, perhaps even sooner. Another important short-term investment is accounts receivable. Accounts receivable will be collected within a month or so. These two short-term investments turn over relatively quickly. The capital invested in inventories and accounts receivable is recovered in a short period of time. The capital is then reinvested in the assets in order to continue in business. The cycle of capital investment, capital recovery, and capital reinvestment is repeated several times during the year.

In contrast, a business makes long-term investments in many different operating assets—land and buildings, machinery and equipment, furniture, fixtures, tools, computers, vehicles, and so on. A business also may make long-term investments in intangible assets—patents and copyrights, customer lists, computer software, established brand names and trademarks developed by other companies, and so on. The capital invested in long term business operating assets is gradually recovered and converted back into cash over three to five years (or longer for buildings and heavy machinery and equipment).

The annual sales revenue of a business includes a component to recover the cost of using its long-term operating assets. (Of course, sales revenue also has to recover the cost of the goods sold and other operating costs to make a profit for the period.) The cost of using long-term assets is recorded as depreciation expense each year. Depreciation expense is not a cash outlay—in fact, just the opposite.

Depreciation is one of the costs embedded in sales revenue; therefore the cash inflow from sales includes a component that reimburses the business for the use of its fixed assets during the year. A sliver of the cash inflow from the annual sales revenue of a business provides recovery of part of the total capital invested in its long-term operating assets. What to do with this cash inflow is one of the most important decisions facing a business.

To continue as a going concern, a business has to purchase or construct new long-term operating assets to replace the old ones that have reached the end of their useful economic lives. In deciding whether to make capital investments in long-term operating assets, managers should determine whether the new assets are really needed, of course, and how they will be used in the operations of the business. They should look at how the new assets blend into the present mix of operating assets. Managers should focus primarily on how well all assets work together to achieve the financial goals of the business. These long-term capital investments of a business are just one part, though an important part to be sure, of a business's overall profit strategy and planning.

THE WHOLE BUSINESS VERSUS SINGULAR CAPITAL INVESTMENTS

From the cost-of-capital viewpoint, the key criterion for guilding investment decisions for the replacement and expansion of long-term assets is whether the business will be able to maintain and improve its return on assets (ROA) performance. Suppose a business has been able to earn an annual 20 percent ROA consistently over several years. In other words, its annual EBIT divided by the total capital invested in its assets has hovered around 20 percent for the past several years. And assume that the business does not plan any significant change in its capital structure in the foreseeable future.

Assume that this level of financial performance is judged to be acceptable by both management and the shareowners of the business. Therefore, in making decisions on capital expenditures to carry on and to grow the business, its managers should apply a 20 percent cost of capital test: Will EBIT in future years be sufficient to maintain its 20 percent ROA performance? This is the key question from the cost-of-capital point of view.

ROA is an investment performance measure for the business as a whole. The entire business is the focus of the analysis. Its entire assemblage of assets is treated as one investment portfolio. Its earnings before interest and income tax (EBIT) for the year is divided by this amount of capital to determine the overall ROA performance of the business.

In contrast, specific capital investments can be isolated and analyzed as singular projects, each like a tub standing on its own feet. Each individual asset investment opportunity is analyzed on its own merits. One important criterion is whether the investment passes muster from the cost-of-capital point of view.

CAPITAL INVESTMENT EXAMPLE

Suppose that a retailer is considering buying new, state-of-the-art electronic cash registers. These registers read bar-coded information on the products it sells. The registers would be connected with the company's computers to track information on sales and inventory stock quantities. The main purpose of switching to these cash registers is to avoid marking sales prices on products. Virtually all the products sold by the retailer are already bar-coded by the manufacturers of the products. The retailer would avoid the labor cost of marking initial sales prices and sales price changes on its products, which takes many hours. The new cash registers would provide better control over sales prices, which is another important advantage. Some of the company's cashiers frequently punch in wrong prices in error; worse, some cashiers intentionally enter lower-than-marked prices for their friends and relatives coming through the checkout line.

Investing in the new cash registers would generate labor cost savings in the future. The company's future annual cash outlays for wages and fringe benefits would decrease if the new cash registers were used. Avoiding a cash outlay is as good as a cash inflow; both increase the cash balance. The cost of the new cash registers—net of the trade-in allowance on its old cash registers and including the cost of installing the new cash registers—would be $500,000, which would be paid immediately.

The company would tap its general cash reserve to invest in the new cash registers. The retailer would not use direct financing for this investment, such as asking the vendor to lend the company a large part of the purchase price. The retailer would not arrange for a third-party loan or seek a lease-purchase arrangement to acquire the cash registers. As the old expression says, the business would pay "cash on the barrelhead" for the purchase of the cash registers.

KEY CONCEPT The manager in charge of making the decision decides to adopt a *five-year planning horizon* for this capital investment. In other words, the manager limits the recognition of cost savings to five years, even though there may be benefits beyond five years. Labor-hour savings and wage rates are difficult to forecast beyond five years, and other factors can change as well. At the end of five years the cash registers are assumed to have no residual value, which is very conservative.

The future labor cost savings depend mainly on how many work hours the new cash registers would save. Of course, estimating the annual labor cost savings is no easy matter. Instead of focusing on the precise forecasting of future labor cost savings, the manager takes a different approach. The manager asks how much annual labor cost savings would have to be to justify the investment.

For example, would future labor cost savings of $160,000 per year for five years be enough? The labor cost savings would occur throughout the year. For convenience of analysis, however, assume that the cost savings occur at each year-end. The company's cash balance would be this much higher at each year-end due to the labor cost savings.

KEY CONCEPT The retailer's capital structure is that presented in the earlier example. As shown in Figure 14.1 and explained previously, the company's before-tax annual cost of capital rate is 22.3 percent ($2,230,000 required annual EBIT ÷ $10 million total capital invested in assets = 22.3% annual cost of capital rate). However, this cost-of-capital rate cannot be simply multiplied by the $500,000 cost of the cash registers to determine the future returns needed from the investment. The cost-of-capital factors must be applied in a different manner.

KEY CONCEPT Furthermore, the future returns from the investment have to recover the $500,000 capital invested in the cash registers. After five years of use the cash registers will be at the end of their useful lives to the business and will have no residual salvage value. In summary, the future returns have to be sufficient to recover the cost of the cash registers and to provide for the cost of capital each year over the life of the investment.

Before moving on to the analysis of this capital investment, I should mention that there would be several incentives to invest in the cash registers. As already stated, the new cash registers would eliminate data entry errors by cashiers and would prevent cashiers from deliberately entering low prices for their friends and relatives. Employee fraud is a common and expensive problem, unfortunately. Also, the company may anticipate that it will be increasingly difficult to hire qualified employees over the next several years. Furthermore, the new cash registers would enable the company to collect marketing data on a real-time basis, which it cannot do at present. In short, there are several good reasons for buying the cash registers. However, the following discussion focuses on the financial aspects of the investment decision.

Analyzing the Investment: First Comments

The first step is to make a ballpark estimate of how much the future returns would have to be for the investment. The business has to recover the capital invested in the cash registers, which is $500,000 in the example. The business has five years to recover this amount of capital. But clearly, future returns of just $100,000 per year for five years is not enough. This amount of yearly return would not cover the company's cost of capital each year. So to start the ball rolling, an annual return of $160,000 is used in the analysis, which might seem to be adequate to cover the company's cost of capital. But is $160,000 per year actually enough?

First Pass at Analyzing the Investment

Figure 14.2 presents a spreadsheet analysis of the investment in the new cash registers. (In the old days before personal computers, this two-dimensional layout was called a *worksheet*.) This is only a first pass to see whether $160,000 annual returns on the investment would be sufficient. The analysis may seem complex at first glance, but it is quite straightforward. The method begins with the return for each year and makes demands on the cash return.

KEY CONCEPT The demands are four in number: (1) interest on debt capital, (2) income tax, (3) ROE (return on equity), and (4) recovery of capital invested in the assets. The first three amounts must be calculated by fixed formulas each year. The fourth is a free-floater; these amounts can follow any pattern year to year. But their total over the five years must add to $500,000, which is the amount of capital invested in the assets.

I'll walk down the first-year column in some detail; the other four years are simply repeats of the first year. The first claim on the annual return (in this example, the labor cost savings for the year) is for interest. For year 1, the interest claim is $14,000 ($175,000 debt balance at start of year × 8.0% interest rate = $14,000 annual interest). The second demand is for income tax. The annual labor cost savings increase the company's taxable income each year. Income tax each year depends on the interest for the year, which is deductible and on the depreciation method used for calculating income tax. As shown in Figure 14.2 the straight-line depreciation method is used, which gives a $100,000 depreciation deduction each year for five years using a zero salvage value at the end of five years. (The accelerated depreciation method could be used instead.)

The bottom layer in Figure 14.2 shows the calculation of income tax for each year attributable to the investment. The income tax for the year is entered above as the second takeout from the annual labor cost savings. The third takeout from the annual return is for earnings on equity capital (see Figure 14.2). The deduction for ROE is based on the ROE goal of 18.0 percent per year. ROE for year 1 equals $58,500 ($325,000 equity capital at start of year × 18.0% ROE = $58,500 net income).

Interest rate	8.0%				
ROE	18.0%	← Cost-of-capital factors			
Income tax rate	40.0%				
Debt % of capital	35.0%				
Equity % of capital	65.0%				

	Year 1	Year 2	Year 3	Year 4	Year 5
Annual Returns					
Labor cost savings	$160,000	$160,000	$160,000	$160,000	$160,000
Distribution of Returns					
For interest	($ 14,000)	($ 12,065)	($ 9,872)	($ 7,384)	($ 4,564)
For income tax	($ 18,400)	($ 19,174)	($ 20,051)	($ 21,046)	($ 22,174)
For ROE	($ 58,500)	($ 50,415)	($ 41,249)	($ 30,856)	($ 19,072)
Equals capital recovery	$ 69,100	$ 78,346	$ 88,828	$100,713	$114,189
Cumulative capital recovery at end of year	$ 69,100	$147,446	$236,274	$336,987	$451,176
Capital Invested at Beginning of Year					
Debt	$175,000	$150,815	$123,394	$ 92,304	$ 57,054
Equity	$325,000	$280,085	$229,160	$171,422	$105,958
Total	$500,000	$430,900	$352,554	$263,726	$163,013
Income Tax					
EBIT increase	$160,000	$160,000	$160,000	$160,000	$160,000
Interest expense	($ 14,000)	($12,065)	($ 9,872)	($ 7,384)	($ 4,564)
Depreciation	($100,000)	($100,000)	($100,000)	($100,000)	($100,000)
Taxable income	$ 46,000	$ 47,935	$ 50,128	$ 52,616	$ 55,436
Income tax	$ 18,400	$ 19,174	$ 20,051	$ 21,046	$ 22,174

FIGURE 14.2 *Analysis of investment in cash registers, assuming $160,000 annual returns.*

As mentioned, the $160,000 annual cash returns amount used in Figure 14.2 is just the starting point in the analysis. This amount may not be enough to actually achieve the 18.0 percent annual ROE goal of the business. The purpose of the analysis is to test whether the $160,000 annual returns would be enough to achieve the ROE goal of the business. Of course, if the ROE goal of the business had been lower than 18.0 percent, then the deduction for ROE from the annual return would be a smaller amount.

KEY CONCEPT The fourth and final demand on each year's cash return is for capital recovery. Capital recovery is the *residual* amount remaining after deducting interest, income tax, and the ROE amount for the year. For year 1, capital recovery is $69,100 (see Figure 14.2). This is the residual amount remaining from the annual return after deducting the requirements for interest, income tax, and ROE. The amount of capital recovery is not reinvested in additional cash registers; the company has all the cash registers it needs, at least for the time being.

KEY CONCEPT In the future, the business may consider replacing the cash registers or increasing the number of cash registers it uses. But as far as this particular investment is concerned the capital recovery each year simply goes back to the cash balance of the business. The capital leaves this project (the cash registers investment). The business may put the money in another investment, or may increase its cash balance, or may reduce its debt, or may pay a higher cash dividend.

As shown in Figure 14.2, in the first year the company liquidates $69,100 of its investment in the cash registers; this much of the total capital that was originally invested in the assets is recovered and is no longer tied up in this particular investment. Therefore the amount of capital invested during the second year is reduced by $69,100 ($500,000 initial capital – $69,100 capital recovery = $430,900 capital invested at start of year 2). Debt supplies 35 percent of this capital balance and equity the other 65 percent, as shown in the column for year 2.

 From year to year this investment sizes down, because each year the business recovers part of the original capital invested in the assets. Thus the annual amounts of interest and ROE earnings decrease year to year as the total capital invested decreases from year to year. But note that the income tax increases year to year because the annual interest expense deduction decreases.

The cumulative capital recovery at the end of each year is shown in Figure 14.2. At the end of the fifth and final year of the investment, this amount should equal the initial amount of capital invested in the assets, which is $500,000 in this example. As Figure 14.2 shows, the cumulative capital recovery falls short of $500,000, however.

Why a Second Pass at the Investment Is Needed

Given the annual returns of $160,000 the cumulative capital recovery at the end of the investment is only $451,176 (see Figure 14.2). But the business has to recover $500,000 capital from the investment, which is the initial amount of capital invested in the cash registers. Thus the annual returns of $160,000 are not enough. The $160,000 amount of annual returns does not generate enough capital recovery after taking out interest, income tax, and earnings on equity each year—unless the ROE for each year is lowered so that more would be available for capital recovery each year.

 Suppose the business goes ahead with the investment and it turns out that the annual returns are only $160,000 per year. In this situation the actual ROE rate earned on the investment would be lower than the 18.0 percent used in Figure 14.2. The precise ROE rate, assuming that the annual returns are $160,000, can be solved with the spreadsheet model. Instead of using the preestablished 18.0 percent rate, the ROE rate is lowered until the exact rate is found that makes the total capital recovery over the five years equal to $500,000. The appendix at the end of this chapter (Figure 14.5) shows the solution for the exact ROE rate, which is 14.6613 percent.

At the $160,000 level of annual returns the cash registers investment is not completely attractive, assuming that the business is serious about earning the annual 18.0 percent ROE rate. Clearly, the annual returns have to be higher than $160,000. The manager should ask his or her accountant or other financial staff person to determine the amount of annual labor cost savings that would justify the investment from the cost-of-capital viewpoint.

Determining Exact Amounts for Returns

The investment analysis model shown in Figure 14.2 for the cash registers example is the printout of my personal computer spreadsheet program. One reason for using a spreadsheet for capital investment analysis to is do all the required calculations quickly and accurately. Another reason is that the factors in the analysis can be easily changed for the purpose of investigating different scenarios for the investment.

I changed the annual cash returns in order to find the exact amount required to earn an annual 18.0 percent ROE. Other input variables were held the same; only the amount of the annual labor cost savings was changed. With a change in the amount of annual returns, the output variables for each year change accordingly—in particular, the income tax for each year and the amount of capital invested each year, which in turn change the amounts of interest and earnings on equity for each year. There is a cascade effect on the output variables from changing the amount of annual returns.

Finding the precise answer requires a trial-and-error, or plug-and-chug process that is repeated until the exact amount of future annual cash returns is found that makes total capital recovery $500,000. This may seem to be time-consuming, but it's not. Only a few trials or passes are required to zero in on the exact answer. From Figure 14.2 I already knew that $160,000 was too low. So I bumped up the annual returns figure to $175,000. This proved to be a little too high. After a few trials I converged on the exact amount. Figure 14.3 presents the answer. Annual labor cost savings of $172,463 for five years yield an annual 18.0 percent ROE and recover exactly $500,000 capital from the investment.

Now comes the hard part. The manager must decide whether the business could, realistically, achieve $172,463 annual labor cost savings. This is the really tough part of the decision-making process. But the manager knows that if the annual labor cost savings turn out to be this amount or higher, then the investment will prove to be a good decision from the cost-of-capital point of view.

Note in Figure 14.3 that the annual depreciation tax deduction amounts differ from the annual capital recovery amounts. For instance, the first year's depreciation tax deduction is

Interest rate	8.0%				
ROE	18.0%	Cost-of-capital factors			
Income tax rate	40.0%				
Debt % of capital	35.0%				
Equity % of capital	65.0%				

	Year 1	Year 2	Year 3	Year 4	Year 5
Annual Returns					
Labor cost savings	$172,463	$172,463	$172,463	$172,463	$172,463
Distribution of Returns					
For interest	($ 14,000)	($ 11,856)	($ 9,425)	($ 6,668)	($ 3,543)
For income tax	($ 23,385)	($ 24,243)	($ 25,215)	($ 26,318)	($ 27,568)
For ROE	($ 58,500)	($ 49,540)	($ 39,382)	($ 27,865)	($ 14,806)
Equals capital recovery	$ 76,578	$ 86,824	$ 98,441	$111,612	$126,546
Cumulative capital recovery at end of year	$ 76,578	$163,401	$261,842	$373,454	$500,000
Capital Invested at Beginning of Year					
Debt	$175,000	$148,198	$117,810	$ 83,355	$ 44,291
Equity	$325,000	$275,225	$218,789	$154,803	$ 82,255
Total	$500,000	$423,422	$336,599	$238,158	$126,546
Income Tax					
EBIT increase	$172,463	$172,463	$172,463	$172,463	$172,463
Interest expense	($ 14,000)	($ 11,856)	($ 9,425)	($ 6,668)	($ 3,543)
Depreciation	($100,000)	($100,000)	($100,000)	($100,000)	($100,000)
Taxable income	$ 58,463	$ 60,607	$ 63,038	$ 65,794	$ 68,919
Income tax	$ 23,385	$ 24,243	$ 25,215	$ 26,318	$ 27,568

FIGURE 14.3 *Exact amount of future returns required for investment.*

$100,000 (using the straight-line method) but the capital recovery for the first year is $76,578. Both the total depreciation over the five years and the total capital recovery over the five years are $500,000. But the two amounts differ from year to year. This disparity is typical of capital investments and does not present a problem when using a spreadsheet model for analysis. (The difference between these two factors is much more of a nuisance in using the mathematical analysis techniques discussed in the Chapter 15.)

FLEXIBILITY OF A SPREADSHEET MODEL

As mentioned before, any factor in the analysis can be changed to test how sensitive the annual returns would be to the change. For instance, instead of the straight-line method the accelerated depreciation method could be used in calculating income tax. Instead of uniform labor cost savings across the years, returns could be set lower in the early years and higher in the later years—or vice versa. The debt-to-equity ratio can be shifted. Of course, the interest rate and ROE target rate can be changed. Once a change is entered, the effects of the change are instantly available on screen.

To illustrate an alternative scenario for the cash registers example, assume the following cost of capital situation for the retailer instead of the preceding example:

Capital Structure and Cost of Capital Factors

- No debt; 100 percent equity source of capital
- Annual interest rate on debt—not applicable
- 40 percent income tax rate
- 18.0 percent annual ROE objective

In this alternative scenario, the business uses no debt capital; all its capital comes from equity sources (capital invested by its shareowners and retained earnings). The ROE target rate is the same as before (18 percent annual ROE). Figure 14.4 shows the annual returns that would be needed in this situation. The required annual returns would jump to $199,815 compared with $172,463 in the earlier example, an increase of more than $27,000 per year! This is a rather significant increase. The capital structure of the business makes a difference on the future returns needed from an investment.

LEASING VERSUS BUYING LONG-TERM ASSETS

Business managers have opportunities for leasing instead of buying long-term operating assets. Most long-term operating

Interest rate	0.0%			
ROE	18.0%	← Cost-of-capital factors		
Income tax rate	40.0%			
Debt % of capital	0.0%			
Equity % of capital	100.0%			

	Year 1	Year 2	Year 3	Year 4	Year 5
Annual Returns					
Labor cost savings	$199,815	$199,815	$199,815	$199,815	$199,815
Distribution of Returns					
For interest	$ 0	$ 0	$ 0	$ 0	$ 0
For income tax	($ 39,926)	($ 39,926)	($ 39,926)	($ 39,926)	($ 39,926)
For ROE	($ 90,000)	($ 77,420)	($ 62,576)	($ 45,059)	($ 24,390)
Equals capital recovery	$ 69,889	$ 82,469	$ 97,313	$114,830	$135,499
Cumulative capital recovery at end of year	$ 69,889	$152,358	$249,671	$364,501	$500,000
Capital Invested at Beginning of Year					
Debt	$ 0	$ 0	$ 0	$ 0	$ 0
Equity	$500,000	$430,111	$347,642	$250,329	$135,499
Total	$500,000	$430,111	$347,642	$250,329	$135,499
Income Tax					
EBIT increase	$199,815	$199,815	$199,815	$199,815	$199,815
Interest expense	$ 0	$ 0	$ 0	$ 0	$ 0
Depreciation	($100,000)	($100,000)	($100,000)	($100,000	($100,000)
Taxable income	$ 99,815	$ 99,815	$ 99,815	$ 99,815	$ 99,815
Income tax	$ 39,926	$ 39,926	$ 39,926	$ 39,926	$ 39,926

FIGURE 14.4 *Future returns required from investment for an alternative scenario (all equity, no debt).*

assets (trucks, equipment, machinery, computers, telephone systems, etc.) can be leased, either directly from the manufacturer of the asset or indirectly through a third-party leasing specialist. The cash registers probably could be leased instead of purchased. Leasing may be very appealing if the business is short of cash.

Perhaps the lessor has a lower cost of capital than the business, in which case the business might be better off leasing rather than investing its own capital in the assets. Then again, the lessor's cost of capital may be higher, which means that the lease rents would be higher than the returns needed by the business based on its lower cost-of-capital rate. Complicating matters is the fact that the term of the lease and pattern of lease rents may differ from the stream of returns generated from the assets.

Also, leases typically offer a purchase option at the end of the lease, at which time the business can purchase the assets. And leases are very complicated legal contracts that generally impose all kinds of conditions and constraints on the lessee. Many leases involve front-end cash outlays by the lessee. In short, comparing the purchase of long-term assets against leasing the same assets can be very difficult—like comparing apples and oranges.

But to illustrate certain basic points regarding the lease-versus-buy decision, suppose the retailer had the opportunity to lease the cash registers instead of buying them. Suppose the lessor quotes monthly rents of $14,372 for five years, which equals a total annual rent of $172,463. I selected this rent amount to equal the amount of the annual labor cost savings for the business to earn 18.0 percent ROE (see Figure 14.3). Also assume that the business would have the option to purchase the cash registers for a nominal amount at the end of the five-year lease. Thus the business would end up in the same position as if it had purchased the assets to begin with.

Generally, the lessee (the retailer) bears all costs of possession and use of the assets as if it had bought them outright. For example, the retailer would pay the fire and theft insurance on the assets whether they are owned or leased. By leasing the cash registers, the retailer would reduce its annual labor costs by $172,463, but would pay annual lease rents of the same amount. From the financial point of view, leasing versus buying is a standoff in this case. The retailer may not have any other investment opportunities that would generate an annual 18.0 percent ROE. So if it has the money, the retailer may prefer to make the investment instead of leasing the cash registers, thus employing its capital and earning an annual 18.0 percent ROE on the investment.

Leases involve certain considerations beyond just the financial aspects. For one thing, the retailer may prefer not to assume the economic risks of owning the cash registers. In a fast-changing technological environment, a business may be reluctant to assume the risks making long-term investments in assets that may become obsolete in two or three years. So a business may shop around for a two- or three-year lease.

The simplest analysis situation for comparing leasing with buying assets is this. Suppose a business has identified a promising opportunity for which it needs to acquire certain assets that would generate a stream of future returns for so many years, say $150,000 per year for seven years. (This forecast of future returns may turn out to be too optimistic, of course.) Assume that the business is short of cash and that it has tapped out its capital sources. It would be difficult for the business to raise additional capital. Assume that a leasing specialist is willing to rent the assets to the business for $10,000 per month, or $120,000 per year for five years. At the end of the lease the business would have the option to purchase the assets for a nominal amount.

In this scenario the lease makes sense, keeping in mind the risk that the future returns may turn out to be lower than $150,000 per year. The business would realize a $30,000 gain in its operating profit each year ($150,000 annual returns from using the assets – $120,000 annual lease rents = $30,000 net gain). This is the simplest way to analyze leases. In actual situations the analysis is much more complicated. In any case, a business should determine the stream of future returns from acquiring the assets. If the assets are purchased, the returns provide the money to recover the capital invested in the assets and cover the business's cost of capital along the way. If the assets are leased, the returns provide the money to pay the lease rents.

A WORD ON CAPITAL BUDGETING

In theory, a business should assemble all its possible investment opportunities, compare them, and rank-order them. The business should select the one with the highest ROE first, and so on. In allocating scarce capital among competing investment opportunities, ROE is the key criterion. According to this view of the world, the job of the business manager is to ration a limited amount of capital among competing investment alternatives.

The premise of rationing scarce capital resources is why the general topic of capital investment analysis is sometimes called *capital budgeting*. The term *budgeting* here is used in the allocation or apportionment sense, not in the sense of overall business management planning and goal setting. The comparative analysis of competing investment alternatives is beyond the scope of this book. Corporate financial management books cover this topic in depth.

END POINT

Business managers make many long-term capital investment decisions. The analysis of capital investments hinges on the cost-of-capital requirements of the business, which depend on the company's mix of debt and equity capital, the cost of each, and the income tax situation of the business. The cost of equity capital is not a contractual rate like interest. Management decides on the ROE (return on equity) objective for the business.

Based on the amount of capital invested, a manager can determine the amounts of future returns that will be needed to satisfy the cost-of-capital requirements of the business. The manager has to judge whether these future returns can actually be achieved. The chapter explains how to apply the cost-of-capital imperatives of a business in making capital investment decisions. A spreadsheet model is used to analyze and illustrate a prototype capital investment. A spreadsheet model has two important advantages: It is an excellent device for organizing and presenting the relevant information for an investment, and it is a versatile tool for examining different scenarios of an investment.

Analysis is important, to be sure. But we should not get carried away. More important is the ability of managers to find good capital investment opportunities and blend them into the overall strategic plan of the business.

CHAPTER APPENDIX

Interest rate	8.0%
ROE	14.6613%
Income tax rate	40.0%
Debt % of capital	35.0%
Equity % of capital	65.0%

Exact ROE rate solved for in this figure

	Year 1	Year 2	Year 3	Year 4	Year 5
Annual Returns					
Labor cost savings	$160,000	$160,000	$160,000	$160,000	$160,000
Distribution of Returns					
For interest	($ 14,000)	($ 11,761)	($ 9,272)	($ 6,503)	($ 3,424)
For income tax	($ 18,400)	($ 19,295)	($ 20,291)	($ 21,399)	($ 22,630)
For ROE	($ 47,649)	($ 40,030)	($ 31,557)	($ 22,134)	($ 11,654)
Equals capital recovery	$ 79,951	$ 88,913	$ 98,880	$109,964	$122,291
Cumulative capital recovery at end of year	$ 79,951	$168,864	$267,744	$377,709	$500,000
Capital Invested at Beginning of Year					
Debt	$175,000	$147,017	$115,898	$ 81,290	$ 42,802
Equity	$325,000	$273,032	$215,238	$150,966	$ 79,489
Total	$500,000	$420,049	$331,136	$232,256	$122,291
Income Tax					
EBIT increase	$160,000	$160,000	$160,000	$160,000	$160,000
Interest expense	($ 14,000)	($ 11,761)	($ 9,272)	($ 6,503)	($ 3,424)
Depreciation	($100,000)	($100,000)	($100,000)	($100,000)	($100,000)
Taxable income	$ 46,000	$ 48,239	$ 50,728	$ 53,497	$ 56,576
Income tax	$ 18,400	$ 19,295	$ 20,291	$ 21,399	$ 22,630

FIGURE 14.5 *Exact ROE rate for cash registers capital investment with $160,000 annual returns.*

Discounting Investment Returns Expected

This chapter and Chapter 14 are like a set of bookends. Chapter 14 explains the analysis of long-term investments in operating assets by businesses. This chapter continues the topic, with one key difference.

The time line of analysis in the previous chapter goes like this:

Present —————————————→ Future

Starting with a given amount of capital invested today, the analysis looks forward in time to determine the amounts of future returns that would be needed in order to satisfy the cost-of-capital requirements of the business.

The time line of analysis in this chapter goes like this:

Present ←————————————— Future

Starting with the amounts of future returns from an investment (which are treated as fixed) the analysis travels backward in time to determine an amount called the *present value* of the investment. The present value is the most that a business should be willing to invest today to receive the future returns from the investment, based on its cost-of-capital requirements. The present value is compared with the entry cost of an investment.

 **TIME VALUE OF MONEY AND COST OF CAPITAL**

The pivotal idea in this and the previous chapter is the *time value of money*. This term refers not only to money but also more broadly to capital and economic wealth in general. Capital should generate income, gain, or profit over the time it is used. The ratio of earnings on the capital invested over a period of time, one year being the standard time period of reference, is the measure for the time value of money. Karl Marx said that capital is "dead labor" and argued that capital should be publicly owned for the good of everyone. I won't pursue this economic philosophy any further. Quite clearly, in our economic system capital does have a time value—or a time cost depending on whose shoes you're standing in.

The business example in Chapter 14 has the following capital structure and cost-of-capital factors:

Capital Structure and Cost-of-Capital Factors

- 35 percent debt and 65 percent equity mix of capital sources
- 8.0 percent annual interest rate on debt
- 40 percent income tax rate (combined federal and state)
- 18.0 percent annual ROE objective

The same business example is continued this chapter. The debt and equity mix and the cost-of-capital factors differ from business to business, of course. But for a large swath of businesses this scenario is in the middle of the fairway.

Chapter 14 focuses on a decision of a retailer regarding investing in cash registers that would generate labor cost savings in the future. The analysis reveals that $160,000 annual returns from the cash registers investment wouldn't be enough to justify the investment; the annual returns would have to be $172,463. Figures 14.2 and 14.3 illustrate these important points. Assuming that annual returns of $172,463 could be earned for five years by using the cash registers, the present value of the investment would be exactly $500,000. The entry cost of the investment is $500,000; this is the initial amount of capital that would be invested in the cash registers.

 When the present value exactly equals the entry cost of an investment, the future returns are the exact amounts needed to recover the total capital invested in the

assets and to satisfy the business's cost-of-capital requirements each year during the life of the investment. The present
value of an investment is found by discounting its future
returns.

BACK TO THE FUTURE: DISCOUNTING
INVESTMENT RETURNS

The first pass in analyzing the cash registers investment by
the retailer in Chapter 14 is a scenario in which the future
annual returns would be $160,000 for five years. Relative to
the business's cost-of-capital requirements, this stream of
future returns would be too low. The business would not
recover the full $500,000 amount of capital that would be
invested in the cash registers. Looking at it another way, if the
business invested $500,000 and realized only $160,000 labor
cost savings for five years, the annual return on equity (ROE)
for this investment would fall short of its 18.0 percent goal.

Suppose the seller of the cash registers is willing to dicker
on the price. The $500,000 asking price for the cash registers
is not carved in stone; the seller will haggle over the price. At
what price would the cash registers investment be acceptable
relative to the company's cost-of-capital requirements? Using
the spreadsheet model explained in Chapter 14, I lowered the
purchase price so that the total capital recovered over the life
of the investment equals the purchase price. I kept the cost-of-
capital factors the same, and I kept the future annual returns
at $160,000. Finding the correct purchase price required only
a few iterations using the spreadsheet model.

Figure 15.1 presents the solution to the question. Suppose
the retailer could negotiate a purchase price of $463,868. At
this price the investment makes sense from the cost-of-capital
point of view. The total capital recovered over the five years is
exactly equal to this purchase price. By the way, note that the
annual depreciation amounts for income tax purposes are
based on this lower purchase cost.

One important advantage of using a spreadsheet model for
capital investment analysis is that any of the variables for the
investment can be changed to explore a variety of questions
and to examine a diversity of scenarios. The scenario presented in Figure 15.1 is, "What if the purchase price were
only $463,868?"

Interest rate	8.0%	
ROE	18.0%	Cost-of-capital factors
Income tax rate	40.0%	
Debt % of capital	35.0%	
Equity % of capital	65.0%	

	Year 1	Year 2	Year 3	Year 4	Year 5
Annual Returns					
Labor cost savings	$160,000	$160,000	$160,000	$160,000	$160,000
Distribution of Returns					
For interest	($12,988)	($10,999)	($8,744)	($6,187)	($3,287)
For income tax	($21,695)	($22,491)	($23,393)	($24,416)	($25,576)
For ROE	($54,273)	($45,960)	($36,536)	($25,851)	($13,736)
Equals capital recovery	$71,044	$80,550	$91,327	$103,547	$117,401
Cumulative capital recovery at end of year	$71,044	$151,593	$242,921	$346,467	$463,868
Capital Invested at Beginning of Year					
Debt	$162,354	$137,488	$109,296	$77,332	$41,090
Equity	$301,514	$255,336	$202,978	$143,616	$76,310
Total	$463,868	$392,824	$312,275	$220,947	$117,401
Income Tax					
EBIT increase	$160,000	$160,000	$160,000	$160,000	$160,000
Interest expense	($12,988)	($10,999)	($8,744)	($6,187)	($3,287)
Depreciation	($92,774)	($92,774)	($92,774)	($92,774)	($92,774)
Taxable income	$54,238	$56,227	$58,483	$61,040	$63,939
Income tax	$21,695	$22,491	$23,393	$24,416	$25,576

Variable solved for in this analysis

FIGURE 15.1 *Purchase cost of cash registers that would justify the investment relative to the business's cost-of-capital requirements.*

Solving for the present value is called *discounting* the future returns. This analysis technique is also called the *discounted cash flow* (DCF) method and usually is explained in a mathematical context using equations applied to the future stream of returns.

SPREADSHEETS VERSUS EQUATIONS

The DCF method is very popular. However, I favor a spreadsheet model to determine the present value of an investment. Spreadsheet programs are very versatile. Furthermore, a spreadsheet does all the irksome calculations involved in investment analysis. Different scenarios can be examined quickly and efficiently, which I find to be an enormous advantage. In business capital investment situations, managers have to make several critical assumptions and forecasts. The manager is well advised to test the sensitivity of each critical input factor. A spreadsheet model is an excellent device for doing this.

Even if you are not a regular spreadsheet user, the logic and layout of the spreadsheet presented in Figure 15.1 are important to understand. Figure 15.1 provides the relevant information for the management decision-making phase and for management follow-through after a decision is made. The year-by-year data points shown in Figure 15.1 are good benchmarks for monitoring and controlling the actual results of the investment as it plays out each year. In short, a spreadsheet model is a very useful analysis tool and is a good way for organizing the relevant information about an investment.

Frankly, another reason for using a spreadsheet model is to avoid mathematical methods for analyzing capital investments. In Chapter 14 not one equation is presented, and so far in this chapter not one equation is presented. In my experience, managers are put off by a heavy-handed mathematical approach loaded with arcane equations and unfamiliar symbols. However, in the not-so-distant past, personal computers were not as ubiquitous as they are today, and spreadsheet programs were not nearly so sophisticated.

In the old days (before personal computers came along), certain mathematical techniques were developed to do capital investment analysis computations. These techniques have become entrenched in the field of capital investment analysis. Indeed, the techniques and terminology are household words that are used freely in the world of business and finance—such as *present value, discounted cash flow,* and *internal rate of return.* Business managers should have at least a nodding acquaintance with these terms and a general idea of how the techniques are applied.

The remainder of this chapter presents a quick, introductory tour of the mathematical techniques for capital investment analysis. To the extent possible, I avoid going into detailed explanations of the computational equations, which I believe have little interest to business managers. These quantitative techniques are just different ways of skinning the cat. I think a spreadsheet model is a better tool of analysis, which reminds me of a personal incident several years ago.

I was shopping for a mortgage on the new house we had just bought. One loan officer pulled out a well-worn table of columns and rows for different interest rates and different loan amount modules. He took a few minutes to determine the monthly payment amount for my mortgage loan. I had brought a business/financial calculator to the meeting. I double-checked his answer and found that it was incorrect. He was somewhat offended and replied that he had been doing these sorts of calculations for many years, and perhaps I had made a mistake. It took me only five seconds to check my calculation. I was right. He took several minutes to compute the amount again and was shocked to discover that his first amount was wrong. I thought better of suggesting that he should use a calculator to do these sorts of calculations.

DISCOUNTED CASH FLOW (DCF)

To keep matters focused on bare-bones essentials, suppose that a business has no debt (and thus no interest to pay) and is organized as a pass-through entity for income tax purposes. The business does not pay income tax as a separate entity. Its only cost-of-capital factor is its annual return on equity (ROE) goal. Assume that the business has established an annual 15 percent ROE goal. (Of course, the ROE could be set lower or higher than 15 percent.) Assume that the business has an

investment opportunity that promises annual returns at the
end of each year as follows:

At End of Year	Returns
1	$115,000.00
2	$132,250.00
3	$152,087.50

What is the value of this investment to the business today, at
the present time? This is called the *present value* (PV) of the
investment.

The discounted cash flow (DCF) method of analysis com-
putes the present value as follows:

Present Value Calculations

Year 1 $115,000.00 \div (1 + 15\%)^1 = $100,000

Year 2 $132,250.00 \div (1 + 15\%)^2 = $100,000

Year 3 $152,087.50 \div (1 + 15\%)^3 = \underline{$100,000}

Present value   = $300,000

I rigged the future return amounts for each year so that the
calculations are easier to follow. Of course, a business should
forecast the actual future returns for an investment. The future
returns represent either increases of cash inflows from making the investment or decreases of cash outflows (as in the
cash registers investment example). Each future return is discounted, or divided by a number greater than 1. Thus, the
term *discounted* cash flow.

KEY CONCEPT The divisor in the DCF calculations equals $(1 + r)^n$, in
which r is the cost-of-capital rate each period and n
is the number of periods until the future return is realized.
Usually r is constant from period to period over the life of the
investment, although a different cost-of-capital rate could be
used for each period.

In summary, the present value of this investment equals
$300,000. This means that if the business went ahead and put
$300,000 capital into the investment and at the end of each
year realized a future return according to the preceding

schedule, then the business would earn exactly 15 percent annual ROE on the investment. To check this present value, I used my spreadsheet model. Figure 15.2 shows the printout of the spreadsheet model, as adapted to the circumstances of this investment. At the end of the third year the full $300,000 capital invested is recovered, which proves that the present value of the investment equals $300,000, using the 15 percent cost-of-capital discount rate.

KEY CONCEPT The DCF method can be used when the future returns from an investment are known or can be predicted fairly accurately. The purpose is to determine the present value (PV) of an investment, which is the maximum amount that a business should invest today in exchange for the future

			Year 1	Year 2	Year 3
Interest rate	0.0%	Cost-of-capital factors			
ROE	15.0%				
Income tax rate	0.0%				
Debt % of capital	0.0%				
Equity % of capital	100.0%				

	Year 1	Year 2	Year 3
Annual Returns			
Labor cost savings	$115,000.00	$132,250.00	$152,087.50
Distribution of Returns			
For interest	$ 0.00	$ 0.00	$ 0.00
For income tax	$ 0.00	$ 0.00	$ 0.00
For ROE	($ 45,000.00)	($ 34,500.00)	($ 19,837.50)
Equals capital recovery	$ 70,000.00	$ 97,750.00	$132,250.00
Cumulative capital recovery at end of year	$ 70,000.00	$167,750.00	$300,000.00
Capital Invested at Beginning of Year			
Debt	$ 0.00	$ 0.00	$ 0.00
Equity	$300,000.00	$230,000.00	$132,250.00
Total	$300,000.00	$230,000.00	$132,250.00

FIGURE 15.2 *Check on the present value calculated by the DCF method.*

returns. The DCF technique is correct, of course. But it has one problem. Well, actually two problems—one not so serious and one more serious.

The not-so-serious problem concerns how to do the computations required by the DCF method. One way is to use a handheld business/financial calculator. These are very powerful, relatively cheap, and fairly straightforward to use (assuming you read the owner's manual). Another way is to use the financial functions included in a spreadsheet program. (Excel® includes a complete set of financial functions.)

The second problem in using the DCF method is more substantive and has nothing to do with the computations for present value. The problem concerns the lack of information in using the DCF technique. The unfolding of the investment over the years is not clear from the present value (PV) calculation. Rather than opening up the investment for closer inspection, the PV computation closes it down and telescopes the information into just one number. The method doesn't reveal important information about the investment over its life.

Figure 15.2 presents a more complete look at the investment. It shows that the cash return at the end of year one is split between $45,000 earnings on equity and $70,000 capital recovery. The capital recovery aspect of an investment is very important to understand. The capital recovery portion of the cash return at the end of the first year reduces the amount of capital invested during the second year. Only $230,000 is invested during the second year ($300,000 initial amount invested – $70,000 capital recovered at end of year one = $230,000 capital invested at start of year 2). Business investments are self-liquidating over the life of the investment; there is capital recovery each period, as in this example.

Managers should anticipate what to do with the $70,000 capital recovery at the end of the first year. (For that matter, managers should also plan what to do with the $45,000 net income.) Will the capital be reinvested? Will the business be able to reinvest the $70,000 and earn 15 percent ROE? To plan ahead for the capital recovery from the investment, managers need information as presented in Figure 15.2, which tracks the earnings and capital recovery year by year. The DCF technique does not generate this information.

NET PRESENT VALUE AND INTERNAL RATE OF RETURN (IRR)

Suppose the business has an investment opportunity that would cost $300,000 to enter today. (Recall that in this example the business has no debt and is a pass-through tax entity that does not pay income tax.) The manager forecasts the future returns from the investment would be as follows:

At End of Year	Returns
1	$118,000.00
2	$139,240.00
3	$164,303.20

The present value and the net present value for this stream of future returns is calculated as follows:

Present Value Calculations

Year 1 $118,000.00 \div (1 + 15\%)^1 = \$102,608.70$

Year 2 $139,240.00 \div (1 + 15\%)^2 = \$105,285.44$

Year 3 $164,303.20 \div (1 + 15\%)^3 = \underline{\$108,032.02}$

Present value	= $315,926.16
Entry cost of investment	($300,000.00)
Net present value	= $15,926.16

The present value is $15,926.16 more of the amount of capital that would have to be invested. The difference between the calculated present value (PV) and the entry cost of an investment is called its *net present value* (NPV). Net present value is negative when the PV is less than the entry cost of the investment. The NPV has informational value, but it's not an ideal measure for comparing alternative investment opportunities. For this purpose, the internal rate of return (IRR) for each investment is determined and the internal rates of return for all the investments are compared.

KEY CONCEPT   The IRR is the precise discount rate that makes PV exactly equal to the entry cost of the investment. In the example, the investment has a $300,000 entry cost. The

IRR for the stream of future returns from the investment is 18.0 percent, which is higher than the 15.0 percent cost-of-capital discount rate used to compute the PV. The IRR rate is calculated by using a business/financial calculator or by entering the relevant data in a spreadsheet program using the IRR financial function.

Figure 15.3 demonstrates that the IRR for the investment is 18.0 percent. This return-on-capital rate is used to calculate the earnings on capital invested each year that is deducted from the return for that year. The remainder is the capital recovery for the year. The total capital recovered by the end of the third year equals the $300,000 entry cost of the investment (see Figure 15.3). Thus the internal rate of return (IRR) is 18.0 percent.

Interest rate	0.0%	← Internal rate of return (IRR)	
ROE	18.0%		
Income tax rate	0.0%		
Debt % of capital	0.0%		
Equity % of capital	100.0%		

	Year 1	Year 2	Year 3
Annual Returns			
Labor cost savings	$118,000.00	$139,240.00	$164,303.20
Distribution of Returns			
For interest	$ 0.00	$ 0.00	$ 0.00
For income tax	$ 0.00	$ 0.00	$ 0.00
For ROE	($ 54,000.00)	($ 42,480.00)	($ 25,063.20)
Equals capital recovery	$ 64,000.00	$ 96,760.00	$139,240.00
Cumulative capital recovery at end of year	$ 64,000.00	$160,760.00	$300,000.00
Capital Invested at Beginning of Year			
Debt	$ 0.00	$ 0.00	$ 0.00
Equity	$300,000.00	$236,000.00	$139,240.00
Total	$300,000.00	$236,000.00	$139,240.00

FIGURE 15.3 *Illustration that internal rate of return (IRR) is 18.0 percent.*

A business should favor investments with higher IRRs in preference to investments with lower IRRs—all other things being the same. A business should not accept an investment that has an IRR less than its hurdle rate, that is, its cost-of-capital rate. Another way of saying this is that a business should not proceed with an investment that has a negative net present value. Well, this is the theory.

 Capital investment decisions are complex and often involve many nonquantitative, or qualitative, factors that are difficult to capture fully in the analysis. A company may go ahead with an investment that has a low IRR because of political pressures or to accomplish social objectives that lie outside the profit motive. The company might make a capital investment even if the numbers don't justify the decision in order to forestall competitors from entering its market. Long-run capital investment decisions are at bottom really survival decisions. A company may have to make huge capital investments to upgrade, automate, or expand; if it doesn't, it may languish and eventually die.

AFTER-TAX COST-OF-CAPITAL RATE

So far I have skirted around one issue in discussing discounted cash flow techniques for analyzing business capital investments—income tax. DCF analysis techniques were developed long before personal computer spreadsheet programs became available. The DCF method had to come up with a way for dealing with the income tax factor, and it did, of course. The trick is to use an after-tax cost-of-capital rate and to separate the stream of returns from an investment and the depreciation deductions for income tax.

An example is needed to demonstrate how to use the after-tax cost of capital rate. The cash registers investment examined in the previous chapter is a perfect example for this purpose. To remind you, the retailer's sources of capital and its cost of capital factors are as follows:

Capital Structure and Cost-of-Capital Factors

- 35 percent debt and 65 percent equity mix of capital sources
- 8.0 percent annual interest rate on debt

- 40 percent income tax rate (combined federal and state)
- 18.0 percent annual ROE objective

The after-tax cost of capital rate for this business is calculated as follows:

After-Tax Cost-of-Capital Rate

Debt	$35\% \times [(8.0\%)(1 - 40\% \text{ tax rate})] =$	1.68%
Equity	$[65\% \times 18.0\%] =$	<u>11.70%</u>
After-tax cost-of-capital rate		= 13.38%

KEY CONCEPT ROE is an after-tax rate; net income earned on the owners' equity of a business is after income tax. To put the interest rate on an after-tax basis, the interest rate is multiplied by (1 – tax rate) because interest is deductible to determine taxable income. The debt weight (35 percent in this example) is multiplied by the after-tax interest rate, and the equity weight (65 percent in this example) is multiplied by the after-tax ROE rate. The after-tax cost of capital, therefore, is 13.38 percent for the business.

Recall that the entry cost of investing in the cash registers is $500,000. Assume that the future annual returns from this investment are $172,463 for five years. Figure 14.3 in the previous chapter shows that for this stream of future returns the company's cost of capital requirements are satisfied exactly. Therefore, the present value of the investment must be exactly $500,000, which is the entry cost of the investment. Using the after-tax cost-of-capital rate to discount the returns from the investment proves this point.

As just calculated, the company's after-tax cost-of-capital rate is 13.38 percent. Instead of applying this discount rate directly to the $172,463 returns (labor cost savings) from the investment, the annual returns are first converted to an after-tax basis, as though the returns were fully taxable at the 40 percent income tax rate. However, income tax is overstated because the depreciation deduction based on the cost of the assets is ignored. The depreciation tax effect is brought into the analysis as follows.

In this example, the straight-line depreciation method is used, so the company deducts $100,000 depreciation each year for income tax purposes. This reduces its taxable income and thus its income tax by $40,000 each year ($100,000 annual depreciation × 40% tax rate = $40,000 income tax savings). The depreciation tax savings are added to the $103,478 after-tax returns each year, which gives a total of $143,478 for each year. These annual amounts are discounted using the after-tax cost-of-capital rate as follows:

Present Value Calculations

Year 1 $143,478 ÷ (1 + 13.38%)^1 = $126,546

Year 2 $143,478 ÷ (1 + 13.38%)^2 = $111,612

Year 3 $143,478 ÷ (1 + 13.38%)^3 = $ 98,441

Year 4 $143,478 ÷ (1 + 13.38%)^4 = $ 86,824

Year 5 $143,478 ÷ (1 + 13.38%)^5 = $ 76,577

Present value = $500,000

The present value calculated in this manner equals the entry cost of the investment. (When the stream of future returns consists of uniform amounts, only one global calculation is required, but I show them for each year to leave a clear trail regarding how present value is calculated.) The company would earn exactly its cost of capital, because the present value equals the entry cost of the investment. This point also is demonstrated in Figure 14.3 in the previous chapter.

As I've said before, I favor a spreadsheet model for capital investment analysis over the equation-oriented DCF method. A spreadsheet model is more versatile and provides more information for management analysis. Also, I think it is a more intuitive and straightforward approach.

 REGARDING COST-OF-CAPITAL FACTORS

Most discourses on business capital investment analysis assume a constant mix, or ratio, of debt and equity over the life of an investment. And the cost of each source of capital is held constant over the life of the investment. Also, the income tax rate is held constant. Before spreadsheets came along, there were very practical reasons for making these assumptions, mainly to avoid using more than one cost-of-capital rate in the analysis. Today these constraints are no longer necessary.

If the situation calls for it, the manager should change the ratio of debt and equity from one period to the next or change the interest rate and/or the ROE rate from period to period. Each period could be assigned its own cost-of-capital rate, in other words. Sometimes this is appropriate for particular capital investments. For instance, a capital investment may involve direct financing, in which a loan is arranged and tailor-made to fit the specific features of the investment.

One example of direct financing is when a business offers its customers the alternative of leasing products instead of buying them. The business makes an investment in the assets leased to its customers. The business borrows money to provide part of the capital invested in the assets leased to customers. The leased assets are used as collateral for the loan, and the terms of the loan are designed to parallel the terms of the lease. Over the life of the lease, the mix of debt and equity capital invested in the assets changes from period to period. Furthermore, the interest rate on the lease loan and the ROE goal for lease investments very likely are different from the cost-of-capital factors for the company's main line of business.

END POINT

This and the previous chapter explain the analysis of a business's long-term investments in operating assets. The capital to make these investments comes from two basic sources— debt and owners' equity. A business should carefully analyze capital investments to determine whether the investment will yield sufficient operating profit to provide for its cost of capital during the life of the investment. This chapter demonstrates how to use the spreadsheet model developed in the previous chapter for discounting the future returns from an investment to determine its present value. The chapter also presents a succinct survey of the commonly used mathematical techniques for analyzing business capital investments.

Discounted cash flow is the broad generic name, or umbrella term, for the traditional equation-oriented capital investment analysis methods. A stream of future cash returns from an investment is discounted to calculate the present value, or the net present value, of the investment. Alternatively, the internal rate of return that the future returns would yield is determined. The IRR of an investment is compared against the company's cost-of-capital rate and with the internal rates of return of alternative investments. These mathematical analysis techniques are explained in the chapter, while keeping the computational equations to a minimum.

The equation-oriented techniques were developed before sophisticated spreadsheet programs were available for personal computers. In my view, the spreadsheet model is a better analysis tool. Spreadsheets are more versatile, easier to follow, and make it possible to display all the relevant information for decision-making analysis and management control. Nevertheless, the traditional capital investment analysis methods probably will be around for some time.

PART 5

End Topics

16

Service Businesses

Ask business consultants and I'd bet most would say that one of the first things new clients tell them is: "Our business is different." Which is true, of course; every business is unique. On the other hand, all businesses draw on a common core of concepts, principles, and techniques. Take people: Every individual is different and unique. Yet basic principles of behavior and motivation apply to all of us. Take products: Breakfast cereals are different from computers, which are different from autos, and so on. Yet basic principles of marketing apply to all products and services.

 Applying basic business concepts and principles is the difficult part that managers are paid to do and do well. The manager must adapt the basic concepts and general principles to the specific circumstances of her or his particular business. Likewise, the tools and techniques of analysis demonstrated in previous chapters must be adapted and modified to fit the characteristics and problems of each particular business.

This chapter applies the profit analysis tools and techniques discussed in previous chapters to service businesses. These business entities do not sell a product, or if a product is sold it is quite incidental to the service. There are very interesting differences in profit behavior between product and service businesses.

FINANCIAL STATEMENT DIFFERENCES OF SERVICE BUSINESSES

Service businesses range from dry cleaners to film processors, from hotels to hospitals, from airlines to freight haulers, from CPAs to barbers, from rental firms to photocopying stores, from newspapers to television networks, and from movie theaters to amusement parks. The service sector is the largest general category in the economy—although extremely diverse.

Nevertheless, a general example serves as a relevant framework for a large swath of service businesses. You can modify and tailor-fit this benchmark example to the particular characteristics of any service business.

I use a typical example for a product-oriented company in Chapter 4 to demonstrate the interpretation of externally reported financial statements. Instead of introducing a new example, the product business example is converted to a service company example to point out the basic differences between these two types of business. Figure 16.1 presents the income statement and balance sheet (statement of financial condition) for the product business with certain accounts crossed out. You don't find these accounts in the financial statements of a service company.

 A service company does not sell a product, so the inventories account and the inventory-dependent accounts are also crossed out. Accounts payable for inventories in the balance sheet is crossed out, but accounts payable for operating expenses remains. (In externally reported balance sheets, these two sources of accounts payable are blended into just one accounts payable liability account, but they are shown separately in Figure 16.1.) Minor differences in the statement of cash flows between product-based and service businesses are not shown in Figure 16.1.

In the income statement, the cost-of-goods-sold expense account and the gross margin profit line are crossed out. Instead of cost of goods sold, most service businesses have comparatively larger fixed operating expenses relative to sales revenue than do product-based businesses.

 As just mentioned, service businesses have no inventories. In the example shown in Figure 16.1, inven-

Income Statement for Year Just Ended

Sales revenue	$39,661,250
~~Cost of goods sold expense~~	~~$24,960,750~~
~~Gross margin~~	~~$14,700,500~~
Selling and administrative expenses	$11,466,135
Earnings before interest and income tax	$ 3,234,365
Interest expense	$ 795,000
Earnings before income tax	$ 2,439,365
Income tax expense	$ 853,778
Net income	$ 1,585,587
Earnings per share	$ 3.75

Balance Sheet at Close of Year Just Ended

Assets

Cash	$ 2,345,675
Accounts receivable	$ 3,813,582
~~Inventories~~	~~$ 5,760,173~~
Prepaid expenses	$ 822,899
Total current assets	$12,742,329
Property, plant, and equipment	$20,857,500
Accumulated depreciation	($ 6,785,250)
Cost less accumulated depreciation	$14,072,250
Total assets	$26,814,579

Liabilities and Owners' Equity

~~Accounts payable—inventories~~	~~$ 1,920,058~~
Accounts payable—operating expenses	$ 617,174
Accrued expenses payable	$ 1,280,214
Income tax payable	$ 58,650
Short-term debt	$ 2,250,000
Total current liabilities	$ 6,126,096
Long-term debt	$ 7,500,000
Total liabilities	$13,626,096
Capital stock (422,823 shares)	$ 4,587,500
Retained earnings	$ 8,600,983
Total Owners' equity	$13,188,483
Total Liabilities and owners' equity	$26,814,579

FIGURE 16.1 *Items deleted for a service business (financial statements from Figures 4.1 and 4.2 for a product-based business).*

tories are almost $6 million, so if this were a service business its total assets would be $6 million less and its liabilities and owners' equity would be $6 million less.

Some service businesses (airlines, gas and electric utilities, railroads) make heavy investments in long-term, fixed operating assets. These businesses are said to be *capital-intensive*. In the past, all three of these examples were regulated industries, but more recently they have been deregulated. In contrast, other types of service businesses (e.g., professional legal firms) make relatively light investments in fixed operating assets. Many service businesses are in the middle regarding capital invested in property, plant, and equipment. Examples are movie theater chains, newspapers, and book publishers. They invest in long-term operating assets, but not huge amounts.

MANAGEMENT PROFIT REPORT
FOR A SERVICE BUSINESS

Figure 16.2 presents internal management reports for three profit modules of a service business, which are used throughout the rest of the chapter. You may notice that this example closely follows the three-profit module example for the product business in Chapter 9. My purpose is to provide comparisons between a middle-of-the-road source of revenue with an average profit margin (the standard service in Figure 16.2), a no-frills basic service with a slim profit margin, and a top-of-the-line premier service with relatively high profit margin.

Just as product-based businesses sell different products with different margins, many service businesses offer different services at different prices. For example, airline companies offer first class, standard class, and tourist class. Entertainment businesses charge different prices depending on where seats are located, as do football and baseball teams. Hotels charge different prices for rooms with a better view. And so on.

Compared with the management profit reports in Figure 9.1 for the product business example, the major changes in Figure 16.2 are the absences of cost-of-goods-sold expense and gross margin. As mentioned earlier, service businesses don't sell products and therefore they don't have a cost-of-goods-sold expense or gross margin (sales revenue less cost of

Standard Service

	100,000 units	
	Per Unit	Totals
Sales revenue	$100.00	$10,000,000
Revenue-driven expenses @ 8.5%	$ 8.50	$ 850,000
Unit-driven expenses	$ 6.50	$ 650,000
Contribution margin	$ 85.00	$ 8,500,000
Fixed operating expenses	$ 75.00	$ 7,500,000
Profit	$ 10.00	$ 1,000,000

Basic Service

	150,000 units	
	Per Unit	Totals
Sales revenue	$ 75.00	$11,250,000
Revenue-driven expenses @ 4.0%	$ 3.00	$ 450,000
Unit-driven expenses	$ 5.00	$ 750,000
Contribution margin	$ 67.00	$10,050,000
Fixed operating expenses	$ 60.33	$ 9,050,000
Profit	$ 6.67	$ 1,000,000

Premier Service

	50,000 units	
	Per Unit	Totals
Sales revenue	$150.00	$ 7,500,000
Revenue-driven expenses @ 7.5%	$ 11.25	$ 562,500
Unit-driven expenses	$ 8.75	$ 437,500
Contribution margin	$130.00	$ 6,500,000
Fixed operating expenses	$110.00	$ 5,500,000
Profit	$ 20.00	$ 1,000,000

FIGURE 16.2 *Management profit reports for service business example.*

goods sold). Note that each service profit module earned $1 million for the year just ended. The purpose of this is twofold.

The three sources of sales added together provide $3 million profit, which is approximately equal to the earnings before interest and income tax shown in the income statement in Figure 16.1. The main reason for showing three different profit modules, however, is to contrast and compare the effects from changes in profit factors among the three.

The amount of the cost-of-goods-sold expense amounts shown in Figure 9.1 for the product-based business are moved to fixed operating expenses in this example for the three service profit modules. In other words, the entire amount of the cost-of-goods-sold expense amount is moved down to the fixed operating expense account, which is the largest expense for each service line. Notice the relatively high amounts of fixed costs for each module in Figure 16.2.

 By definition, a service business sells services and not products. Even so, incidental products are often sold along with the services. For example, a copying business (such as Kinko's) sells paper to its customers. Of course, the main thing sold is the copying service, not the paper. Airlines sell transportation but also provide in-flight food and beverages. Hotels are not really in the business of selling towels and ashtrays, but they know that many guests take these with them on the way out. Many personal and professional service firms (e.g., CPA and architect firms) sell no product at all. (Although come to think of it, our architect charged us a small amount for blueprint copies of our home remodeling project.)

Some expenses of a service business vary with total sales revenue. Credit card discounts and sales commissions come to mind. Service businesses also have some expenses that vary with sales volume—for example, the number of passengers flown by an airline. The number of hotel guests directly affects certain variable expenses of this business.

Most service businesses are saddled with large annual fixed expenses. Service takes people to render it: Most service businesses have a large number of employees on fixed salaries or who are paid fixed hourly rates based on a 40-hour workweek. Also, many service businesses, such as gas and electric utilities and airlines, make large capital investments in buildings and equipment and record large depreciation expense each year. Therefore, the service business example includes a large amount of fixed expenses for each of the three profit modules.

In contrast to product-based businesses, the contribution margins of service-based businesses are relatively large percents of their sales revenue. For the service business example shown in Figure 16.1, the contribution margins are as follows:

Standard
service $85.00 unit margin ÷ $100.00 sales price = 85%

Basic
service $67.00 unit margin ÷ $75.00 sales price = 89%

Premier
service $130.00 unit margin ÷ $150.00 sales price = 87%

The annual sales volumes in the three profit modules are expressed in *units of service,* whatever these units might be—billable hours for a law firm, number of tickets for a movie theater, or passenger miles for an airline. For a long-distance trucking company it is ton-miles hauled. Most service businesses adopt a common denominator to measure their sales volume activity.

SALES PRICE AND VOLUME CHANGES

The profit impacts of increasing sales prices 10 percent versus increasing sales volumes 10 percent are compared in Figure 16.3. Please keep in mind that the baseline profit for each of the three profit modules is $1 million. The amount of the profit increase is divided by $1 million to determine the percentage increases shown in Figure 16.3. For all three service lines, note the relatively small difference in profit increase between the sales volume and the sales price increase scenarios.

Looking back at the profit effects for a product-based business (refer to Figure 10.2), there is a huge advantage to increasing sales price versus increasing sales volume by the same percent. But as Figure 16.3 shows, this is not true for a service business because price increases on top of the relatively high unit margins of a service business don't pack the same wallop as price increases for a product business.

For instance, consider the standard product line (Figure 9.1) versus the standard service line (Figure 16.2). In both, the sales price is $100.00 per unit. The unit margin for the standard product line is $20.00 versus $85.00 for the standard service line. A 10 percent sales price increase yields a $9.15 unit margin increase (net of revenue-driven variable expenses). This

Standard Service

| | Sales Volume Increase | | Sales Price Increase | |
| | 110,000 units | | 100,000 units | |
	Per Unit	Totals	Per Unit	Totals
Sales revenue	$100.00	$11,000,000	$110.00	$11,000,000
Revenue-driven expenses @ 8.5%	$ 8.50	$ 935,000	$ 9.35	$ 935,000
Unit-driven expenses	$ 6.50	$ 715,000	$ 6.50	$ 650,000
Contribution margin	$ 85.00	$ 9,350,000	$ 94.15	$ 9,415,000
Fixed operating expenses	$ 68.18	$ 7,500,000	$ 75.00	$ 7,500,000
Profit	$ 16.82	$ 1,850,000	$ 19.15	$1,915,000
Profit increase (compared with Figure 16.2)		85%		92%

Basic Service

| | 165,000 units | | 150,000 units | |
	Per Unit	Totals	Per Unit	Totals
Sales revenue	$ 75.00	$12,375,000	$ 82.50	$12,375,000
Revenue-driven expenses @ 4.0%	$ 3.00	$ 495,000	$ 3.30	$ 495,000
Unit-driven expenses	$ 5.00	$ 825,000	$ 5.00	$ 750,000
Contribution margin	$ 67.00	$11,055,000	$ 74.20	$11,130,000
Fixed operating expenses	$ 54.85	$ 9,050,000	$ 60.33	$ 9,050,000
Profit	$ 12.15	$ 2,005,000	$ 13.87	$ 2,080,000
Profit increase (compared with Figure 16.2)		101%		108%

Premier Service

| | 55,000 units | | 50,000 units | |
	Per Unit	Totals	Per Unit	Totals
Sales revenue	$150.00	$ 8,250,000	$165.00	$ 8,250,000
Revenue-driven expenses @ 7.5%	$ 11.25	$ 618,750	$ 12.37	$ 618,750
Unit-driven expenses	$ 8.75	$ 481,250	$ 8.75	$ 437,500
Contribution margin	$130.00	$ 7,150,000	$143.88	$ 7,193,750
Fixed operating expenses	$100.00	$ 5,500,000	$110.00	$ 5,500,000
Profit	$ 30.00	$ 1,650,000	$ 33.88	$ 1,693,750
Profit increase (compared with Figure 16.2)		65%		69%

FIGURE 16.3 *Comparison of 10 percent increases in sales volume versus sales price.*

equals a 46 percent leap in unit margin for the product business ($9.15 ÷ $20.00 = 46%), but only an 11 percent gain for the service business ($9.15 ÷ $85.00 = 11%). For a service business, a price increase is better than a volume increase, but the advantage is much less than for a product business.

KEY CONCEPT — WHAT ABOUT FIXED COSTS?

One key issue concerns the large amount of fixed operating expenses for a typical service business. The profit increases shown in Figure 16.3 are based on the premise that fixed costs remain constant at the higher sales volumes. However, if the business were already operating at or close to its capacity limits, its fixed costs probably would have to be increased to enable higher sales volumes. Keep in mind that basically fixed costs provide *capacity,* or the ability to handle a certain level of sales activity during the period.

Capacity for a service business is measured by the total number of hours its employee workforce could turn out during the year, the number of passenger miles that an airline could fly, the number of energy units a utility could deliver over the period, and so on. Always a key question is whether capacity is being fully used or not. Some slack, or unused capacity, is normal, which allows for a modest growth in sales volume. When sales volume is too far below capacity and top management sees no way to rebuild sales volume, the option is to downsize the capacity of the business.

Looking at Figure 16.3 again, the business could afford to expand capacity and increase its fixed costs to support a 10 percent gain in sales volume for its service lines—but not by more than the projected profit increase. Increasing sales prices generally does not require a business to increase its fixed costs. So the clear advantage is on the side of increasing sales prices. Of course, the key question is whether a business could pass along a 10 percent sales price increase without adversely affecting the demand for its services.

TRADE-OFF DECISIONS

Suppose the business is considering cutting sales prices 10 percent on all three of its service lines. One question the managers should ask is this: How much would the increases in sales volumes have to be simply to maintain the same profit? Of course, the business would really prefer to stimulate demand to *increase* profit, not just keep it the same. But calculating these same-profit sales volumes provides very useful points of reference. Each manager should forecast sales demand at the lower prices and compare the predicted sales volume against the same-profit volumes.

The profit report format presented in Figure 16.4 is a good tool for this sort of analysis. (This is the same profit pathway used in Chapter 11 for analyzing trade-off decisions for a product-based business, except that cost-of-goods-sold expense is deleted.)

Figure 16.5 shows the unit margins at the lower sales prices and the required sales volumes needed just to maintain the same profit. The required sales volumes are determined by dividing the contribution margin targets (from Figure 16.4) by the lower unit margins caused by the lower sales prices. Fixed costs are held the same, but as previously mentioned, one should be very careful in making this assumption when sales volumes are increased.

What about the opposite trade-off? Suppose sales prices were increased 10 percent, causing decreases in sales volume. The same method of analysis can be used to determine how far sales volume could drop and profit remain the same. (If you do these calculations the answers are standard = 9,719 units

	Service Line		
	Standard	**Basic**	**Premier**
Sales price	$100.00	$75.00	$150.00
Revenue-driven expenses	$8.50	$3.00	$11.25
Unit-driven expenses	$6.50	$5.00	$8.75
Unit margin	$85.00	$67.00	$130.00
Sales volume	100,000	150,000	50,000
Contribution margin	$8,500,000	$10,050,000	$6,500,000
Fixed operating expenses	$7,500,000	$9,050,000	$5,500,000
Profit	$1,000,000	$1,000,000	$1,000,000

FIGURE 16.4 *Profit model for a service business.*

| | Service Line | | |
	Standard	Basic	Premier
Sales price	$90.00	$67.50	$135.00
Revenue-driven expenses	$7.65	$2.70	$10.12
Unit-driven expenses	$6.50	$5.00	$8.75
Unit margin	$75.85	$59.80	$116.13
Contribution margin target	$8,500,000	$10,050,000	$6,500,000
Required sales volume	112,063	168,060	55,974
Present sales volume	100,000	150,000	50,000
Sales volume increase needed	12,063	18,060	5,974

FIGURE 16.5 *Sales volumes needed at 10 percent lower sales prices.*

decrease, basic = 14,555 units decrease, and premier = 4,822 units decrease.) Whether a service business would willingly sacrifice sales volume and market share in order to increase its sales prices is another matter.

END POINT

In most ways, the financial statements of service businesses are not all that different from those of product companies (though there are some differences, of course). In a service business income statement, there is no cost-of-goods-sold expense or gross margin. In a service business balance sheet, there are no inventories or accounts payable for inventories.

Having said this, a service business may sell incidental products with its services (popcorn and candy at a movie theater, for example) and therefore report a relatively small amount of inventories. Some service businesses are very capital-intensive (e.g., transportation companies, telephone companies, and gas and electricity utilities). Other service companies need relatively little in the way of long-term operating assets (e.g., CPAs and law firms).

The tools of financial analysis are essentially the same for both product and service businesses. Naturally the models and tools of analysis have to be adapted to fit the characteristics of each business. The chapter demonstrates techniques of profit analysis for service businesses. The profit consequences for a change in sales volume versus a change in sales price for service businesses are not nearly as divergent as those of product businesses. Sales price improvements have an edge over sales volume improvements for both types of businesses, but the advantage is not nearly so pronounced for service businesses.

I should mention in closing that the ratios used for interpreting profit performance and financial condition (Chapter 4) and the techniques for analyzing capital investments (Chapters 14 and 15) apply with equal force to service businesses and product businesses.

17

Management Control

Management decisions constitute a plan of action for accomplishing a business's objectives. Establishing the objectives for the period may be done through a formal budgeting process or without a budget. In either case, actually achieving the objectives for the period requires management control. In the broadest sense, *management control* refers to everything managers do in moving the business toward its objectives. Decisions start things in motion; control brings things to a successful conclusion. Good decisions with bad control can turn out as disastrously as making bad decisions in the first place. Good tools for making management decisions should be complemented by good tools for management control.

Previous chapters concentrate on models of profit, cash flow, and capital investment that are useful in decision-making analysis. This chapter shifts attention to management control and explores how managers keep a steady hand on the helm during the business's financial voyage, often across troubled waters. This chapter also presents a brief overview of business budgeting. This short summary on budgeting is not an exhaustive treatise on the topic, of course.

FOLLOW-THROUGH ON DECISIONS

Management control is both preventive and positive in nature. Managers have to prevent, or at least minimize, wrong things from happening. Murphy's Law is all too true; if something can go wrong, it will. Equally important, managers have to make sure right things are happening and happening on time. Managers shouldn't simply react to problems; they should be proactive and push things along in the right direction. Management control is characterized not just by the absence of problems, but also by the presence of actions to achieve the goals and objectives of the business.

One of the best definitions of the management control process that I've heard was by a former student. I challenged the students in the class to give me a very good but very concise description of management control—one that captured the essence of management control in very few words. One student answered in two words: "Watching everything." This pithy comment captures a great deal of what management control is all about.

Management theorists include control in their conceptual scheme of the functions of managers, although there's no consensus regarding the exact meaning of *control.* Most definitions of *management control* emphasize the need for *feedback information* on actual performance that is compared against goals and objectives for the purpose of detecting deviations and variances. Based on the feedback information, managers take corrective action to bring performance back on course.

Management control is an information-dependent process, that's for sure. Managers need actual performance information reported to them on a timely basis. In short, feedback information is the main ingredient for management control. And managers need this information quickly. Information received too late can result in costly delays before problems are corrected.

MANAGEMENT CONTROL INFORMATION

In general, management control information can be classified as one of three types:

1. *Regular periodic comprehensive coverage reports* (e.g., financial statements to managers on the profit performance, cash flows, financial condition of the business as a whole and major segments of the business)
2. *Regular periodic limited-scope reports* that focus on critical factors (e.g., bad-debt write-offs, inventory write-downs, sales returns, employee absenteeism, quality inspection reports, productivity reports, new customers)
3. *Ad hoc reports* triggered by specific problems that have arisen unexpectedly, which are needed in addition to regular control reports

Feedback information divides naturally into either good news or bad news. Good news is when actual performance is going according to plan or better than plan. Management's job is to keep things moving in this direction. Management control information usually reveals bad news as well—problems that have come up and unsatisfactory performance areas that need attention.

Managers draw on a very broad range of information sources to keep on top of things and to exercise control. Managers monitor customer satisfaction, employee absenteeism and morale, production schedules, quality control inspection results, and so on. Managers listen to customers' complaints, shop the competition, and may even decide that industrial intelligence and espionage are necessary to get information about competitors. The accounting system of a business is one of the most important sources of control information.

Managers are concerned with problems that directly impact the financial performance of the business, of course—such as sales quotas not being met, sales prices discounted lower than predicted, product costs higher than expected, expenses running over budget, and cash flow running slower than planned. Or perhaps sales are over quota, sales prices are higher than predicted, and product costs are lower than expected. Even when things are moving along very close to plan, managers need control reports to inform them of conformity with the plan.

 Control reports should be designed to fit the specific areas of authority and responsibility of individual managers. The purchasing (procurement) manager gets control

reports on inventory and suppliers; the credit manager gets control reports on accounts receivable and customers' payment histories; the sales manager gets control reports on sales by product categories and salespersons, and so on.

Periodic control reports are rich in detail. For example, the monthly sales report for a territory may include breakdowns on hundreds and perhaps more than a thousand different products and customers. Moving up in the organization to a brand manager or a division manager, for example, the span of management authority and responsibility becomes broader and broader. At the top level (president or chief executive officer), the span of authority and responsibility encompasses the whole business. At the higher rungs on the organizational ladder, managers need control information in the form of comprehensive financial and other reports.

Financial statements for management control are much more detailed and are supplemented by many supporting schedules and analyses compared with the profit and cash flow models explained in earlier chapters, which are used primarily for decision-making analysis. For instance, management control financial reports include detailed schedules of customers' receivables that are past due, products that have been held in inventory too long, lists of products that have unusually high rates of return from customers (probably indicating product defects), particular expenses that are out of control relative to the previous period or the goals for the current period, and so on. The profit and cash flow models illustrated in earlier chapters are like executive summaries compared with the enormous amount of detail in management control reports.

In addition to comprehensive control reports, a manager may select one or several specific factors, or key items, for special attention. I read about an example of this approach a couple of years ago. During a cost-cutting drive, the chief executive of a business asked for a daily count on the number of company employees. He was told he couldn't get it. Some data kept by divisions were difficult to gather together in one place. Some were in a payroll database accessible only to programmers. But the CEO persisted, and now the data are at his fingertips whenever he wants them: A specially designed executive information system links personnel data directly to a personal computer in his office. "Management knows I'm watching the count very closely," he said. "Believe me, they don't add staff carelessly."

It's a good idea to identify a few relatively critical success factors and keep a close watch on them. Knowing what these factors are is one secret of good management. Product quality is almost always one such key success factor. Customer loyalty is another.

By their very nature, management control reports are confidential and are not discussed outside the company. Management control reports contain very sensitive information; these reports disclose the "mistakes" of decisions that went wrong.

Often, unexpected and unpredictable developments upset the apple cart of good decisions. Some degree of inherent uncertainty surrounds all business decisions, of course. Nevertheless, management control reports do have a strong element of passing judgment on managers' decisions and their ability to make good predictions.

INTERNAL ACCOUNTING CONTROLS

KEY CONCEPT

A business relies heavily on its accounting system to supply essential information for management control. The reliability of accounting information depends heavily on specially designed procedures called *internal accounting controls* and how well these controls are working in actual practice.

Forms and Procedures

Specific forms are required to carry out the activities of the business, and certain established procedures must be followed. One fundamental purpose of these forms and procedures is to eliminate (or at least minimize) data processing errors in capturing, processing, storing, retrieving, and reporting the large amount of information needed to operate a business.

Forms and procedures are not too popular, but without them an organization couldn't function. Without well-designed forms and clear-cut procedures for doing things, an organization couldn't function very well, if at all. On the other side of the coin, there's a danger that filling out the forms becomes perfunctory and careless, and some employees may bypass them or take shortcuts instead of faithfully following official procedures.

DANGER! Internal accounting controls also are instituted for another extremely important reason—to protect against theft and fraud by employees, suppliers, customers, and managers themselves. Unfortunately, my father-in-law was right. He told me many years ago that, based on his experience, "There's a little bit of larceny in everyone's heart." He could have added that there's a lot of larceny in the hearts of a few. It's an unpleasant fact of business life that some customers will shoplift, some vendors and suppliers will overcharge or short-count on deliveries, some employees will embezzle or steal assets, and some managers will commit fraud against the business or take personal advantage of their position of authority. Newspapers and the financial press report stories of employee and management fraud with alarming frequency.

KEY CONCEPT In summary, internal controls have two primary purposes: (1) to ensure the accuracy, completeness, and timeliness of information collected, processed, and reported by the accounting system, and (2) to deter and detect dishonest, illegal, and other behaviors counter to the policies of the business by its employees, managers, customers, and others. This is a tall order, but any business manager you ask about this will attest to the need for effective internal accounting controls.

The ideal internal accounting control is one that ensures the integrity of the information being recorded and processed, one that deters or at least quickly detects any fraud and dishonesty, and one that is cost-effective. Some controls are simply too costly or are too intrusive on personal privacy. Body searches of employees leaving work might qualify, though diamond and gold mines take these precautions, I understand, and a recent article in the *New York Times* indicated that some of General Electric's employees must go through a search on exiting from work.

INDEPENDENT AUDITS AND INTERNAL AUDITING

The national organization of CPAs, the American Institute of Certified Public Accountants (AICPA), is a good source for useful publications that deal with internal accounting controls.* These are superb summaries and reflect the long experience of CPAs in auditing a wide range of businesses. The AICPA's guidelines are an excellent checklist for the types of internal accounting controls that a business should establish and enforce with due diligence.

KEY CONCEPT Speaking of CPAs, financial statement audits by independent public accountants can be viewed as one type of internal control. Based on its annual audit, the CPA firm expresses an opinion on the external financial statements issued by a business. Business managers should understand the limits of audits by CPAs regarding the discovery of errors and fraud. Auditors are responsible for discovering material errors and fraud that would cause the financial statements to be misleading. However, it is not cost-effective to have the outside auditor firm do a thoroughgoing examination that would catch all errors and fraud. It would take too long and cost too much. The first line of defense is the business's internal accounting controls. Having an audit by an independent CPA firm provides an independent appraisal and check on its internal controls, but the business itself has the primary responsibility to design and establish effective internal accounting controls.

Many larger business organizations establish an internal auditing function in the organization structure of the business. Although the internal auditors are employees of the organization, they are given autonomy to act independently. Internal auditors report to the highest levels of management, often directly to the board of directors of the corporation. Internal auditors monitor and test the organization's internal accounting

---

*A good place to start is *Statement on Auditing Standards No. 55,* "Consideration of the Internal Control Structure in a Financial Statement Audit" (American Institute of Certified Public Accountants, Inc., New York, originally issued in 1988 and later amended). Also, the AICPA has put out an *Audit Guide* on this topic, and the Committee of Sponsoring Organizations of the Treadway Commission issued a series of influential publications dealing with internal control in 1992.

controls regularly. They also carry out special investigations, either on their own or at the request of top management and the board of directors. Different departments and areas of operation are audited on a surprise basis or on a regular rotation basis.

FRAUD

Business fraud is like adultery. It shouldn't happen, but those who do it make every attempt to hide it, although it often comes out eventually. The same holds true for business fraud. Businesses handle a lot of money, have many valuable assets, and give managers and other employees a great deal of authority. So it's not surprising that a business is vulnerable to fraud and other dishonest schemes. Fraud, in contrast to theft, involves an element of deception. The guilty person is in a position of trust and authority. The perpetrator of fraud owes a duty to his or her employer, but deliberately violates this duty and covers up the scheme.

Many books have been written on business fraud. Many seminars and training programs are offered that deal with fraud in the business world. Indeed, developments are under way to make the control and detection of business fraud a professional specialty. Keep in mind that audits and internal accounting controls are not foolproof. A disturbing amount of fraud still slips through these preventive measures. High-level management fraud is particularly difficult to prevent and detect. By their very nature, high-level managers have a great deal of authority and discretion. Their positions of trust and power give high-level managers an unparalleled opportunity to commit fraud and the means to conceal it.

A few years ago several investment banks and other financial institutions revealed huge losses caused by employees making unauthorized trades in financial derivatives. In virtually all of these cases there was a breakdown in important internal controls. Many of these cases violated one of the most important of all internal controls—requiring two or more persons to authorize significant expenditures and major risk exposures. Many of these cases also revealed another key internal control that was violated: *separation of duties*. The authority for making a decision and carrying it out should always be separated from its accounting and record keeping functions. One person should never do both.

One prime example of a high-risk fraud area in business comes to mind. The purchasing agents of a business are vulnerable to accepting bribes, kickbacks, under-the-table payments, and other favors from vendors. A purchasing agent I know very well made me aware of how serious a problem this is. He didn't say that all purchasing agents are corrupt, but he certainly suggested that the temptation is there and that many succumb.

Keeping a close watch on cash flows is a good way to catch signs of possible fraud, which is evidently overlooked by most managers. Most fraud schemes and scams go after the money. As Willie Sutton said when asked why he robbed banks, "Because that's where the money is." To get the money and conceal the fraud as long as possible, a perpetrator must manipulate and misstate an asset or a liability—most often accounts receivable, inventories, or sometimes accounts payable. (Other assets and liabilities may also be involved.)

In particular, managers should keep alert to increases in accounts receivable and inventories. Not only do these increases cause negative cash flow effects, such increases could signal a suspicious change that is not consistent with changes in sales activity and other facts and information known to the manager.

It may be argued that businesses should aggressively prosecute offenders. The record shows, however, that most businesses are reluctant to do this, fearing the adverse publicity surrounding legal proceedings. Many businesses adopt the policy that fraud is just one of the many costs of doing business. They don't encourage it, of course, and they do everything practical to prevent it. But in the final analysis, a majority of businesses appear to tolerate some amount of normal loss from fraud.

As an example, suppose an employee or midlevel manager steals inventory and sells the products for cash, which goes into his or her pocket. A good management control reporting system keeps a very close watch on inventory levels and cost-of-goods-sold expense ratios. If a material amount of inventory is stolen, the inventory shrinkage and/or profit margin figures should sound alarms. The sophisticated thief realizes this and will cover up the missing inventory. Indeed, this is exactly what is done in many fraud cases.

 In one example, a company's internal controls were not effective in preventing the coverup; the accounting system reported inventory that in fact was not there. Thus, inventory showed a larger increase (or a smaller decrease) than it should have. You might think that managers would be alert to any inventory increase. But in the majority of fraud cases, managers have not pursued the reasons for the inventory increase. If they had, they might have discovered the inventory theft.

In similar fashion, fraud may involve taking money out of collections on accounts receivable, which is covered up by overstating the accounts receivable account. Other fraud schemes may use accounts payable to conceal the fraud. Managers should keep in mind that the reported profit performance of the business will be overstated as the result of undiscovered fraud. This is terribly embarrassing when it is discovered and prior financial statements have to be revised and restated. But fraud can be disastrous. Furthermore, it may lead to firing the executive who failed to discover the theft or fraud; one responsibility of managers is to prevent fraud by subordinates and to devise ways and means of ensuring that no fraud is going on.

MANAGEMENT CONTROL REPORTING GUIDELINES

The design of effective and efficient management control reports is a real challenge. This section presents guidelines and suggestions for management control reporting. Unfortunately, there is no one best format and system for control reporting. There is no one-size-fits-all approach for communicating the vital control information needed by managers, no more than there are simple answers in most areas of business decision making. One job of managers is to know what they need to know, and this includes the information they should get in their control reports.

Control Reports and Making Decisions

The first rule for designing management control reports is that they should be based on the decision-making analysis methods and models used by managers. This may sound straightforward, but it's not nearly as easy as it sounds. This first rule for control reports is implicit in the concept of feedback information discussed at the beginning of the chapter. One problem is that control reports include a great deal of detail, whereas the profit and cash flow models that are best for decision-making analysis are condensed and concise.

Nevertheless, control reports should resonate as much as possible with the logic and format of the models used by managers in their decision-making analysis. For example, the reports each period on the actual results of a capital investment decision should be structured the same as the manager's capital investment analysis. If the manager uses the layout shown in Figures 14.2 and 14.3, for instance, then the control report should be in the same format and include comparison of actual returns with the forecast returns from the investment.

Need for Comparative Reports

More than anything else, management control is directed toward achieving profit goals and meeting the other financial objectives of the business. Goals and objectives are not established in a vacuum. Prior-period performance is one reference for comparison, of course. Ideally, however, the business should adopt goals and objectives for the period that are put into a framework of clear-cut benchmarks and standards against which actual performance is compared. Budgeting, discussed later in the chapter, is one way of doing this.

In practice, many companies simply compare actual performance for the current period against the previous period. This is certainly better than no comparison at all, and it does focus attention on trends, especially if several past periods are used for comparison and not just the most recent period. However, this approach may sidetrack one of management's main responsibilities, which is to look ahead and forecast changes in the economic environment that will affect the business.

Changes from previous period may have been predictable and should have been built into the plan for the current period. The changes between the current period and the previous period don't really present any new information relative to what should have been predicted. The manager should get into a forward-planning mode. Based on forecasts of broad average changes for the coming period, profit and cash flows budgets are developed, which serve as the foundation for planning the capital needs of the business during the coming period. One danger of using the previous period for comparison is that the manager gets into a rear-view style of management—looking behind but not ahead.

Management by Exception

KEY CONCEPT One key concept of management control reporting is referred to as *management by exception.* Managers have limited time to spend on control reports and therefore they focus mainly on deviations and variances from the plan (or budget). Departures and detours from the plan are called *exceptions.* The premise is that most things should be going according to plan but some things will not. Managers need to pay the most attention to the things going wrong and the things that are off course.

Frequency of Control Reports

A tough question to answer is how frequently to prepare control reports for managers. They cannot wait until the end of the year for control reports, of course, although a broad-based and overall year-end review is a good idea to serve as the platform for developing next year's plan. Daily or weekly control reports are not practical for most businesses, although some companies, such as airlines and banks, monitor sales volume and other vital operating statistics on a day-to-day basis.

 Monthly or quarterly management control reports are the most common. Each business develops its own practical solution to the frequency question; there's no single general answer that fits all companies. The main thing is to strike a balance between preparing control reports too frequently versus too seldom. With computers and other electronic means of communication today, it is tempting to bombard managers with too much control information too often. Sorting out the truly relevant from the less relevant and truly irrelevant information is at the core of the manager's job.

Profit Control Reports

The type of management profit report illustrated in previous chapters is a logical starting point for designing reports to managers for profit control. First and foremost, profit margins and total contribution margin should be the main focus of attention and should be clear and easy to follow. These two key measures of performance should be reported for each major product or product line (backed up with detailed schedules for virtually every individual product) in management profit performance reports. These are very confidential data, which are not divulged in external income statements—or, for that matter, very widely within the business organization.

KEY CONCEPT Variable expenses should be divided between those that depend on sales volume and those that depend on sales revenue and broken down into a large number of specific accounts. Sales volumes for each product and product line should be reported. Fixed expenses should be broken down into major components—salaries, advertising, occupancy costs, and so on. Sales and/or manufacturing capacity should be reported. Any significant change in capacity due to changes in fixed expenses should be reported.

Management control reports should analyze changes in profit. In particular, the impact of sales volume changes should be separated from changes in sales price, product cost, and variable expenses as explained in earlier chapters (see Chapters 9 and 10). If trade-off decisions were made—for example, cutting sales price to increase sales volume—there should be follow-up analysis in the management control profit reports that track how the decision actually worked out. Did sales volume increase as much as expected?

As this chapter explains later in more detail, a fringe of negative factors constantly threaten profit margins and bloat fixed expenses. Each of these negative factors should be singled out for special attention in management profit control reports. Inventory shrinkage, for example, should be reported on a separate line, as should sales returns, unusually high bad debts, and any extraordinary losses or gains recorded in the period (with adequate explanations).

 If there is a general fault with internal profit reports for management control purposes, it is in my opinion the failure of the accounting staff to explain and analyze why profit increased or decreased relative to the previous period or relative to the budget for the period. Such profit-change analysis would be very useful to include in the profit reports. But managers generally are left on their own to do this. The analysis tools discussed in previous chapters are very helpful for this.

Sales Price Negatives

When eating in a restaurant, you don't argue about the menu prices. And you don't bargain over the posted prices at the gas pump or in the supermarket. In contrast, sales price negotiation is a way of life in many industries. Many businesses advertise or publish list prices. Examples are sticker prices on new cars, manufacturer's suggested retail prices on consumer products, and standard price sheets for industrial products.

List prices are not the final prices; they are only the point of reference for negotiating the final terms of the sale. In some cases, such as new car sales, neither the seller nor the buyer takes the list price as the real price—the list price simply sets the stage for bargaining. In other cases, the buyer agrees to pay list price, but demands other types of price concessions and reductions or other special accommodations.

Prompt-payment discounts are offered when one business sells to another business on credit. For example a 2 percent discount may be given for payment received within 10 days after the sales invoice date. These are called *sales discounts*. Buyers should view these as penalties for delayed payment. Also, businesses commonly give their customers quantity discounts for large orders, and most businesses offer special discounts in making sales to government agencies and educational institutions.

Many consumer product companies offer their customers rebates and coupons, which lower the final net sales price received by the seller, of course. Businesses also make allowances or adjustments to sales prices after the point of sale when customers complain about the quality of the product or discover minor product flaws after taking delivery. Instead of having the customer return the product, the company reduces the original sales price.

Managers must decide how these sales price negatives should be handled in their internal management control reports. One alternative is to report sales revenue net of all such sales price reductions. I don't recommend this method. The better approach is to report sales revenue at established list prices. All sales price negatives should be recorded in sales revenue contra accounts that are deducted from gross (list price) sales revenue.

Figure 17.1 illustrates the reporting sales price negatives to managers. Seven different reductions from sales revenue are shown in this figure. A business may not have all the sales contra accounts shown, but three or four are not unusual. The amounts of each contra account may not be as large as shown (hopefully not).

In the external income statement of the business, only net sales revenue ($8,303,000 in Figure 17.1) is reported, as a general rule. For internal management control reporting, however, gross (list price) sales revenue before all sales price reductions should be reported to give managers the complete range of information they need for controlling sales prices. Sales price negatives should be accumulated in contra (deduction) accounts so that managers can monitor each one relative

Gross sales revenue, at list prices		$10,000,000
Sales price negatives:		
Sales price discounts—normal	($150,000)	
Sales price discounts—special	($200,000)	
Sales returns	($175,000)	
Quantity discounts	($275,000)	
Rebates	($650,000)	
Coupons	($165,000)	
Sales price allowances	($ 82,000)	($ 1,697,000)
Net sales revenue		$ 8,303,000

FIGURE 17.1 *Sales revenue negatives in a management control report.*

to established sales pricing policies and so they can make comparisons with previous periods and with the goals (or budget) for the current period.

Inventory Shrinkage

DANGER! Inventory shrinkage is a serious problem for many businesses, especially retailers. These inventory losses are due to shoplifting by customers, employee theft, and short counting from suppliers. Many businesses also suffer inventory obsolescence, which means they end up with some products that cannot be sold or have to be sold below cost. When this becomes apparent, inventory should be decreased by write-down entries. The inventories asset account is decreased and an expense account is increased.

Losses caused by damage to and deterioration of products being held in inventory and inventory write-downs to recognize product obsolescence should be separated from losses due to theft and dishonesty—but sometimes the term *inventory shrinkage* is used to include any type of inventory disappearance and loss. Inventory shrinkage of 1.5 to 2.0 percent of retail sales is not unusual.

Inventory loss due to theft is a particularly frustrating expense. The business buys (or manufactures) products and then holds them in inventory, which entails carrying costs, only to have them stolen by customers or employees. On the other hand, inventory shrinkage due to damage from handling and storing products, product deterioration over time, and product obsolescence is a normal and inescapable economic risk of doing business.

TiP Internal management control reports definitely should separate inventory shrinkage expense and not include it in the cost-of-goods-sold expense. Inventory shrinkage is virtually never reported as a separate expense in external income statements; it is combined with cost-of-goods-sold or some other expense. However, managers need to keep a close watch on inventory shrinkage, and they cannot do so if it is buried in the larger cost-of-goods-sold expense.

Another reason for separating inventory shrinkage in management control reports is that this expense does not behave the same way as cost-of-goods-sold expense. Cost-of-goods-sold expense varies with sales volume. Inventory shrinkage may include both a fixed amount that is more or less the same regardless of sales volume and an amount that may vary with sales volume.

Strong internal controls help minimize inventory shrinkage. But even elaborate and expensive inventory controls do not eliminate inventory shrinkage. Almost every business tolerates some amount of inventory shrinkage. For instance, most businesses look the other way when it comes to minor employee theft; they don't encourage it, of course, but they don't do anything about it, either. Preventing all inventory theft would be too costly or might offend innocent customers and hurt sales volume. Would you shop in retail stores that carried out body searches on all customers leaving the store? I doubt it. Many retailers even hesitate to require customers to check bags before entering their stores. On the other hand, closed-circuit TV monitors are common in many stores. Retailers are constantly trying to find controls that do not offend their customers. As you know, product packages are often designed to make it difficult to shoplift (e.g., oversized packages that are difficult to conceal).

In internal management control reports, the negative factors just discussed should be set out in separate expense accounts if they are relatively material or listed separately in a supplementary schedule. Managers may have to specifically instruct their accountants to isolate these expenses. In external income statements, these costs are grouped in a larger expense account (e.g., cost of goods sold, general and administrative expenses).

Sales Volume Negatives

Sales returns can be a problem, although this varies from industry to industry quite a bit. Many retailers accept sales returns without hesitation as part of their overall marketing strategy. Customers may be refunded their money, or they may exchange for a different product. On the other hand, products such as new cars are seldom returned (even when recalled).

 Sales returns definitely should be accumulated in a separate sales contra account that is deducted from gross sales revenue (see Figure 17.1 again). The total of sales returns is very important control information. On the other hand, in external income statements only the amount of net sales revenue (gross sales revenue less sales returns and all other sales revenue negatives) is reported.

Lost sales due to temporary *stock-outs* (zero inventory situations) are important for managers to know about. Such non-sales are not recorded in the accounting system. No sales transaction takes place, so there is nothing to record in the sales revenue account. However, missed sales opportunities should be captured and kept track of in some manner, and the amount of these lost sales should be reported to managers even though no sales actually took place. Managers need a measure of how much additional contribution margin could have been earned on these lost sales.

Customers may be willing to back-order products, or sales may be made for future delivery when customers do not need immediate delivery; these are called *sales backlogs*. Information about sales backlogs should be reported to managers, but not as sales revenue, of course. If a customer refuses to back-order or will not wait for future delivery, the sale may be lost. As a practical matter, it is difficult to keep track of lost sales. The manager may have to rely on other sources of information, such as complaints from customers and the company's sales force.

Key Sales Ratios

Many retailers keep an eye on measures such as sales revenue per employee and sales revenue per square foot of retail space. Most retailers have general rules ($300 to $400 sales per square foot of retail space, $250,000 sales per employee, etc.). These amounts vary widely from industry to industry. Trade associations collect data from their members and publish industry averages. Retailers can compare their performances against local and regional competition and against national averages. Hotels and motels carefully watch their occupancy rates, which is an example of a useful ratio to measure actual sales against capacity.

When sales ratios are lagging, the business probably has too much capacity—too many employees, too much space, too many machines, and so on. The obvious solution is to reduce the fixed operating costs of the business. However, reducing these fixed expenses is not easy, as you probably know. Employees may have to be fired (or temporarily laid off), major assets may have to be sold, contracts may have to be broken, and so on. Downsizing decisions are extremely difficult to make. For one thing, they are an admission of the inability of the business to generate enough sales volume to justify its fixed expenses. Nonetheless, part of the manager's job is to make these painful decisions.

The tendency is to put off the decision, to delay the tough choices that have to be made. In an article in the *Wall Street Journal,* the former CEO of Westinghouse observed that one of the biggest failings of U.S. chief executives is one of procrastinating—executives are reluctant to face up to making these decisions at the earliest possible time.

In Closing

I would like to show you examples of management control reports. But control reports are highly confidential; companies are not willing to release them outside the business. In some situations, control reports contain proprietary information that a business is not willing to give out without payment (e.g., customer lists). Management control reports are like income tax returns in this regard—neither is open for public inspection.

However, you may be able to get your hands on one type of management control report—those that are required in a franchise contract between the franchisee and the parent company that owns the franchise name. These contracts usually require that certain accounting reports be prepared and sent to the home office of the company that operates the chain. These reports are full of management control information that is very interesting. Perhaps you could secure a blank form of such an accounting control report.

Last, I should point out that management control reports vary a great deal from business to business. Compare in your mind, if you would, the following types of businesses—a gambling casino, a grocery store, an auto manufacturer, an electric utility, a bank, a hotel, and an airline. Each type of business is unique in the types of control information its managers need. The preceding comments offer general obser-vations and suggestions for management control reports with-out going into the many details for particular industries.

SALES MIX ANALYSIS AND ALLOCATION OF FIXED COSTS

Typically, two or more products share a common base of fixed operating expenses. For instance, consider the sales of a department store in one building. There are many building occupancy expenses, including rent (or depreciation), utilities, property taxes, fire and hazard insurance, and so on. All products sold in the store benefit from the fixed expenses. Or consider a sales territory managed by a sales manager whose salary and other office costs cover all the products sold in the territory. Should such fixed expenses be allocated among the different products?

Allocation may appear to be logical. The more basic question is whether or not allocation really helps management decision making and control. Allocation is a controversial issue, espe-cially where product lines (or other product groupings) are organized as separate profit centers for which different man-agers have profit responsibility (and whose compensation may depend, in part at least, on the profit performance of the orga-nizational unit).

If a company sold only one product, there would be no cost allocation problems between products—although there may be common costs extending over two or more separate sales regions (territories). The main concern in the following discus-sion is the allocation of fixed expenses among products.

Sales Mix Analysis

Suppose you're the general manager of a business's major division, which is one of the several autonomous profit cen-ters in the organization. (I treat this as a profit module in the following discussion.) Your division sells one basic product line consisting of four products sold under the company's brand names plus one product sold as a generic product (no brand name is associated with the product) to a supermarket chain. Figure 17.2 presents your management profit report for the most recent year.

	Generic	Economy	Standard	Deluxe	Premier	Units	Dollars
		Products				**Product Line Totals**	
Sales price	$28.25	$42.50	$60.00	$75.00	$95.00		$5,261,000
Product cost	($20.05)	($26.65)	($32.00)	($36.00)	($40.60)		($2,886,500)
Variable expenses	($1.13)	($6.80)	($11.80)	($16.50)	($21.15)		($922,390)
Unit margin	$7.07	$9.05	$16.20	$22.50	$33.25		$1,452,110
% of sales price	25%	21%	27%	30%	35%		28%
Sales volume	28,000	18,000	35,000	10,000	9,000	100,000	
% of total sales volume	28%	18%	35%	10%	9%	100%	
Contribution margin	$197,960	$162,900	$567,000	$225,000	$299,250	100%	$1,452,110
% of contribution margin	14%	11%	39%	15%	21%		
Fixed expenses	?	?	?	?	?		($766,000)
Profit	?	?	?	?	?		$686,110

The question is whether or not to allocate the total fixed expenses among the five products to determine profit attributable to each product line.

FIGURE 17.2 *Management profit report.*

All five products are earning a contribution margin—though these unit profit margins vary in dollar amount and by percent of sales price across the five products. The premier product has the highest percent of profit margin (35 percent), as well as the highest dollar amount of unit margin ($33.25). You might notice that the generic model has a higher percent of contribution margin and generates more total contribution margin than the economy model.

Production costs are cut to the bone on the generic product, and no advertising or sales promotion of any type is done on the product—the variable expenses are mainly delivery costs. Product cost is highest for the premier product because the best raw materials are used and additional labor time is required to produce top-of-the-line quality. Also, variable advertising and sales promotion costs are very heavy for this product; variable expenses are 22 percent of sales price for this product ($21.15 variable expenses ÷ $95.00 sales price = 22%).

The economy model accounts for 18 percent of sales volume but only 11 percent of total contribution margin. The premier model accounts for only 9 percent of sales volume but yields 21 percent of total contribution margin. Which brings up the very important issue of determining the best, or optimal, sales mix. The comparative information presented in Figure 17.2 is very useful for making marketing decisions. Shifts in sales mix and trade-offs among the products are important to understand.

The marketing strategy of many businesses is to encourage their customers to trade up, or move up to the higher-priced items in their product line. As a rule, higher-priced products have higher unit margins. This general rule applies mainly to mature products, which are those products in the middle-age or old phases of their life cycles.

 Newer products in the infant and adolescent stages of their life cycles often have a competitive advantage. During the early phases of their life cycle, new products may enjoy high profit margins until competition catches up and forces sales price and/or sales volume down. In fact, the CEO of Kodak made this very point a few years ago in an article in the *New York Times*.

Compare the following two products: standard versus deluxe. You make a $6.30 higher unit contribution profit margin on the deluxe product ($22.50 deluxe – $16.20

standard = $6.30). Giving up one unit of standard in trade-off for one unit of deluxe would increase total contribution margin without any change in your total fixed expenses. Marketing strategies should be based on contribution margin information such as that presented in Figure 17.2.

The position of the economy model is interesting because its contribution margin is by far the lowest of the company-brand products and not much more than the generic model. The economy model may be in the nature of a loss leader or, more accurately, a *minimum-profit leader*—a product on which you don't make much margin but one that is necessary to get the attention of customers and that serves as a spring-board or stepping-stone for customers to trade up to higher-priced products.

DANGER! But the opposite may happen. In tough times, many customers may trade down from higher-priced models and buy products that yield lower profit margins. Large numbers of customers may trade down to the standard or the economy models. Dealing with this downscaling is a challenging marketing problem. Perhaps the sales prices on the lower-end products could be raised to increase their unit margins; perhaps not.

Should you be making and selling the generic product? On the one hand, this product brings in 28 percent of your total sales volume and 14 percent of total contribution margin. On the other hand, these units may be taking sales away from your other four products—though this is hard to know for certain. This question has to be answered by market research.

If the generic product were not available in supermarkets, would these customers buy one of your other models? If all these customers would buy the economy model, you would be better off; you'd be giving up sales on which you make a unit contribution profit margin of $7.07 for replacement sales on which you would earn $9.05, or almost $2.00 more per unit. If customers shifted to the standard or higher models you would be ahead that much more, though it would seem that customers who tend to buy generic products are not likely to trade up.

Many different marketing questions can be raised. Indeed, the job of the manager is to consider the whole range of marketing strategies, including the positioning of each product, setting sales prices, the most effective means of advertising, and so on. Deciding on sales strategy requires information on contribution profit margins and sales mix such as that presented in Figure 17.2. The exhibit is a good tool of analysis for making marketing decisions regarding the optimal sales mix.

Fixed Expenses: To Allocate or Not?

When selling two or more products, inevitably there are fixed operating expenses that cannot be directly matched or coupled with the sales of each product or each separate stream of sales revenue. The unavoidable question is whether or not to allocate the total fixed operating expenses among the products. Refer to Figure 17.2, please; notice that fixed expenses are not allocated. Should these fixed expenses be distributed among the five different products in some manner?

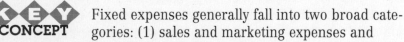 Fixed expenses generally fall into two broad categories: (1) sales and marketing expenses and (2) general and administrative expenses. Most fixed operating expenses are *indirect;* the expenses cannot be directly associated with particular products. The example here assumes there are no direct fixed expenses for any of the products. On the other hand, there could be some direct fixed expenses.

For example, an advertising campaign may feature only one product. Suppose you bought a one-time insertion in the *Wall Street Journal* for the premier product. The cost of this one-time ad should be deducted from the contribution margin of the premier product as a direct fixed expense. Typically, however, most fixed expenses are indirect; they cannot be directly matched to any one product.

Indirect fixed expenses can be allocated to products, although the purposes and methods of allocation are open to much debate and differences of opinion. For instance, the allocation can be done on the basis of sales volume, which means each unit sold would be assigned an equal amount of the total fixed expense. Or fixed costs can be allocated on the basis of sales revenue, which means that each dollar of sales revenue would be assigned an equal amount of total fixed expense. Alternatively, fixed costs can be allocated according to a more complex formula.

Figure 17.3 shows two alternative profit reports for the example—one in which total fixed expenses are allocated on

Method A: Fixed Expenses Allocated on Basis of Sales Volume

	Generic	Economy	Standard	Deluxe	Premier
Sales revenue	$791,000	$765,000	$2,100,000	$750,000	$855,000
Cost-of-goods-sold expense	($561,400)	($479,700)	($1,120,000)	($360,000)	($365,400)
Gross margin	$229,600	$285,300	$980,000	$390,000	$489,600
Variable expenses	($31,640)	($122,400)	($413,000)	($165,000)	($190,350)
Contribution margin	$197,960	$162,900	$567,000	$225,000	$299,250
Fixed expenses	($214,480)	($137,880)	($268,100)	($76,600)	($68,940)
Profit (loss)	($16,520)	$25,020	$298,900	$148,400	$230,310

Method B: Fixed Expenses Allocated on Basis of Sales Revenue

	Generic	Economy	Standard	Deluxe	Premier
Sales revenue	$791,000	$765,000	$2,100,000	$750,000	$855,000
Cost-of-goods-sold expense	($561,400)	($479,700)	($1,120,000)	($360,000)	($365,400)
Gross margin	$229,600	$285,300	$980,000	$390,000	$489,600
Variable expenses	($31,640)	($22,400)	($413,000)	($165,000)	($190,350)
Contribution margin	$197,960	$162,900	$567,000	$225,000	$299,250
Fixed expenses	($115,169)	($111,384)	($305,759)	($109,200)	($124,488)
Profit (loss)	$82,791	$51,516	$261,241	$115,800	$174,762

FIGURE 17.3 Two common methods for allocating fixed expenses.

basis of sales volume (method A), and the second on the basis of sales revenue of each product (method B). Total profit for the product line is the same for both, but the operating profit reported for each product differs between the two allocation methods.

Both sales volume and sales revenue for allocating fixed costs have obvious shortcomings; furthermore, both methods are rather arbitrary. Either method rests on a dubious premise. Method A assumes that each and every unit has the same fixed cost. Method B assumes that each and every sales revenue dollar has the same fixed cost. Recent attention has been focused on the theory of *cost drivers* to allocate fixed expenses, which goes under the rubric of *activity based costing* (ABC). This approach should really be called activity based cost *allocation,* because it's a method to allocate indirect costs to products.

Activity Based Costing (ABC)

The ABC method challenges the premise that fixed expenses are truly and completely indirect. Total fixed expenses are subdivided into separate cost pools; a separate cost pool is determined for each basic activity or support service. Instead of lumping all fixed costs into one conglomerate pool of general support, each basic type of support activity is identified with its own separate cost pool. Each product is then analyzed to determine and measure the usage the product makes of each activity for which separate fixed-expense pools are established.

In this example, for instance, all products except the generic model are advertised, and all advertising is done through the advertising department of the corporation. The advertising department is defined as one separate fixed-cost pool, and its activity is measured according to some common denominator of activity, such as number of ad pages run in the print media (newspapers and magazines). Each product is allocated a share of the total advertising department's cost pool based on the number of ad pages run for that product. The number of ad pages is called a *cost driver.* This activity drives, or determines, the amount of the fixed-cost subpool to be allocated to each product.

Alternatively, different types of advertising (print versus

electronic media, for example) could be identified and each product line charged with its share of the advertising department's cost based on two separate cost drivers—one for the number of print media pages and a second for the number of minutes on television or radio.

Some fixed expenses are quite indirect and far removed from particular products. Examples include the accounting department, the legal department, the annual CPA audit fee, the cost of security guards, general liability insurance, and many more. The cost driver concept would get stretched to its limit for these fixed expenses. Also, the number of separate activities having their own expense pools can get out of hand. Three to five, perhaps even seven to ten separate cost drivers for fixed-cost allocation may be understandable and feasible, but there is a limit.

KEY CONCEPT Returning to the title of this section, the fundamental management question is whether *any* allocation scheme is worth the effort. What's the purpose? Does allocation help decision making? The basic management purpose should not be to find the true or actual profit for each product or other sales revenue source. The fundamental question is whether management is making optimal use of the resources and potential provided by the division's fixed operating expenses.

The bottom line is finding which sales mix maximizes total contribution margin. Allocation of indirect fixed expenses in and of itself doesn't help to do this. Indirect fixed expenses may have to be allocated for legal or contract purposes. If so, the method(s) for such allocation should be spelled out in advance rather than waiting until after the fact to select the allocation rationale.

Sometimes a business may allocate fixed expenses to minimize the apparent profit on a product. I was hired to be an expert witness for the plaintiff in a patent infringement lawsuit against a well-known corporation. The defendant had already lost in the first stage, having been found guilty of patent infringement. For three years the defendant corporation had manufactured and sold a product on which the plaintiff owned the patent without compensating the plaintiff. The second stage was to assess the amount of damages to be awarded to the plaintiff.

The plaintiff was suing for recovery of the profit made by the defendant corporation on sales of the product. The defendant allocated every indirect fixed cost it could think of to the product—including part of the CEO's annual salary—to minimize the profit that was allegedly earned from sales of the product. The jury threw out this heavy-handed allocation and awarded $16 million to the plaintiff.

BUDGETING OVERVIEW

It goes without saying that managers should plan ahead and formulate strategy and tactics for the coming year—and longer. The future does not take care of itself. Any manager will tell you of the importance of forecasting major changes, adapting the core strategy of the business to the new environment, developing and implementing initiatives, and in general keeping ahead of the curve. One tool for planning is budgeting. The technical aspects and detailed procedures of a comprehensive budgeting system are beyond the scope of this book. The following discussion focuses on fundamentals.

Reasons for Budgeting

Management decisions taken as a whole should constitute an integrated and coordinated strategy and an overarching plan of action for achieving the profit and financial objectives of a business. Decisions are like the blueprint for a building; control should be carried out in the context of the decision blueprint. Budgeting is one very good means of integrating management decision making and management control, akin to constructing a building according to its blueprint.

Decisions are made explicit in a budget, which is the concrete plan of action for achieving the profit and financial objectives of the business according to a timetable. Actual results are then evaluated against budget, period by period, line by line, and item by item. Variances have to be explained. They serve as the catalyst for taking corrective action or for revising the plan as needed.

Lack of budgeting doesn't necessarily mean that there is no management control. Budgeting is certainly helpful but not absolutely essential for management control. Many businesses do little or no budgeting, yet they make a good profit and remain solvent and financially healthy. They depend on the management control reports to track their actual profit performance, financial position, and cash flows. But they have no formal or explicit budget against which to compare actual results. More than likely they use the previous year as the reference for comparison.

The master budget is made up of the separate profit and other budgets for each organizational unit—such as sales territories, departments, product lines, branches, divisions, or subsidiaries. Each subunit's budget is like a building stone in a large pyramid that leads up to the master budget at the top. Starting at the bottom end, sales and expense budgets dovetail into larger-scale profit budgets, which in turn are integrated with cash flow and financial condition (balance sheet) budgets.

The larger the organization, the more likely you'll find a formal and comprehensive financial budgeting process in place. And the more bureaucratic the organization, the more likely that it uses a budgeting system. The budget is one primary means of communication and authorization down the line in the organization. The budget provides the key benchmarks for evaluating performance of managers at all levels. Actual is compared against budget, and significant variances are highlighted, investigated, and reported up the line. Managers are rewarded for meeting or exceeding the budget, and they are held accountable for unfavorable variances.

A complete budget plan requires a profit budget (income statement) and cash flow budget for the coming period and a budgeted financial condition report (balance sheet) at the end of the period. As explained in previous chapters, the financial condition of the business is driven mainly by the profit-making operations of the business. Capital expenditures for replacements and expansions of long-term operating assets of the business must be included in the cash flow budget and the budgeted year-end financial condition.

A total financial plan in which a profit budget is integrated with the financial condition and cash flow budgets is a very convincing package when you're applying for a loan or renewing an existing line of credit. It shows that the company's total financial plan has been thought out.

Costs and Disadvantages of Budgeting

There are persuasive reasons for and advantages of budgeting. On the other side of the coin, budgeting is costly and may lead to a lot of game playing and dysfunctional behavior. Some reasons for budgeting are not highly applicable to smaller businesses or even to midsized businesses. Smaller businesses do not need budgets for communication and coordination purposes, functions that are much more important in larger organizations, where top management is distant from its far-flung, day-to-day operations.

Profit budgeting depends heavily on the ability of managers to provide detailed and accurate forecasts of changes in the key factors that drive profit. Nothing is more counterproductive and discouraging than an unrealistic profit budget built on flimsy sales projections. If no one believes the sales budget numbers, the budget process becomes a lot of wasted motion or, worse, an exercise in hypocrisy.

The profit budget should be accepted as realistically achievable by those managers responsible for meeting the objectives and goals of the profit plan and as a realistic benchmark against which actual performance can be compared. If budget goals are too unrealistic, managers may engage in all sorts of manipulations and artificial schemes to meet their budget profit targets. There are enormous pressures in a business organization to make budget, even if managers think the budget is unfair and unrealistic.

Then there are always unexpected developments—events that simply cannot be foreseen at the time of putting together a budget. The budget should be adjusted for such developments, but making budget revisions is not easy; it's like changing horses in the middle of the stream. Once adopted, budgets tend to become carved in stone. Higher levels of management quite naturally are suspicious that requests for budget adjustments may be attempts to evade budget goals or excuses for substandard performance. Budgeting works best in a stable and predictable environment.

As mentioned previously, management control entails thousands of details. Control deals with detail, detail, and more detail. Day to day and month to month the manager has to pay attention to an avalanche of details. Keeping all the details in perspective is a challenge, to say the least. Control reports comparing actual with budget should not let the details take over, which can easily cause managers to lose sight of the overall progress toward profit goals.

The whole point of budgeting, which is easy to lose sight of, is to achieve profit and other financial objectives. Budgeting is not an end but a means. Detailed expense and cost reporting is required so that managers can keep close watch on the total effect of the key expense and cost factors that were forecast in the profit budget. Often, managers ask for reams of detailed expense and cost reports, but they do not necessarily read all the detail.

END POINT

Managers do not simply make decisions and then assume that their decisions put into motion everything that has to be done to achieve the goals of the business. Managers must follow through and exercise management control throughout the period. There is no such thing as putting a business on automatic pilot. Managers have to watch everything. Management control depends on feedback information about actual performance, which managers compare against the plan.

Management control begins with a solid foundation of internal accounting controls. These forms and procedures are absolutely essential to ensure the reliability of the information recorded by a business's accounting system. Internal accounting controls also serve a second duty—to deter and detect fraud and other dishonest behavior. Most fraud can be traced to the absence or breakdown of internal accounting controls. These controls should be enforced vigilantly. Many larger business organizations use internal auditors to evaluate and improve their internal accounting controls and to perform other functions.

The chapter offers guidelines for management control reports. These reports should resonate with the decision-making analysis methods and models used by managers. These reports should provide the most relevant benchmarks against which actual performance is compared. Control reports contain a great amount of detail, but key factors and variances should be highlighted and not lost in the avalanche of details. Control reports should focus on several negative factors that adversely affect sales prices, sales volume, and expenses.

Budgeting provides useful yardsticks and standards for management control. But budgeting is done for more than just control purposes. Budgeting is a broader management practice that encompasses strategic planning, communication throughout the organization, motivation of managers, and more. The brief overview in the chapter looks at the reasons for budgeting, as well as its inherent disadvantages.

18

Manufacturing Accounting

If you're in the manufacturing business, this chapter is an absolute must. The chapter presents a concise explanation of the accounting methods used by virtually all manufacturers to determine and measure product cost. To set sales prices, to control costs, and to plan for the future, a business must know the costs of manufacturing its products.

But suppose you're not in the business of manufacturing the products you sell. You may have your enthusiasm under control for this chapter. I would point out, however, that all managers use product cost information and that all products begin their life by being manufactured. Even if your company does not manufacture products, it's important to understand how manufacturing costs are accumulated, how they are allocated to products, and how certain accounting problems are dealt with by manufacturers.

PRODUCT MAKERS VERSUS PRODUCT RESELLERS

Manufacturers are producers—they make the products they sell. Retailers (as well as wholesalers and distributors) do not make the products they sell; they are channels of distribution. Product cost is purchase cost for retailers; it comes on a purchase invoice. Product cost is much different for manufacturers;

it's the composite of diverse costs of production. It has to be computed.

The manufacturing process may be simple and short or complex and long. It may be either labor-intensive or capital-(asset-) intensive. Products (e.g., breakfast cereal) may roll nonstop off the end of a continuous mass-production assembly line. These are called *process cost systems*. Or production may be discontinuous and done on a one-batch-at-a-time basis; these are called *job order systems*. Printing and binding 10,000 copies of a book is an example of a job order system.

The example in this chapter is for an established manufacturing business, one that has been operating for several years. Its managers have already assembled and organized machines, equipment, tools, and employees into a smooth-running production process that is dependable and efficient—a monumental task, to say the least. Plant location is critical; so is plant layout, employee training, materials procurement, complying with an ever broadening range of governmental regulations, employee safety laws, environmental protection laws, and so on. These points are mentioned only in passing to make you aware of the foundation that precedes product cost determination.

 MANUFACTURING BUSINESS EXAMPLE

Some manufacturers determine their product costs monthly, others quarterly. There is no one standard period. It could be done weekly or even daily. The year is a natural time period for management planning and financial reporting. Thus, one year is the time period for this example.

In this example, the business manufactures one product in its one production plant. Figure 18.1 presents the company's profit report for the year down through its operating profit line (earnings before interest and income tax expenses). It includes the manufacturing cost report, which is a supporting schedule that has not been presented before.

Manufacturing costs consist of four basic cost components or natural groupings. *Raw materials* are purchased parts and materials that become part of the finished product. *Direct labor* refers to those employees who work on the production

Management Profit Report for Year

Sales Volume = 11,000 Units

	Per Unit	Total
Sales revenue	$1,400	$15,400,000
Cost-of-goods-sold expense	($ 685)	($ 7,535,000)
Gross margin	$ 715	$ 7,865,000
Variable operating expenses	($ 305)	($ 3,355,000)
Contribution margin	$ 410	$ 4,510,000
Fixed operating expenses		($ 2,300,000)
Operating profit (earnings before interest and income tax)		$ 2,210,000

Manufacturing Costs for Year

Annual Production Capacity = 12,000 Units
Actual Output = 12,000 Units

Basic Cost Components	Per Unit	Total
Raw materials	$ 215	$ 2,580,000
Direct labor	$ 260	$ 3,120,000
Variable overhead	$ 35	$ 420,000
Fixed overhead	$ 175	$ 2,100,000
Total manufacturing costs	$ 685	$ 8,220,000

Distribution of Manufacturing Costs		
11,000 units sold (see above)	$ 685	$ 7,535,000
1,000 units inventory increase	$ 685	$ 685,000
Total manufacturing costs		$ 8,220,000

FIGURE 18.1 *Profit report and manufacturing costs schedule for year.*

line. Direct labor costs include fringe benefits, which typically add 30 to 40 percent to basic wages. For instance, employer Social Security and Medicare tax rates presently are 7.65 percent of base wages; also, there are unemployment taxes, employee retirement and pension plan contributions, health and medical insurance, worker's compensation insurance, and paid vacations and sick leaves.

The company recorded $8,220,000 total manufacturing costs and produced 12,000 units during the year. Of this amount $7,535,000 is charged to cost-of-goods-sold expense for the 11,000 units sold during the year and $685,000 is allocated to the 1,000-unit inventory increase.* Thus $685,000 of the manufacturing costs for the year will not be expensed until next year or sometime further into the future when the inventory is sold.†

Manufacturing *overhead* refers to all other production costs. Some of these costs vary with total output, such as electricity that powers machinery and equipment. These *variable overhead* costs are separated from *fixed overhead* costs. Over the short run, many manufacturing overhead costs are fixed in amount and do not depend on the level of production activity. Examples are property taxes, fire insurance on the production plant, and plant security guards who are paid a fixed salary.

In this example, the company's annual production capacity is 12,000 units. Its $2.1 million total fixed overhead costs provide the physical facilities and human resources to produce 12,000 units under normal, practical operating conditions. Actual production output for the year in the example equals the company's production capacity. In actual practice, actual output usually falls somewhat below capacity. How accountants deal with the difference between capacity and output is discussed later in the chapter.

Computation of Unit Product Cost

Unit product cost is determined by dividing the total manufacturing costs for the period by total production output for the period:

*During the production process, which can take several weeks or months, manufacturing costs are first accumulated in an inventory account called *work-in-process*. When production is completed, the cost of the completed units is transferred to the *finished goods* inventory account.

†A manufacturing business may select either the FIFO or the LIFO method for assigning product costs to cost-of-goods-sold expense and to the inventories asset. This choice of costing methods is available to manufacturers as well as retailers and wholesalers. Product costs usually vary from period to period. Thus the cost-of-goods-sold expense and the amount allocated to the inventory increase are different between the two methods. The FIFO and LIFO methods are explained in Chapter 20 of my book, *How to Read a Financial Report*, 5th ed., (New York: John Wiley & Sons, 1999).

$$\frac{\$8,220,000 \text{ total manufacturing costs}}{12,000 \text{ units total output}}$$

$$= \$685 \text{ unit product cost}$$

KEY CONCEPT Notice immediately three things about unit product cost. First, it's a calculated amount. It doesn't exist until it's computed. Clearly, both the numerator and the denominator of the computation must be correct or else the unit product cost would be wrong. Second, unit product cost is an average. Total cost over a period of time is divided by total output over that same period, one year in this example. Costs and quantities may vary daily, weekly, or monthly—but the definition and computation of unit product cost is the average over a certain period of time.* Third, only manufacturing costs are included, not the nonmanufacturing expenses of operating the business such as marketing (sales promotion, advertising, etc.), delivery costs, administration and general management costs, legal costs, and interest expense. A so-called Chinese wall should be built between manufacturing costs and all other, nonmanufacturing costs. The proper classification and separation between costs is critical.

KEY CONCEPT Sales and marketing costs, such as advertising, are not included in product cost; these are viewed as costs of making sales, not making products. Research and development (R&D) costs are not classified as product cost, even though these costs may lead to new products, new methods of manufacture, new compounds of materials, or other technological improvements.

Raw materials and direct labor costs are clearly manufacturing costs. Taken together, they are called *prime costs*. Direct materials and direct labor are matched with or traced to particular products being manufactured. Variable overhead, on the other hand, presents problems of matching with particular products. And fixed overhead is a real headache. The term *overhead* refers to indirect costs of manufacturing the products.

*In job order costing systems, the total cost of each job (one batch or group of products that is manufactured as a separate lot) is divided by the total number of units in the job to determine unit product cost.

Consider, for example, the print order for the production of 10,000 copies of a book. The paper and ink costs (raw materials) can be identified to each production run. Likewise, the employees who set up and operate the presses (direct labor) can be identified and matched to the job. However, variable overhead costs cannot be directly identified with particular press runs; instead, these costs must be allocated. For instance, the cost of electricity to power the presses can be allocated on the basis of the machine hours of each print run.

Much more troublesome are fixed manufacturing overhead costs, which include a wide variety of costs such as property taxes on the production plant, depreciation of the production equipment, fixed salaries of plant nurses and doctors, the fixed salary of the vice president of production, and so on. Fixed manufacturing overhead costs have to be allocated according to some basis for sharing these costs among the different products manufactured by the company. The company in this example makes only one product. So fixed overhead and variable overhead costs are all assigned to this one product. (Cost allocation issues and methods are discussed in Chapter 17.)

MISCLASSIFICATION OF MANUFACTURING COSTS

To minimize taxable income, some manufacturers have been known to intentionally misclassify some of their costs. Certain costs were recorded as marketing or as general and administration expenses that should have been booked as manufacturing costs. These misclassified costs were not included in the calculation of unit product cost. The purpose was to maximize costs that are charged off immediately to expense. By minimizing current taxable income, the business could delay payment of income taxes.

KEY CONCEPT The Internal Revenue Code takes a special interest in the problem of manufacturing overhead cost classification. The Internal Revenue Service noticed that many manufacturers were misclassifying some of their costs. The income tax law spells out in some detail which costs must be classified as manufacturing overhead costs and therefore capitalized. *Capitalize* means to put the cost into an inventories asset account by including the cost in the calculation of unit product cost. Remember that the cost of products held in inventory remains an asset and is not charged to expense until the products are sold.

 The following costs should definitely be classified as manufacturing costs: production employee benefits costs; rework, scrap, and spoilage costs; quality control costs; and routine repairs and maintenance on production machinery and equipment. Of course, depreciation of production machinery and equipment and property taxes on the production plant should be classified as manufacturing overhead costs.

To illustrate the effects of misclassifying manufacturing costs, suppose that $480,000 of the company's manufacturing fixed overhead costs had been recorded in fixed operating expenses instead of in fixed manufacturing overhead costs. Otherwise, everything else remains the same as shown before in the company example. Figure 18.2 shows the effects of this misclassification error. Pay particular attention to the operating profit line, which is taxable income before the interest expense deduction.

In Figure 18.2 fixed operating expenses are inflated by $480,000 (from $2,300,000 to $2,780,000). This amount is shifted from fixed manufacturing overhead costs, which decreases from $2,100,000 to $1,620,000. Thus, $480,000 in manufacturing fixed overhead escapes being charged to the 12,000 units produced, which decreases unit product cost by $40, from $685 to $645.

Remember that 1,000 of the 12,000 units manufactured during the year go into ending inventory, not out the door to customers. Each of the 1,000 units carries $40 less in fixed overhead cost, for a total of $40,000 less in ending inventory. Operating profit, or taxable income before interest, is $40,000 less as the result of the misclassification error, so income tax for the year would be less. In one sense, we have cooked the books to record $40,000 less in operating profit simply by reclassifying some costs away from manufacturing.*

*Although it would be rather unusual, a manufacturer could start and end the period with no inventory, in which case profit would be the same no matter how costs were classified—although for internal management reports the proper classification of costs is always important.

Management Profit Report for Year
Sales Volume = 11,000 Units

	Per Unit	Total
Sales revenue	$1,400	$15,400,000
Cost-of-goods-sold expense	($ 645)	($ 7,095,000)
Gross margin	$ 755	$ 8,305,000
Variable operating expenses	($ 305)	($ 3,355,000)
Contribution margin	$ 450	$ 4,950,000
Fixed operating expenses		($ 2,780,000)
Operating profit (earnings before interest and income tax)		$ 2,170,000

Manufacturing Costs for Year
Annual Production Capacity = 12,000 Units
Actual Output = 12,000 Units

Basic Cost Components	Per Unit	Total
Raw materials	$ 215	$ 2,580,000
Direct labor	$ 260	$ 3,120,000
Variable overhead	$ 35	$ 420,000
Fixed overhead	$ 135	$ 1,620,000
Total manufacturing costs	$ 645	$ 7,740,000

Distribution of Manufacturing Costs		
11,000 units sold (see above)	$ 645	$ 7,095,000
1,000 units inventory increase	$ 645	$ 645,000
Total manufacturing costs		$ 7,740,000

FIGURE 18.2 *Misclassification of manufacturing costs.*

Target sales prices may be determined by marking up unit product cost a certain percent. Thus, managers should be very clear regarding whether all manufacturing overhead costs are included in the calculation of unit product cost. If not, the markup percent should be adjusted since it would be based on an understated unit product cost. The better course of action would seem to be to properly classify all manufacturing overhead costs in the first place.

KEY CONCEPT

IDLE PRODUCTION CAPACITY

Most manufacturers have fairly large fixed manufacturing overhead costs—depreciation of plant and equipment, salaries of a wide range of employees (from the vice president of production to janitors), fire insurance costs, property taxes, and literally hundreds of other costs. Fixed manufacturing overhead costs provide production capacity. Managers should measure or at least make their best estimate of the production capacity provided by their fixed manufacturing overhead costs. Capacity is the maximum potential production output for a period of time provided by the manufacturing facilities that are in place and ready for use.

Suppose the company's annual production capacity were 15,000 units instead of the 12,000 units assumed in the preceding example. The business has correctly classified costs between manufacturing and other operating costs. All other profit and production factors are the same as before. The company manufactured only 12,000 units during the year. The 3,000-unit gap between actual output and production capacity is called *idle capacity.* In short, the company operated at 80 percent of its capacity (12,000 units actual output ÷ 15,000 units capacity = 80%). I should mention that 20 percent idle capacity is not unusual.

Producing below capacity in any one year does not necessarily mean that management should downsize its production facilities. Production capacity has a long-run planning horizon. Most manufacturers have some capacity in reserve to provide for growth and for unexpected surges in demands for its products. Our concern focuses on how to determine unit product cost given the 20 percent idle capacity.

In most situations, 20 percent idle capacity would be considered within the range of normal production output levels. So the company would compute unit product cost the same as shown earlier. The 12,000-unit actual output is divided into the $2.1 million total fixed manufacturing overhead costs to get the fixed overhead cost *burden rate,* which is $175. This is the burden rate included in unit product cost in Figure 18.1.

The theory is that the actual number of units produced should absorb all fixed manufacturing overhead costs for the year even though a fraction of the total fixed manufacturing costs were wasted, as it were, because the company did not produce up to its full capacity. In this way, the cost of idle capacity is buried in the unit product cost, which would have been lower if the company had produced at its full capacity and thus spread its fixed manufacturing costs over 15,000 units.

The main alternative is to divide total fixed manufacturing overhead costs by capacity. This would give a fixed overhead cost burden rate of $140 ($2.1 million total fixed manufacturing overhead costs ÷ 15,000 units annual capacity = $140 burden rate). In terms of total dollars, the company had 20 percent idle capacity during the year, so 20 percent of its $2.1 million total fixed overhead costs, or $420,000, would be charged to an idle capacity expense for the year. This amount would bypass the unit product cost computation and go directly to expense for the year.*

Managers may not like treating idle capacity cost as a separate expense because this draws attention to it. In the manufacturing costs summary, anyone could easily see that the business produced at only 80 percent of its capacity and so would be aware that the unit product cost is higher than if it were based on capacity.

 If, on the other hand, actual output were substantially less than production capacity, the fixed overhead burden rate should not be based on actual output. The idle capacity cost definitely should be reported as a separate expense in the internal management profit report. (External financial reports seldom report the cost of idle capacity as a separate expense.)

The generally accepted accounting rule is that the fixed manufacturing overhead burden rate included in the calculation of unit product cost should be based on a normal output level—not necessarily equal to 100 percent of production capacity, but typically in the 75 to 90 percent range. However, it must be admitted that there are no hard-and-fast guidelines on this. In short, some amount of normal idle capacity cost is

*Cost-of-goods-sold expense would be $7,150,000 (11,000 units sold × $650 unit product cost = $7,150,000); idle capacity expense would be $420,000. The total of these two would be $7,570,000, which is $35,000 more than the $7,535,000 cost-of-goods-sold expense shown in Figure 18.1. In short, operating profit would be $35,000 less and ending inventory would be $35,000 less.

loaded into the unit product cost because the fixed overhead burden rate is based on an output level less than full capacity.

MANUFACTURING INEFFICIENCIES

The ideal manufacturing scenario is one of maximum production efficiency—no wasted materials, no wasted labor, no excessive reworking of products that don't pass inspection the first time through, no unnecessary power usage, and so on. The goal is optimum efficiency and maximum productivity for all variable costs of manufacturing. The current buzz word is TQM, or *total quality management,* as the means to achieve these efficiencies and to maximize quality.

Management control reports should clearly highlight productivity ratios for each factor of the production process—each raw material item, each labor step, and each variable cost factor. One key productivity ratio, for instance, is *direct labor hours per unit.* Ten to fifteen years ago it took 10 hours to make a ton of steel, but today it takes only about 4 hours; a recent article in the *New York Times* commented that the relatively low number of workers on the production floor of the modern steel plant is remarkable.

The computation of unit product cost is based on the essential premise that the manufacturing process is reasonably efficient, which means that productivity ratios for every cost factor are fairly close to what they should be. Managers should watch productivity ratios in their production control reports, and they should take quick action to deal with the problems. Occasionally, however, things spin out of control, and this causes an accounting problem regarding how to deal with gross inefficiencies.

To explain, suppose the company in the example had wasted raw materials during the year. Assume the $2,580,000 total cost of raw materials in the original scenario (see Figure 18.1) includes $660,000 of wastage. These materials were scrapped and not used in the final products. Inexperienced or untrained employees may have caused this. Or perhaps inferior-quality materials not up to the company's normal quality control standards were used as a cost-cutting measure.

This problem should have been stopped before it

amounted to so much; quicker action should have been taken. In any case, assume the problem persisted and the result was that raw materials costing $660,000 had to be thrown away and not used in the production process. The preferred approach is to remove the $660,000 from the computation of unit product cost, which would lower the unit product cost by $55 ($660,000 wasted raw materials cost ÷ 12,000 units output = $55). The $660,000 excess raw materials cost would be deducted as a onetime extraordinary expense, or loss, in the profit report.

The wasted raw materials costs could be included in unit product cost, but this could result in a seriously misleading cost figure. Nevertheless, exposing excess raw materials cost in a management profit report is a touchy issue. Would you want the blame for this laid at your doorstep? It might be better to bury the cost in unit product cost and let it flow against profit that way rather than as a naked item for other top-level managers to see in a report.

Standard Costs

Many manufacturing businesses use a standard cost system. Perhaps the term *system* here is too broad. What is meant is that certain procedures are adopted by the business to establish performance benchmarks, then actual costs are compared against these standards to help managers carry out their control function.

Quantity and price standards for raw materials, direct labor, and variable overhead costs are established as yardsticks of performance, and any variances (deviations) from the standards are reported. Despite the clear advantages of standard cost systems, many manufacturers do not use any formal standard cost system. It takes a fair amount of time and cost to develop and to update standards.

If the standards are not correct and up-to-date, they can cause more harm than good. Nevertheless, actual costs should be compared against benchmarks of performance. If nothing else, current costs should be compared against past performance. Many trade associations collect and publish industry cost averages, which are helpful benchmarks for comparison.

KEY CONCEPT

EXCESSIVE PRODUCTION

Please refer again to Figure 18.1. Notice that the $685 unit product cost includes $175 of fixed manufacturing overhead costs. If the units are sold, the fixed overhead cost ends up in the cost-of-goods-sold expense; if the units were not sold then $175 fixed overhead cost per unit is included in ending inventory. Inventory increased 1,000 units in this example, so ending inventory carries $175,000 of fixed overhead costs that will not be charged off to expense until the products are sold in a future period. The inclusion of fixed manufacturing overhead costs in inventory is called full-cost absorption. This sounds very reasonable, doesn't it?

Growing businesses need enough production capacity for the sales made during the year and to increase inventory in anticipation of higher sales next year. However, sometimes a manufacturer makes too many products and production output rises far above sales volume for the period, causing a large increase in inventory—much more than what would be needed for next year.

Suppose, for example, that the company had sold only 6,000 units during the year even though it manufactured 12,000 units. Figure 18.3 presents the profit and manufacturing cost report for this disaster scenario. Notice that the company's inventory would have increased by 6,000 units—as many units as it sold during the year!

The inventory buildup could be in anticipation of a long strike looming in the near future, which will shut down production for several months. Or perhaps the company predicts serious shortages of raw materials during the next several months. There could be any number of such legitimate reasons for a large inventory buildup. But assume not.

Instead, assume the company fell way short of its sales goals for the year and failed to adjust its production output. And assume the sales forecast for next year is not all that encouraging. The large inventory overhang at year-end presents all sorts of problems. Where do you store it? Will sales price have to be reduced to move the inventory? And what about the fixed manufacturing overhead cost included in inventory? This last question presents a very troublesome accounting problem.

Management Profit Report for Year
Sales Volume = 6,000 Units

	Per Unit	Total
Sales revenue	$1,400	$8,400,000
Cost-of-goods-sold expense	($ 685)	($4,110,000)
Gross margin	$ 715	$4,290,000
Variable operating expenses	($ 305)	($1,830,000)
Contribution margin	$ 410	$2,460,000
Fixed operating expenses		($2,300,000)
Operating profit (earnings before interest and income tax)		$ 160,000

Manufacturing Costs for Year
Annual Production Capacity = 12,000 Units
Actual Output = 12,000 Units

Basic Cost Components	Per Unit	Total
Raw materials	$ 215	$2,580,000
Direct labor	$ 260	$3,120,000
Variable overhead	$ 35	$ 420,000
Fixed overhead	$ 175	$2,100,000
Total manufacturing costs	$ 685	$8,220,000

Distribution of Manufacturing Costs		
11,000 units sold (see above)	$ 685	$4,110,000
1,000 units inventory increase	$ 685	$4,110,000
Total manufacturing costs		$8,220,000

FIGURE 18.3 *Excessive accumulation of inventory.*

If only 6,000 units had been produced instead of the 12,000 actual output, the company would have had 50 percent idle capacity—an issue discussed earlier in the chapter. By producing 12,000 units the company seems to be making full use of its production capacity. But is it, really? Producing excessive inventory is a false and illusory use of production capacity.

A good case can be made that no fixed manufacturing overhead costs should be included in excessive quantities of inventory; the amount of fixed overhead cost that usually would be allocated to the inventory should be charged off as expense to the period. Unless the company is able to slash its fixed overhead costs, which is very difficult to do in the short run, it will have these fixed overhead costs again next year. It should bite the bullet this year, it is argued.

Assume the company will have to downsize its inventory next year, which means it will have to slash production output next year. Unless it can make substantial cuts in its fixed manufacturing overhead costs, it will have substantial idle capacity next year.

The question is whether the excess quantity of ending inventory should be valued at only variable manufacturing costs and exclude fixed manufacturing overhead costs. As a practical matter, it is very difficult to draw a line between excessive and normal inventory levels. Unless ending inventory was extremely large, the full-cost absorption method is used for ending inventory. The fixed overhead burden rate is included in the unit product cost for all units in ending inventory.*

END POINT

Manufacturers must determine their unit product costs; they have to develop relatively complex accounting systems to keep track of all the different costs that go into manufacturing their products. Direct costs of raw materials and labor and variable overhead costs are relatively straightforward. Fixed manufacturing overhead costs are another story. The chapter examines the problems of excess (idle) production capacity, excess manufacturing costs due to inefficiencies, and excess production output. Managers have to stay on top of these situations if they occur and know how their unit product costs are affected by the accounting procedures for dealing with the problems.

---

*One theory is that *no* fixed manufacturing overhead costs should be included in ending inventory—whether normal or abnormal quantities are held in stock. Only variable manufacturing costs would be included in unit product cost. This is called *direct costing,* though more properly it should be called *variable costing.* It is not acceptable for external financial reporting or for income tax purposes.

Glossary for Managers

accelerated depreciation   (1) The estimated useful life of the fixed asset being depreciated is shorter than a realistic forecast of its probable actual service life; (2) more of the total cost of the fixed asset is allocated to the first half of its useful life than to the second half (i.e., there is a front-end loading of depreciation expense).

accounting   A broad, all-inclusive term that refers to the methods and procedures of financial record keeping by a business (or any entity); it also refers to the main functions and purposes of record keeping, which are to assist in the operations of the entity, to provide necessary information to managers for making decisions and exercising control, to measure profit, to comply with income and other tax laws, and to prepare financial reports.

accounting equation   An equation that reflects the two-sided nature of a business entity, assets on the one side and the sources of assets on the other side (assets = liabilities + owners' equity). The assets of a business entity are subject to two types of claims that arise from its two basic sources of capital—liabilities and owners' equity. The accounting equation is the foundation for double-entry bookkeeping, which uses a scheme for recording changes in these basic types of accounts as either debits or credits such that the total of accounts with debit balances equals the total of accounts with credit balances. The accounting equation also serves as the framework for the statement of financial condition, or balance sheet, which is one of the three fundamental financial statements reported by a business.

accounts payable   Short-term, non-interest-bearing liabilities of a business that arise in the course of its activities and operations from purchases on credit. A business buys many things on credit, whereby the purchase cost of goods and services are not paid for immediately. This liability account records the amounts owed for credit purchases that will be paid in the short run, which generally means about one month.

accounts receivable   Short-term, non-interest-bearing debts owed to a business by its customers who bought goods and services from the business on credit. Generally, these debts should be collected within a month or so. In a balance sheet, this asset is listed immediately after cash. (Actually the amount of short-term marketable investments, if the business has any, is listed after cash and before accounts receivable.) Accounts receivable are viewed as a near-cash type of asset that will be turned into cash in the short run. A business may not collect all of its accounts receivable. See also **bad debts.**

accounts receivable turnover ratio   A ratio computed by dividing annual sales revenue by the year-end balance of accounts receivable. Technically speaking, to calculate this ratio the amount of annual *credit* sales should be divided by the *average* accounts receivable balance, but this information is not readily available from external financial statements. For reporting internally to managers, this ratio should be refined and fine-tuned to be as accurate as possible.

accrual-basis accounting   Well, frankly, *accrual* is not a good descriptive term. Perhaps the best way to begin is to mention that accrual-basis accounting is much more than cash-basis accounting. Recording only the cash receipts and cash disbursement of a business would be grossly inadequate. A business has many assets other than cash, as well as many liabilities, that must be recorded. Measuring profit for a period as the difference between cash inflows from sales and cash outflows for expenses would be wrong, and in fact is not allowed for most businesses by the income tax law. For management, income tax, and financial reporting purposes, a business needs a comprehensive record-keeping system—one that recognizes, records, and reports all the assets and liabilities of a business. This all-inclusive scope of financial record keeping is referred to as *accrual-basis accounting.* Accrual-basis accounting records sales revenue when sales are made (though cash is received before or after the sales) and records expenses when costs are incurred (though cash is paid before or after expenses are recorded). Established financial reporting standards require that profit for a period must be recorded using accrual-basis accounting methods. Also, these authoritative standards require that in reporting its financial condition a business must use accrual-basis accounting.

accrued expenses payable   The account that records the short-term, non-interest-bearing liabilities of a business that accumulate over time, such as vacation pay owed to employees. This liability is different than **accounts payable,** which is the liability account for bills that have been received by a business from purchases on credit.

accumulated depreciation   A contra, or offset, account that is coupled with the property, plant, and equipment asset account in which the original costs of the long-term operating assets of a business are recorded. The accumulated depreciation contra account accumulates the amount of depreciation expense that is recorded period by period. So the balance in this account is the cumulative amount of depreciation that has been recorded since the assets were acquired. The balance in the accumulated depreciation account is deducted from the original cost of the assets recorded in the property, plant, and equipment asset account. The remainder, called the *book value* of the assets, is the amount included on the asset side of a business.

acid test ratio (also called the **quick ratio**)   The sum of cash, accounts receivable, and short-term marketable investments (if any) is divided by total current liabilities to compute this ratio. Suppose that the short-term creditors were to pounce on a business and not agree to roll over the debts owed to them by the business. In this rather extreme scenario, the acid test ratio reveals whether its cash and near-cash assets are enough to pay its short-term current liabilities. This ratio is an extreme test that is not likely to be imposed on a business unless it is in financial straits. This ratio is quite relevant when a business is in a liquidation situation or bankruptcy proceedings.

activity based costing (ABC)   A relatively new method advocated for the allocation of indirect costs. The key idea is to classify indirect costs, many of which are fixed in amount for a period of time, into separate activities and to develop a measure for each activity called a *cost driver*. The products or other functions in the business that benefit from the activity are allocated shares of the total indirect cost for the period based on their usage as measured by the cost driver.

amortization   This term has two quite different meanings. First, it may refer to the allocation to expense each period of the total cost of an intangible asset (such as the cost of a patent purchased from the inventor) over its useful economic life. In this sense amortization is equivalent to depreciation, which allocates the cost of a tangible long-term operating asset (such as a machine) over its useful economic life. Second, amortization may refer to the gradual paydown of the principal amount of a debt. *Principal* refers to the amount borrowed that has to be paid back to the lender as opposed to interest that has to be paid for use of the principal. Each period, a business may pay interest and also make a payment on the principal of the loan, which reduces the principal amount of the loan, of course. In this situation the loan is *amortized,* or gradually paid down.

asset turnover ratio   A broad-gauge ratio computed by dividing annual sales revenue by total assets. It is a rough measure of the sales-generating power of assets. The idea is that assets are used to make sales, and the sales should lead to profit. The ultimate test is not sales revenue on assets, but the profit earned on assets as measured by the *return on assets* (ROA) ratio.

bad debts   Refers to accounts receivable from credit sales to customers that a business will not be able to collect (or not collect in full). In hindsight, the business shouldn't have extended credit to these particular customers. Since these amounts owed to the business will not be collected, they are written off. The accounts receivable asset account is decreased by the estimated amount of uncollectible receivables, and the bad debts expense account is increased this amount. These write-offs can be done by the *direct write-off method,* which means that no expense is recorded until specific accounts receivable are identified as uncollectible. Or the *allowance method* can be used, which is based on an estimated percent of bad debts from credit sales during the period. Under this method, a contra asset account is created (called *allowance for bad debts*) and the balance of this account is deducted from the accounts receivable asset account.

balance sheet   A term often used instead of the more formal and correct term—*statement of financial condition*. This financial statement summarizes the assets, liabilities, and owners' equity sources of a business at a given moment in time. It is prepared at the end of each profit period and whenever else it is needed. It is one of the three primary financial statements of a business, the other two being the *income statement* and the *statement of cash flows*. The values reported in the balance sheet are the amounts used to determine book value per share of capital stock. Also, the book value of an asset is the amount reported in a business's most recent balance sheet.

basic earnings per share (EPS)   This important ratio equals the net income for a period (usually one year) divided by the number capital stock shares issued by a business corporation. This ratio is so important for publicly owned business corporations that it is included in the daily stock trading tables published by the *Wall Street Journal,* the *New York Times,* and other major newspapers. Despite being a rather straightforward concept, there are several technical problems in calculating earnings per share. Actually, two EPS ratios are needed for many businesses—basic EPS, which uses the actual number of capital shares outstanding, and diluted EPS, which takes into account additional shares of stock that may be issued for stock options granted by a business and other stock shares that a business is obligated to issue in the future. Also, many businesses report not one but two net income figures—one before extraordinary gains and losses were recorded in the period and a second after deducting these nonrecurring gains and losses. Many business corporations issue more than one class of capital stock, which makes the calculation of their earnings per share even more complicated.

big bath   A street-smart term that refers to the practice by many businesses of recording very large lump-sum write-offs of certain assets or recording large amounts for pending liabilities triggered by business restructurings, massive employee layoffs, disposals of major segments of the business, and other major traumas in the life of a business. Businesses have been known to use these occasions to record every conceivable asset write-off and/or liability write-up that they can think of in order to clear the decks for the future. In this way a business avoids recording expenses in the future, and its profits in the coming years will be higher. The term is derisive, but investors generally seem very forgiving regarding the abuses of this accounting device. But you never know—investors may cast a more wary eye on this practice in the future.

book value and **book value per share**   Generally speaking, these terms refer to the balance sheet value of an asset (or less often of a liability) or the balance sheet value of owners' equity per share. Either term emphasizes that the amount recorded in the accounts or on the books of a business is the value being used. The total of the amounts reported for owners' equity in its balance sheet is divided by the number of stock shares of a corporation to determine the book value per share of its capital stock.

bottom line   A commonly used term that refers to the net income (profit) reported by a business, which is the last, or bottom line, in its income statement. As you undoubtedly know, the term has taken on a much broader meaning in everyday use, referring to the ultimate or most important effect or result of something. Not many accounting-based terms have found their way into everyday language, but this is one that has.

breakeven point   The annual sales volume level at which total contribution margin equals total annual fixed expenses. The breakeven point is only a point of reference, not the goal of a business, of course. It is computed by dividing total fixed expenses by unit margin. The breakeven point is quite useful in analyzing profit behavior and operating leverage. Also, it gives manager a good point of reference for setting sales goals and understanding the consequences of incurring fixed costs for a period.

capital   A very broad term rooted in economic theory and referring to money and other assets that are invested in a business or other venture for the general purpose of earning a profit, or a return on the investment. Generally speaking, the sources of capital for a business are divided between debt and equity. *Debt,* as you know, is borrowed money on which interest is paid. *Equity* is the broad term for the ownership capital invested in a business and is most often called *owners' equity.* Owners' equity arises from two quite different sources: (1) money or other assets invested in the business by its owners and (2) profit earned by the business that is retained and not distributed to its owners (called *retained earnings*).

capital budgeting   Refers generally to analysis procedures for ranking investments, given a limited amount of total capital that has to be allocated among the various capital investment opportunities of a business. The term sometimes is used interchangeably with the analysis techniques themselves, such as calculating *present value, net present value,* and the *internal rate of return* of investments.

capital expenditures   Refers to investments by a business in long-term operating assets, including land and buildings, heavy machinery and equipment, vehicles, tools, and other economic resources used in the operations of a business. The term *capital* is used to emphasize that these are relatively large amounts and that a business has to raise capital for these expenditures from debt and equity sources.

capital investment analysis   Refers to various techniques and procedures used to determine or to analyze future returns from an investment of capital in order to evaluate the capital recovery pattern and the periodic earnings from the investment. The two basic tools for capital investment analysis are (1) spreadsheet models (which I strongly prefer) and (2) mathematical equations for calculating the present value or internal rate of return of an investment. Mathematical methods suffer from a lack of information that the decision maker ought to consider. A spreadsheet model supplies all the needed information and has other advantages as well.

capital recovery   Refers to recouping, or regaining, invested capital over the life of an investment. The pattern of period-by-period capital recovery is very important. In brief, capital recovery is the return *of* capital—not the return *on* capital, which refers to the rate of earnings on the amount of capital invested during the period. The returns from an investment have to be sufficient to provide for both recovery of capital and an adequate rate of earnings on unrecovered capital period by period. Sorting out how much capital is recovered each period is relatively easy if you use a spreadsheet model for capital investment analysis. In contrast, using a mathematical method of analysis does not provide this period-by-period capital recovery information, which is a major disadvantage.

capital stock   Ownership shares issued by a business corporation. A business corporation may issue more than one class of capital stock shares. One class may give voting privileges in the election of the directors of the corporation while the other class does not. One class (called *preferred stock*) may entitle a certain amount of dividends per share before cash dividends can be paid on the other class (usually called *common stock*). Stock shares may have a minimum value at which they have to be issued (called the *par value*), or stock shares can be issued for any amount (called *no-par stock*). Stock shares may be traded on public markets such as the New York Stock Exchange or over the Nasdaq network. There are about 10,000 stocks traded on public markets (although estimates vary on this number). In this regard, I find it very interesting that there are more than 8,000 mutual funds that invest in stocks.

capital structure, or **capitalization**   Terms that refer to the combination of capital sources that a business has tapped for investing in its assets—in particular, the mix of its interest-bearing debt and its owners' equity. In a more sweeping sense, the terms also include appendages and other features of the basic debt and equity instruments of a business. Such things as stock options, stock warrants, and convertible features of preferred stock and notes payable are included in the more inclusive sense of the terms, as well as any debt-based and equity-based financial derivatives issued by the business.

capitalization of costs   When a cost is recorded originally as an increase to an asset account, it is said to be *capitalized*. This means that the outlay is treated as a capital expenditure, which becomes part of the total cost basis of the asset. The alternative is to record the cost as an expense immediately in the period the cost is incurred. Capitalized costs refer mainly to costs that are recorded in the long-term operating assets of a business, such as buildings, machines, equipment, tools, and so on.

cash burn rate   A relatively recent term that refers to how fast a business is using up its available cash, especially when its cash flow from operating activities is negative instead of positive. This term most often refers to a business struggling through its start-up or early phases that has not yet generated enough cash inflow from sales to cover its cash outflow for expenses (and perhaps never will).

cash flow   An obvious but at the same time elusive term that refers to cash inflows and outflows during a period. But the specific sources and uses of cash flows are not clear in this general term. The statement of cash flows, which is one of the three primary financial statements of a business, classifies cash flows into three types: those from operating activities (sales and expenses, or profit-making operations), those from investing activities, and those from financing activities. Sometimes the term *cash flow* is used as shorthand for *cash flow from profit* (i.e., cash flow from operating activities).

cash flow from operating activities, also called **cash flow from profit**
This equals the cash inflow from sales during the period minus the cash outflow for expenses during the period. Keep in mind that to measure net income, generally accepted accounting principles require the use of accrual-basis accounting. Starting with the amount of accrual-basis net income, adjustments are made for changes in accounts receivable, inventories, prepaid expenses, and operating liabilities—and depreciation expense is added back (as well as any other noncash outlay expense)—to arrive at cash flow from profit, which is formally labeled *cash flow from operating activities* in the externally reported statement of cash flows.

cash flows, statement of   One of the three primary financial statements that a business includes in the periodic financial reports to its outside shareowners and lenders. This financial statement summarizes the business's cash inflows and outflows for the period according to a threefold classification: (1) cash flow from operating activities (cash flow from profit), (2) cash flow from investing activities, and (3) cash flow from financing activities. Frankly, the typical statement of cash flows is difficult to read and decipher; it includes too many lines of information and is fairly technical compared with the typical balance sheet and income statement.

contribution margin   An intermediate measure of profit equal to sales revenue minus cost-of-goods-sold expense and minus variable operating expenses—but before fixed operating expenses are deducted. Profit at this point contributes toward covering fixed operating expenses and toward interest and income tax expenses. The breakeven point is the sales volume at which contribution margin just equals total fixed expenses.

conversion cost Refers to the sum of manufacturing direct labor and overhead costs of products. The cost of raw materials used to make products is not included in this concept. Generally speaking, this is a rough measure of the value added by the manufacturing process.

cost of capital Refers to the interest cost of debt capital used by a business plus the amount of profit that the business should earn for its equity sources of capital to justify the use of the equity capital during the period. Interest is a contractual and definite amount for a period, whereas the profit that a business should earn on the equity capital employed during the period is not. A business should set a definite goal of earning at least a certain minimum return on equity (ROE) and compare its actual performance for the period against this goal. The costs of debt and equity capital are combined into either a before-tax rate or an after-tax rate for capital investment analysis.

current assets *Current* refers to cash and those assets that will be turned into cash in the short run. Five types of assets are classified as current: cash, short-term marketable investments, accounts receivable, inventories, and prepaid expenses—and they are generally listed in this order in the balance sheet.

current liabilities *Current* means that these liabilities require payment in the near term. Generally, these include accounts payable, accrued expenses payable, income tax payable, short-term notes payable, and the portion of long-term debt that will come due during the coming year. Keep in mind that a business may roll over its debt; the old, maturing debt may be replaced in part or in whole by new borrowing.

current ratio Calculated to assess the short-term solvency, or debt-paying ability of a business, it equals total current assets divided by total current liabilities. Some businesses remain solvent with a relatively low current ratio; others could be in trouble with an apparently good current ratio. The general rule is that the current ratio should be 2:1 or higher, but please take this with a grain of salt, because current ratios vary widely from industry to industry.

debt-to-equity ratio A widely used financial statement ratio to assess the overall debt load of a business and its capital structure, it equals total liabilities divided by total owners' equity. Both numbers for this ratio are taken from a business's latest balance sheet. There is no standard, or generally agreed on, maximum ratio, such as 1:1 or 2:1. Every industry is different in this regard. Some businesses, such as financial institutions, have very high debt-to-equity ratios. In contrast, many businesses use very little debt relative to their owners' equity.

depreciation   Refers to the generally accepted accounting principle of allocating the cost of a long-term operating asset over the estimated useful life of the asset. Each year of use is allocated a part of the original cost of the asset. Generally speaking, either the *accelerated method* or the *straight-line method* of depreciation is used. (There are other methods, but they are relatively rare.) Useful life estimates are heavily influenced by the schedules allowed in the federal income tax law. Depreciation is not a cash outlay in the period in which the expense is recorded—just the opposite. The cash inflow from sales revenue during the period includes an amount to reimburse the business for the use of its fixed assets. In this respect, depreciation is a source of cash. So depreciation is added back to net income in the statement of cash flows to arrive at cash flow from operating activities.

diluted earnings per share (EPS)   This measure of earnings per share recognizes additional stock shares that may be issued in the future for stock options and as may be required by other contracts a business has entered into, such as convertible features in its debt securities and preferred stock. Both basic earnings per share and, if applicable, diluted earnings per share are reported by publicly owned business corporations. Often the two EPS figures are not far apart, but in some cases the gap is significant. Privately owned businesses do not have to report earnings per share. See also **basic earnings per share.**

discounted cash flow (DCF)   Refers to a capital investment analysis technique that discounts, or scales down, the future cash returns from an investment based on the cost-of-capital rate for the business. In essence, each future return is downsized to take into account the cost of capital from the start of the investment until the future point in time when the return is received. *Present value* (PV) is the amount resulting from discounting the future returns. Present value is subtracted from the entry cost of the investment to determine *net present value* (NPV). The net present value is positive if the present value is more than the entry cost, which signals that the investment would earn more than the cost-of-capital rate. If the entry cost is more than the present value, the net present value is negative, which means that the investment would earn less than the business's cost-of-capital rate.

dividend payout ratio   Computed by dividing cash dividends for the year by the net income for the year. It's simply the percent of net income distributed as cash dividends for the year.

dividend yield ratio   Cash dividends paid by a business over the most recent 12 months (called the *trailing* 12 months) divided by the current market price per share of the stock. This ratio is reported in the daily stock trading tables in the *Wall Street Journal* and other major newspapers.

double-entry accounting   See **accrual-basis accounting**.

earnings before interest and income tax (EBIT)   A measure of profit that equals sales revenue for the period minus cost-of-goods-sold expense and all operating expenses—but before deducting interest and income tax expenses. It is a measure of the operating profit of a business before considering the cost of its debt capital and income tax.

earnings per share (EPS)   See **basic earnings per share** and **diluted earnings per share**.

equity   Refers to one of the two basic sources of capital for a business, the other being debt (borrowed money). Most often, it is called *owners' equity* because it refers to the capital used by a business that "belongs" to the ownership interests in the business. Owners' equity arises from two quite distinct sources: capital invested by the owners in the business and profit (net income) earned by the business that is not distributed to its owners (called *retained earnings*). Owners' equity in our highly developed and sophisticated economic and legal system can be very complex—involving stock options, financial derivatives of all kinds, different classes of stock, convertible debt, and so on.

extraordinary gains and losses   No pun intended, but these types of gains and losses are extraordinarily important to understand. These are nonrecurring, onetime, unusual, nonoperating gains or losses that are recorded by a business during the period. The amount of each of these gains or losses, net of the income tax effect, is reported separately in the income statement. Net income is reported before and after these gains and losses. These gains and losses should not be recorded very often, but in fact many businesses record them every other year or so, causing much consternation to investors. In addition to evaluating the regular stream of sales and expenses that produce operating profit, investors also have to factor into their profit performance analysis the perturbations of these irregular gains and losses reported by a business.

financial condition, statement of   See **balance sheet.**

financial leverage   The equity (ownership) capital of a business can serve as the basis for securing debt capital (borrowing money). In this way, a business increases the total capital available to invest in its assets and can make more sales and more profit. The strategy is to earn operating profit, or earnings before interest and income tax (EBIT), on the capital supplied from debt that is more than the interest paid on the debt capital. A financial leverage gain equals the EBIT earned on debt capital minus the interest on the debt. A financial leverage gain augments earnings on equity capital. A business must earn a rate of return on its assets (ROA) that is greater than the interest rate on its debt to make a financial leverage gain. If the spread between its ROA and interest rate is unfavorable, a business suffers a financial leverage loss.

financial reports and statements   *Financial* means having to do with money and economic wealth. *Statement* means a formal presentation. Financial reports are printed and a copy is sent to each owner and each major lender of the business. Most public corporations make their financial reports available on a web site, so all or part of the financial report can be downloaded by anyone. Businesses prepare three primary financial statements: the statement of financial condition, or balance sheet; the statement of cash flows; and the income statement. These three key financial statements constitute the core of the periodic financial reports that are distributed outside a business to its shareowners and lenders. Financial reports also include footnotes to the financial statements and much other information. Financial statements are prepared according to generally accepted accounting principles (GAAP), which are the authoritative rules that govern the measurement of net income and the reporting of profit-making activities, financial condition, and cash flows. Internal financial statements, although based on the same profit accounting methods, report more information to managers for decision making and control. Sometimes, financial statements are called simply *financials*.

financing activities   One of the three classes of cash flows reported in the statement of cash flows. This class includes borrowing money and paying debt, raising money from shareowners and the return of money to them, and dividends paid from profit.

fixed assets   An informal term that refers to the variety of long-term operating resources used by a business in its operations—including real estate, machinery, equipment, tools, vehicles, office furniture, computers, and so on. In balance sheets, these assets are typically labeled *property,* *plant, and equipment.* The term *fixed assets* captures the idea that the assets are relatively fixed in place and are not held for sale in the normal course of business. The cost of fixed assets, except land, is depreciated, which means the cost is allocated over the estimated useful lives of the assets.

fixed expenses (costs)   Expenses or costs that remain the same in amount, or fixed, over the short run and do not vary with changes in sales volume or sales revenue or other measures of business activity. Over the longer run, however, these costs increase or decrease as the business grows or declines. Fixed operating costs provide capacity to carry on operations and make sales. Fixed manufacturing overhead costs provide production capacity. Fixed expenses are a key pivot point for the analysis of profit behavior, especially for determining the breakeven point and for analyzing strategies to improve profit performance.

free cash flow   Generally speaking, this term refers to cash flow from profit (cash flow from operating activities, to use the more formal term). The underlying idea is that a business is free to do what it wants with its cash flow from profit. However, a business usually has many ongoing commitments and demands on this cash flow, so it may not actually be free to decide what do with this source of cash. *Warning:* This term is not officially defined anywhere and different persons use the term to mean different things. Pay particular attention to how an author or speaker is using the term.

generally accepted accounting principles (GAAP)   This important term refers to the body of authoritative rules for measuring profit and preparing financial statements that are included in financial reports by a business to its outside shareowners and lenders. The development of these guidelines has been evolving for more than 70 years. Congress passed a law in 1934 that bestowed primary jurisdiction over financial reporting by publicly owned businesses to the Securities and Exchange Commission (SEC). But the SEC has largely left the development of GAAP to the private sector. Presently, the Financial Accounting Standards Board is the primary (but not the only) authoritative body that makes pronouncements on GAAP. *One caution:* GAAP are like a movable feast. New rules are issued fairly frequently, old rules are amended from time to time, and some rules established years ago are discarded on occasion. Professional accountants have a heck of time keeping up with GAAP, that's for sure. Also, new GAAP rules sometimes have the effect of closing the barn door after the horse has left. Accounting abuses occur, and only then, after the damage has been done, are new rules issued to prevent such abuses in the future.

gross margin, also called **gross profit**   This first-line measure of profit equals sales revenue less cost of goods sold. This is profit before operating expenses and interest and income tax expenses are deducted. Financial reporting standards require that gross margin be reported in external income statements. Gross margin is a key variable in management profit reports for decision making and control. Gross margin doesn't apply to service businesses that don't sell products.

income statement   Financial statement that summarizes sales revenue and expenses for a period and reports one or more profit lines for the period. It's one of the three primary financial statements of a business. The bottom-line profit figure is labeled *net income* or *net earnings* by most businesses. Externally reported income statements disclose less information than do internal management profit reports—but both are based on the same profit accounting principles and methods. Keep in mind that profit is not known until accountants complete the recording of sales revenue and expenses for the period (as well as determining any extraordinary gains and losses that should be recorded in the period). Profit measurement depends on the reliability of a business's accounting system and the choices of accounting methods by the business. *Caution:* A business may engage in certain manipulations of its accounting methods, and managers may intervene in the normal course of operations for the purpose of improving the amount of profit recorded in the period, which is called *earnings management, income smoothing, cooking the books,* and other pejorative terms.

internal accounting controls   Refers to forms used and procedures established by a business—beyond what would be required for the record-keeping function of accounting—that are designed to prevent errors and fraud. Two examples of internal controls are (1) requiring a second signature by someone higher in the organization to approve a transaction in excess of a certain dollar amount and (2) giving customers printed receipts as proof of sale. Other examples of internal control procedures are restricting entry and exit routes of employees, requiring all employees to take their vacations and assigning another person to do their jobs while they are away, surveillance cameras, surprise counts of cash and inventory, and rotation of duties. Internal controls should be cost-effective; the cost of a control should be less than the potential loss that is prevented. The guiding principle for designing internal accounting controls is to deter and detect errors and dishonesty. The best internal controls in the world cannot prevent most fraud by high-level managers who take advantage of their positions of trust and authority.

internal rate of return (IRR)   The precise discount rate that makes the present value (PV) of the future cash returns from a capital investment exactly equal to the initial amount of capital invested. If IRR is higher than the company's cost-of-capital rate, the investment is an attractive opportunity; if less, the investment is substandard from the cost-of-capital point of view.

inventory shrinkage   A term describing the loss of products from inventory due to shoplifting by customers, employee theft, damaged and spoiled products that are thrown away, and errors in recording the purchase and sale of products. A business should make a physical count and inspection of its inventory to determine this loss.

inventory turnover ratio   The cost-of-goods-sold expense for a given period (usually one year) divided by the cost of inventories. The ratio depends on how long products are held in stock on average before they are sold. Managers should closely monitor this ratio.

inventory write-down   Refers to making an entry, usually at the close of a period, to decrease the cost value of the inventories asset account in order to recognize the lost value of products that cannot be sold at their normal markups or will be sold below cost. A business compares the recorded cost of products held in inventory against the sales value of the products. Based on the lower-of-cost-or-market rule, an entry is made to record the inventory write-down as an expense.

investing activities   One of the three classes of cash flows reported in the statement of cash flows. This class includes capital expenditures for replacing and expanding the fixed assets of a business, proceeds from disposals of its old fixed assets, and other long-term investment activities of a business.

management control   This is difficult to define in a few words—indeed, an entire chapter is devoted to the topic (Chapter 17). The essence of management control is "keeping a close watch on everything." Anything can go wrong and get out of control. Management control can be thought of as the follow-through on decisions to ensure that the actual outcomes happen according to purposes and goals of the management decisions that set things in motion. Managers depend on feedback control reports that contain very detailed information. The level of detail and range of information in these control reports is very different from the summary-level information reported in external income statements.

mark to market   Refers to the accounting method that records increases and decreases in assets based on changes in their market values. For example, mutual funds revalue their securities portfolios every day based on closing prices on the New York Stock Exchange and Nasdaq. Generally speaking, however, businesses do *not* use the mark-to-market method to write up the value of their assets. A business, for instance, does not revalue its fixed assets (buildings, machines, equipment, etc.) at the end of each period—even though the replacement values of these assets fluctuate over time. Having made this general comment, I should mention that accounts receivable are written down to recognize bad debts, and a business's inventories asset account is written down to recognize stolen and damaged goods as well as products that will be sold below cost. If certain of a business's long-term operating assets become impaired and will not have productive utility in the future consistent with their book values, then the assets are written off or written down, which can result in recording a large extraordinary loss in the period.

market capitalization, or **market cap** Current market value per share of capital stock multiplied by the total number of capital stock shares outstanding of a publicly owned business. This value often differs widely from the book value of owners' equity reported in a business's balance sheet.

negative cash flow The cash flow from the operating activities of a business can be negative, which means that its cash balance decreased from its sales and expense activities during the period. When a business is operating at a loss instead of making a profit, its cash outflows for expenses very likely may be more than its cash inflow from sales. Even when a business makes a profit for the period, its cash inflow from sales could be considerably less than the sales revenue recorded for the period, thus causing a negative cash flow for the period. *Caution:* This term also is used for certain types of investments in which the net cash flow from all sources and uses is negative. For example, investors in rental real estate properties often use the term to mean that the cash inflow from rental income is less than all cash outflows during the period, including payments on the mortgage loan on the property.

net income (also called the **bottom line, earnings, net earnings,** and **net operating earnings**) This key figure equals sales revenue for a period less all expenses for the period; also, any extraordinary gains and losses for the period are included in this final profit figure. Everything is taken into account to arrive at net income, which is popularly called the *bottom line.* Net income is clearly the single most important number in business financial reports.

net present value (NPV) Equals the present value (PV) of a capital investment minus the initial amount of capital that is invested, or the entry cost of the investment. A positive NPV signals an attractive capital investment opportunity; a negative NPV means that the investment is substandard.

net worth   Generally refers to the book value of owners' equity as reported in a business's balance sheet. If liabilities are subtracted from assets, the accounting equation becomes: assets – liabilities = owners' equity. In this version of the accounting equation, owners' equity equals net worth, or the amount of assets after deducting the liabilities of the business.

operating activities   Includes all the sales and expense activities of a business. But the term is very broad and inclusive; it is used to embrace all types of activities engaged in by profit-motivated entities toward the objective of earning profit. A bank, for instance, earns net income not from sales revenue but from loaning money on which it receives interest income. Making loans is the main revenue operating activity of banks.

operating cash flow   See **cash flow from operating activities.**

operating leverage   A relatively small percent increase or decrease in sales volume that causes a much larger percent increase or decrease in profit because fixed expenses do not change with small changes in sales volume. Sales volume changes have a lever effect on profit. This effect should be called *sales volume leverage,* but in practice it is called *operating leverage.*

operating liabilities   The short-term liabilities generated by the operating (profit-making) activities of a business. Most businesses have three types of operating liabilities: accounts payable from inventory purchases and from incurring expenses, accrued expenses payable for unpaid expenses, and income tax payable. These short-term liabilities of a business are non-interest-bearing, although if not paid on time a business may be assessed a late-payment penalty that is in the nature of an interest charge.

operating profit   See **earnings before interest and income tax (EBIT).**

overhead costs   Overhead generally refers to indirect, in contrast to direct, costs. Indirect means that a cost cannot be matched or coupled in any obvious or objective manner with particular products, specific revenue sources, or a particular organizational unit. Manufacturing overhead costs are the indirect costs in making products, which are in addition to the direct costs of raw materials and labor. Manufacturing overhead costs include both *variable costs* (electricity, gas, water, etc.), which vary with total production output, and *fixed costs,* which do not vary with increases or decreases in actual production output.

owners' equity   Refers to the capital invested in a business by its share-owners plus the profit earned by the business that has not been distributed to its shareowners, which is called *retained earnings*. Owners' equity is one of the two basic sources of capital for a business, the other being borrowed money, or debt. The book value, or value reported in a balance sheet for owners' equity, is not the market value of the business. Rather, the balance sheet value reflects the historical amounts of capital invested in the business by the owners over the years plus the accumulation of yearly profits that were not paid out to owners.

present value (PV)   This amount is calculated by discounting the future cash returns from a capital investment. The discount rate usually is the cost-of-capital rate for the business. If PV is more than the initial amount of capital that has to be invested, the investment is attractive. If less, then better investment alternatives should be found.

price/earnings (P/E) ratio   This key ratio equals the current market price of a capital stock share divided by the earnings per share (EPS) for the stock. The EPS used in this ratio may be the basic EPS for the stock or its diluted EPS—you have to check to be sure about this. A low P/E may signal an undervalued stock or may reflect a pessimistic forecast by investors for the future earnings prospects of the business. A high P/E may reveal an overvalued stock or reflect an optimistic forecast by investors. The average P/E ratio for the stock market as a whole varies considerably over time—from a low of about 8 to a high of about 30. This is quite a range of variation, to say the least.

product cost   This is a key factor in the profit model of a business. Product cost is the same as purchase cost for a retailer or wholesaler (distributor). A manufacturer has to accumulate three different types of production costs to determine product cost: direct materials, direct labor, and manufacturing overhead. The cost of products (goods) sold is deducted from sales revenue to determine gross margin (also called *gross profit*), which is the first profit line reported in an external income statement and in an internal profit report to managers.

profit   The general term *profit* is not precisely defined; it may refer to net gains over a period of time, or cash inflows less cash outflows for an investment, or earnings before or after certain costs and expenses are deducted from income or revenue. In the world of business, profit is measured by the application of generally accepted accounting principles (GAAP). In the income statement, the final, bottom-line profit is generally labeled *net income* and equals revenue (plus any extraordinary gains) less all expenses (and less any extraordinary losses) for the period. Internal management profit reports include several profit lines: gross margin, contribution margin, operating profit (earnings before interest and income tax), and earnings before income tax. External income statements report gross margin (also called *gross profit*) and often report one or more other profit lines, although practice varies from business to business in this regard.

profit and loss statement (P&L statement)   This is an alternative moniker for an income statement or for an internal management profit report. Actually, it's a misnomer because a business has *either* a profit *or* a loss for a period. Accordingly, it should be profit *or* loss statement, but the term has caught on and undoubtedly will continue to be profit and loss statement.

profit module   This concept refers to a separate source of revenue and profit within a business organization, which should be identified for management analysis and control. A profit module may focus on one product or a cluster of products. Profit in this context is not the final, bottom-line net income of the business as a whole. Rather, other measures of profit are used for management analysis and decision-making purposes—such as gross margin, contribution margin, or operating profit (earnings before interest and income tax).

profit ratios   Ratios based on sales revenue for a period. A measure of profit is divided by sales revenue to compute a profit ratio. For example, gross margin is divided by sales revenue to compute the *gross margin profit ratio*. Dividing bottom-line profit (net income) by sales revenue gives the profit ratio that is generally called *return on sales*.

property, plant, and equipment   This label is generally used in financial reports to describe the long-term assets of a business, which include land, buildings, machinery, equipment, tools, vehicles, computers, furniture and fixtures, and other tangible long-lived resources that are not held for sale but are used in the operations of a business. The less formal name for these assets is **fixed assets,** which see.

quick ratio   See **acid test ratio.**

return on assets (ROA)   Although there is no single uniform practice for calculating this ratio, generally it equals operating profit (before interest and income tax) for a year divided by the total assets that are used to generate the profit. ROA is the key ratio to test whether a business is earning enough on its assets to cover its cost of capital. ROA is used for determining financial leverage gain (or loss).

return on equity (ROE) This key ratio, expressed as a percent, equals net income for the year divided by owners' equity. ROE should be higher than a business's interest rate on debt because the owners take more risk.

return on investment (ROI) A very general concept that refers to some measure of income, earnings, profit, or gain over a period of time divided by the amount of capital invested during the period. It is almost always expressed as a percent. For a business, an important ROI measure is its return on equity (ROE), which is computed by dividing its net income for the period by its owners' equity during the period.

return on sales This ratio equals net income divided by sales revenue.

revenue-driven expenses Operating expenses that vary in proportion to changes in total sales revenue (total dollars of sales). Examples are sales commissions based on sales revenue, credit card discount expenses, and rents and franchise fees based on sales revenue. These expenses are one of the key variables in a profit model. Segregating these expenses from other types of expenses that behave differently is essential for management decision-making analysis. (These expenses are not disclosed separately in externally reported income statements.)

Securities and Exchange Commission (SEC) The federal agency that oversees the issuance of and trading in securities of public businesses. The SEC has broad powers and can suspend the trading in securities of a business. The SEC also has primary jurisdiction in making accounting and financial reporting rules, but over the years it has largely deferred to the private sector for the development of generally accepted accounting principles (GAAP).

solvency Refers to the ability of a business to pay its liabilities on time when they come due for payment. A business may be *insolvent,* which means that it is not able to pay its liabilities and debts on time. The current ratio and acid test ratio are used to evaluate the short-term solvency prospects of a business.

spontaneous liabilities See **operating liabilities.**

stockholders' equity, statement of changes in Although often considered a financial statement, this is more in the nature of a supporting schedule that summarizes in one place various changes in the owners' equity accounts of a business during the period—including the issuance and retirement of capital stock shares, cash dividends, and other transactions affecting owners' equity. This statement (schedule) is very helpful when a business has more than one class of stock shares outstanding and when a variety of events occurred during the year that changed its owners' equity accounts.

straight-line depreciation   This depreciation method allocates a uniform amount of the cost of long-lived operating assets (fixed assets) to each year of use. It is the basic alternative to the accelerated depreciation method. When using the straight-line method, a business may estimate a longer life for a fixed asset than when using the accelerated method (though not necessarily in every case). Both methods are allowed for income tax and under generally accepted accounting principles (GAAP).

sunk cost   A cost that has been paid and cannot be undone or reversed. Once the cost has been paid, it is irretrievable, like water over the dam or spilled milk. Usually, the term refers to the recorded value of an asset that has lost its value in the operating activities of a business. Examples are the costs of products in inventory that cannot be sold and fixed assets that are no longer usable. The book value of these assets should be written off to expense. These costs should be disregarded in making decisions about what to do with the assets (except that the income tax effects of disposing of the assets should be taken into account).

times interest earned   A ratio that tests the ability of a business to make interest payments on its debt, which is calculated by dividing annual earnings before interest and income tax by the interest expense for the year. There is no particular rule for this ratio, such as 3 or 4 times, but obviously the ratio should be higher than 1.

unit margin   The profit per unit sold of a product after deducting product cost and variable expenses of selling the product from the sales price of the product. Unit margin equals profit before fixed operating expenses are considered and before interest and income tax are deducted. Unit margin is one of the key variables in a profit model for decision-making analysis.

unit-driven expenses   Expenses that vary in close proportion to changes in total sales volume (total quantities of sales). Examples of these types of expenses are delivery costs, packaging costs, and other costs that depend mainly on the number of products sold or the number of customers served. These expenses are one of the key factors in a profit model for decision-making analysis. Segregating these expenses from other types of expenses that behave differently is essential for management decision-making analysis. The cost-of-goods-sold expense depends on sales volume and is a unit-driven expense. But product cost (i.e., the cost of goods sold) is such a dominant expense that it is treated separately from other unit-driven operating expenses.

variable expenses   Expenses that change with changes in either sales volume or sales revenue, in contrast to fixed expenses that remain the same over the short run and do not fluctuate in response to changes in sales volume or sales revenue. See also **revenue-driven expenses** and **unit-driven expenses.**

weighted-average cost of capital   *Weighted* means that the proportions of debt capital and equity capital of a business are used to calculate its average cost of capital. This key benchmark rate depends on the interest rate(s) on its debt and the ROE goal established by a business. This is a return-on-capital rate and can be applied either on a before-tax basis or an after-tax basis. A business should earn at least its weighted-average rate on the capital invested in its assets. The weighted-average cost-of-capital rate is used as the discount rate to calculate the present value (PV) of specific investments.

Topical Guide to Figures

Accounting functions and system   1.1

Accrual-basis accounting versus cash flows   2.1

Balance sheet (statement of financial condition)   2.3, 4.2, 5.2, 5.4, 6.4, 7.2, 16.1

Breakeven point (sales volume)   8.1

Budget profit plan for coming period   7.1

Capital investment analysis   14.2, 14.3, 14.4, 14.5, 15.1, 15.2, 15.3

Cash flow changes from profit changes   13.2, 13.3

Cash flows, statement of   2.4, 2.5, 4.3, 7.3

Contribution margin analysis   3.4

Cost changes   10.4, 12.1, 12.2, 12.3

Cost of capital   14.1

Discounted cash flow   15.2

Expenses connected with their operating assets and liabilities   5.3, 5.4

Financial leverage   6.3

Fixed expenses (costs) allocation   17.2

Gross margin analysis   3.2

Income statement   2.2, 3.1, 4.1, 5.1, 5.4, 6.1, 7.1, 16.1

Internal rate of return   15.3

Inventories, excessive accumulation of   18.3

Management profit report	3.3, 8.1, 9.1, 9.2, 9.3, 10.1, 10.3, 10.4, 12.4, 12.5, 12.6, 12.7, 13.1, 16.2, 17.2, 18.1
Manufacturing costs summary	18.1
Manufacturing costs, misclassification of	18.2
Operating profit (earnings before interest and income tax) and cost of capital	14.1
Price/volume trade-offs	11.2, 11.3, 11.4
Profit model	11.1, 11.2, 11.3, 11.4, 12.4, 12.5, 12.6, 12.7, 16.4
Profit ratios	4.5
Profit report (*see* Management profit report; Income statement)	
Return on assets	6.2
Return on equity	6.2
Sales price changes	10.1, 10.2, 10.3, 12.2, 13.3, 16.3, 16.4
Sales revenue "negatives"	17.1
Sales revenue connected with its operating asset	5.3, 5.4
Sales volume changes	9.2, 9.3, 10.2, 12.1, 12.3, 13.1, 13.2, 16.3, 16.4
Service businesses	16.1
Spreadsheet model (for capital investment analysis)	14.2, 14.3, 14.5, 15.1, 15.2, 15.3
Stockholders' equity, statement of changes in	4.4

Absorption costing method, 383–384

Accelerated depreciation method, 33, 206

Account (record-keeping element), 4, 18

Accounting, external functions, 4–5, 6, 11–12

Accounting, internal functions, 4–5, 6

Accounting equation, 65

Accounting methods, 8, 19, 33, 40

Accounting system, 4–5, 247

Accounts payable, 20, 70, 71, 75, 79, 104, 183, 184, 232–233, 241

Accounts receivable, 18, 20, 34, 40, 69, 76–77, 81, 143, 165, 251–252

Accounts receivable turnover ratio, 58

Accrual-basis accounting, 13–15, 16, 21, 24, 179–180, 184–185

Accrued expenses payable, 20, 70, 72, 75, 79, 184

Accumulated depreciation, 20, 103–104, 114

Acid test ratio (also called *quick ratio*), 56

Activity-based costing (ABC), 140n, 268–269

Advance payments from customers, 20

Advertising expense, 34, 129, 149, 279

After-tax cost of capital, 224–226

American Institute of Certified Public Accountants (AICPA), 249

Amortization (of debt principal), 83–84

Apple Computer, 29

Assets, 7, 12, 18, 20, 22, 40, 63, 66, 76, 81, 191
  as capital investments, 195–197
  connections with sales revenue and expenses, 69–73, 100, 101–102

Asset turnover ratio, 59, 64

Auditing, internal, 249–250

Audit of external financial statements by CPA, 7, 9, 34, 41, 249

Bad debts expense, 34, 40, 143, 255–256

Balance sheet (also called *statement of financial condition*), 12, 18–21, 44–45, 74–76, 232–233, 271

Basic earnings per share, 51–52

Big bath, 47

Book value of assets, 18, 154

Book value of owners' equity and stock shares, 49–50

Bottom line. *See* Net income

Breakeven point (volume), 118, 120–121, 122, 170, 173

Budgeting, 101, 270–273, 274

Burden rate (for fixed manufacturing overhead costs), 283–284

Business valuation, 82

Capacity, 112–113, 130, 133, 150, 170, 239, 260. *See also* Production capacity

Capital, sources of, 67–69, 76, 99, 100, 191–192, 227

Capital budgeting, 210

Capital expenditures, 98, 100, 103, 271

Capital invested in assets, 80, 95, 99, 100, 165, 192, 202–203

Capital investment, 191–192, 195–199, 213, 215–224

Capitalization of costs, 280–281

Capital needs planning, 97, 99–105, 165

Capital recovery (return of invested capital), 199–206, 220, 221, 223

Capital stock (shares, or units of ownership), 85–86

Capital structure (capitalization), 82–83, 192, 193, 206, 214

Capital structure model, 88

Cash dividends. *See* Dividends

Cash flow, 3, 7, 251

Cash flow breakeven volume, 119–120

Cash flow from operating activities (also called *cash flow from profit, and operating cash flow*), 14, 16–17, 23, 100, 101, 104–106, 179, 184–185, 196

Cash flow from profit. *See* Cash flow from operating activities

Cash flows, statement of, 7, 12, 21–24, 45, 271

Cash working balance, 18, 73–74, 81, 83, 100, 103

Coca-Cola Company, 29

Common stock, 85

Contribution margin, 31, 33, 35–36, 111, 132, 143, 152, 236–237, 255, 260

Control. *See* Management control

Corporation (type of business entity), 85–86

Cost allocation, 171–172, 262, 266–270, 280

Cost driver, 140n, 268–269

Cost of capital, 192–195, 206, 210, 214, 215, 218, 219, 224–227

Cost of equity capital, 194

Cost of goods sold, 17, 28, 29, 30, 77, 140, 182–183, 232–233, 234, 241, 258, 259, 278n

Cost/sales volume trade-offs, 164–165, 167–169

Current assets, 55–56

Current liabilities, 55–56

Current ratio, 55–56

Current replacement value of assets, 40

Debt (interest-bearing liabilities), 20, 55, 68, 76, 79, 81–84, 92, 94, 95, 98, 192, 193, 226, 227

Debt-to-equity ratio, 57, 206

Depreciation expense, 20, 24, 33, 40, 70, 73, 103–104, 113–115, 129, 146, 172–173, 180, 196, 204–205, 283

Diluted earnings per share, 52–53

Direct (variable) costing, 289n

Direct labor costs of manufacturing, 276–277, 289

Direct method (for reporting cash flow from operating activities), 23

Disclosure in financial reports, 9, 17, 22, 39–40, 48, 118,

255, 257, 258, 260. *See also* External versus internal financial report-ing
Discounted cash flow (DCF), 217, 218–221, 224, 227
Dividends, 51, 82, 86, 89, 104
Dividend yield ratio, 53–54
Double-entry bookkeeping, 65

Earnings. *See* Net income
Earnings before interest and income tax (EBIT), 17, 68, 88–89, 90, 93, 95, 109, 112, 116, 192, 194
Earnings multiplier, 94
Earnings per share (EPS). *See* Basic earnings per share; Diluted earnings per share
Equity. *See* Owners' equity
Ethics, 10
Expenses (in general), 12, 14, 16, 17, 20, 28, 76
External versus internal financial reporting, 25
Extraordinary gains and losses, 46–47, 256

Feedback information, 244, 245, 253. *See also* Management control information
Financial condition, 3, 12. *See also* Balance sheet
Financial condition, statement of. *See* Balance sheet
Financial leverage (and financial leverage gain or loss), 79, 92–94, 95
Financial reporting and reports, 4–8, 9, 24. *See also* Financial statements
Financial statement manipulation, 40–41
Financial statement ratios, 39, 47–53, 59–60, 242
Financial statements, nature,

purposes and types, 7–8, 11–12, 24, 39–46, 241, 246
Financing activities (basic type of cash flows), 22
Finished goods inventory account, 278n
Fixed assets, 70, 81, 114. *See also* Property, plant, and equipment
Fixed manufacturing overhead costs, 278, 283, 289
Fixed operating expenses (costs), 31, 33, 35–36, 112–113, 117, 122, 123, 129, 133, 134, 136, 139–140, 143, 146, 149, 150, 155, 159, 169, 171–172, 236, 239, 255, 266
Footnotes (to financial state-ments), 7, 29, 43
Fraud, 41, 79, 248, 250–252, 273

Generally accepted accounting principles (GAAP), 7, 8, 28, 41
Going-concern premise of finan-cial statement accounting, 50
Graham, Benjamin, and Dodd, David (authors of *Security Analysis*), 49
Gresham, Sir Thomas, 10
Gross margin (profit), 17, 28–31, 232–233, 234, 241
Gross margin ratio, 29, 30, 49

How to Read a Financial Report (John A. Tracy), 43, 278n
Hurdle rate, 224

Idle capacity, 283–285, 288
Income statement (external profit report), 12, 17, 24, 27–28, 32, 36, 40, 42, 43, 232–233, 271

Income statement, connections with balance sheet, 75–76

Income tax (factor in capitalization structure of business), 89–91, 193–194, 218

Income tax expense, 33, 116–117, 192

Index, *The Fast Forward MBA in Finance,* 2nd edition, Tracy, 11

Indirect method (for reporting cash flow from operating activities), 23–24

Interest expense, 12, 33, 67, 68, 81, 83, 88–89, 98–99, 116, 192, 210, 225

Internal accounting controls, 247–249, 259, 273

Internal rate of return (IRR), 218, 222–224, 227

Inventories (inventory), 12, 19, 20, 34, 66, 70–71, 77, 81, 104, 165, 183, 188, 232, 241, 251–252, 278, 281

Inventory, excessive accumulation, 287–289

Inventory shrinkage, 34, 258–259

Inventory stock-outs, 260

Inventory turnover and inventory turnover ratio, 29, 58–59

Inventory write-down, 40, 154

Investing activities (basic type of cash flows), 21–22

Job order costing, 276

Land (cost not depreciated), 113–114

Leasing (alternative to purchase), 206, 208–209

Liabilities, 12, 18, 65
connections with expenses, 69–73, 100, 101–102

Limited liability company (type of business entity), 85

Lower of cost or market (LCM), 154n

Management by exception, 254

Management control, 4, 243–274

Management control information, 244–247

Management control reports, 4–5, 6, 243–274, 285

Management discussion and analysis (MD&A), 9

Management (internal) profit reports, 4–5, 6, 31–32, 36, 109–110, 119, 126–127, 140, 170–171, 234–235

Management responsibility for external financial reports, 40–42

Management stewardship responsibility, 9

Manufacturers and manufacturing processes, 275, 276, 285

Manufacturing accounting, 275–289

Manufacturing capacity. *See* Production capacity

Manufacturing costs, 276–278, 281

Manufacturing costs, misclassification of, 280–282

Manufacturing overhead costs, 278, 279–280

Margin of safety, 120

Market cap (capitalization), 83

Market share, 36, 137, 157, 159, 160

Melicher, Ron, 94

Nasdaq, 42

Net earnings. *See* Net income

Net income, 13, 16–17, 23, 32, 33, 40, 48, 68, 76, 81–82, 104, 192

Net income available for common stockholders, 51
Net present value (NPV), 222
Net worth, 82
New York Stock Exchange, 42
Notes payable, 13, 20, 76

Operating activities (basic type of cash flows), 23
Operating cash flow. *See* Cash flow from operating activities
Operating earnings (profit). *See* Earnings before interest and income tax (EBIT)
Operating expenses, 28, 31, 140–142, 146
Operating leverage, 132–133
Operating liabilities, 20, 23, 63, 66, 67, 69, 71–72, 75, 76, 79–80, 81, 95, 99–100
Opportunity cost of capital, 92
Overhead costs, 112. *See also* Manufacturing overhead costs
Owners' equity, 20, 65, 68, 76, 80, 81, 84–86, 91, 192, 226, 227

Partnership (type of business entity), 84–85
Preferred stock, 51, 52, 85–86
Prepaid expenses, 20, 70, 72–73
Present value (PV), 213, 214–215, 218, 219, 221, 222, 226
Price/earnings (P/E) ratio, 54
Prime costs of manufacturing, 279
Process costing, 276
Product cost, 30, 146, 149, 161, 162–163, 166, 177, 275–276, 278–279, 282, 284, 285–286, 289
Production capacity, 278, 283

Profit and loss statement, 12. *See also* Income Statement
Profit and profit accounting, 3, 7, 8, 9–10, 12, 32, 76, 109, 180, 188, 255. *See also* Net income
Profit center, 126. *See also* Profit module
Profit change analysis, 256
Profit improvement planning and analysis, 98–99, 170–177
Profit margin, 155, 255
Profit module, 126, 127
Profit pathways and models, 116–122, 128, 150–151
Profit ratios, 47–49, 97
Profit reporting:
    external (*see* Income statement)
    internal (*see* Management profit reports)
Property, plant, and equipment, 19, 20, 70, 81, 103–104, 114. *See also* Fixed assets

Quick ratio. *See* Acid test ratio

Raw materials manufacturing costs, 183, 276, 289
Research and development costs, 28, 279
Retained earnings, 20, 68
Return on assets (ROA), 65, 87–89, 95, 196–197
Return on equity (ROE), 88–89, 91–92, 97, 174–175, 192, 193, 210, 225
Return on investment (ROI), 86–87
Return on sales, 47, 97
Returns (from capital investment), 87, 191, 199–206, 210, 213, 214, 220, 225, 227

Revenue-driven expenses and costs, 31–33, 149, 163

Sales backlog, 260
Sales capacity, 112–113, 173
Sales commission expense, 142, 149
Sales mix, 111, 262–266, 269
Sales price and revenue negatives, 256–258
Sales price changes:
    cash flow impact, 185–188
    profit impact, 140–142, 144–146, 148, 237–239
Sales prices and pricing, 27, 130, 139, 144, 149, 150, 155, 157, 159, 161–162, 163, 165–166, 177, 188, 282
Sales price/volume trade-offs, 150–158, 239, 241
Sales ratios, 260–261
Sales revenue, 12, 13, 14, 15–16, 17, 20, 28, 29, 30, 69, 76, 180–182, 255, 260
Sales revenue contra accounts, 257–258
Sales volume, 27, 109, 110–111, 129–130, 137, 149, 255, 259–260
Sales volume changes:
    cash flow impact, 180–185
    profit impact, 130–132, 133–136, 142, 148, 237–239
Securities and Exchange Commission (SEC), 42
Service businesses, 231–237
Sole proprietorship (type of business entity), 84
Solvency, 3, 55–57
Spontaneous liabilities. See Operating liabilities

Spreadsheet (model for capital investment analysis), 191, 215, 217, 226, 228
Standard costs, 286
Statement of financial condition. See Balance sheet
Stockholders' equity, statement of changes in, 46
Stock options, 52
Straight-line depreciation method, 33, 205, 206, 225–226
Sunk costs, 154

Tax returns, 4–5, 6, 261
Times interest earned, 57
Time value of money, 214
Total quality control (TQM), 167, 285
Trading on the equity, 92. See also Financial leverage

Unit-driven expenses and costs, 31–33
Unit margin (contribution margin per unit), 111, 144, 146, 152, 157, 160, 167–169, 175–176, 177, 183, 236, 255
Units-of-production depreciation method, 115

Variable expenses and costs, 30, 31, 32–33, 128, 140, 146, 163–164, 166, 177, 183, 236, 255. See also Revenue-driven expenses; Unit-driven expenses
Variable manufacturing overhead costs, 278, 289
Volume-driven expenses. See Unit-driven expenses and costs

Work-in-process inventory account, 278n